Investigating Education and Training

Investigating Education and Training

Paul Trowler

Collins Educational
An Imprint of Harper Collins Publishers

Published by Collins Educational
An imprint of HarperCollins*Publishers*
77–85 Fulham Palace Road
Hammersmith, London W6 8JB

First published in 1995
Reprinted 1996

ISBN 0-00-322406-6   OO42811

Commissioned by Emma Dunlop
Edited by Louise Wilson and Kay Wright
Cover artwork and design by Derek Lee
Illustrations by Oxford Illustrators
Typeset by Harper Phototypesetters Ltd, Northampton
Printed and bound by Scotprint Ltd, Musselburgh

Contents

Acknowledgements

The author and publisher are indebted to the following:

For permission to reproduce photographs and illustrations:

BBC Photograph Library and Archive (Figs 5.1, 5.2, 5.5, pp138, 139, 147); Blackwell Publishers (Figs 2.11, 2.12, pp59, 63); British Film Institute (Fig 5.10, p170); Cassell PLC (Implementation Staircase, p90); CSO (Tabs 5.6, 6.1, pp168, 178; Figs 6.1, 6.2, p175); Express News and Services (Fig 5.4, p143); Format Partners Picture Library (Fig 4.1, p104); Harcourt Brace and Company (Figs 1.6, 1.7, 2.6, 2.8, pp21, 23, 44, 49); *Higher Education Quarterly* (Fig 2.11, p59); HMSO (Figs 3.3, 3.4, 3.7, 4.5, 4.6, 6.3, 6.4, 6.5, 6.6, 6.9, 6.10, 7.2, pp71, 75, 132, 176, 178, 199, 217); Holt Education (Fig 1.9, p30); Hulton Deutsch Collection (Fig 5.3, p140); Ken Pyne (Fig 7.1, p207); Lord Callaghan (Fig 3.2, p70); Knight Features (Fig 1.8, p24); *New Community* (Figs 4.7, 4.8, 4.9, pp134, 135); Newham Monitoring Project (Fig 4.4, p217); Nigel Paige (Figs 1.4, 3.1, 3.8, 5.9, 6.8, pp5, 68, 76, 167, 196) Open University Press (Fig 2.7, 5.6, pp45, 149); Press Association Photos (Fig 1.2, p2); Policy Studies Institute (Table 4.2, p113); Routledge Publishers (Fig 2.1, p. 32); Steve Bell (Fig 1.3, p4); Stanley Thornes (Fig 1.5, p20); Tony Hall (Fig 5.7, p158); Universal Pictorial Press & Agency (Fig 3.6, p74); University of Central Lancashire (Figs 2.9, 7.5, pp50, 225); Will & Denni McIntyre (Fig 2.5, p44)

While every effort has been made to contact copyright-holders, this has not proved possible in every case. The publishers would be pleased to hear from any copyright-holders not acknowledged.

Biographies of Contributors

The authors are all members of the Department of Education Studies at the University of Central Lancashire.

Stuart Billingham taught for nine years in further education before becoming a senior lecturer in the Racial Equality Unit at Lancashire Polytechnic (now the University of Central Lancashire). Since 1992 he has been senior lecturer in education at the University. He has written several articles, international conference papers and acted as consultant to colleges and universities on issues of racial inequality and equality of opportunity since the early 1980s. He is currently working on a book, Racism and Education in Europe (provisional title) with Metin Alkan at the University of Amsterdam. Stuart spends his spare time supporting West Bromwich Albion F.C.

Ken Foster is currently co-ordinator of Teaching and Training Studies at the University where he has a central role in the provision of in-service teacher education. He has an interest in classroom research, the culture of the classroom and the ethnography of teacher-pupil relationships. He teaches sociology of education on undergraduate courses, with particular reference to social class and equality of opportunity. Recent projects include international programmes of study for student teachers and management training for teachers in primary and secondary schools.

Gary Heywood-Everett is senior lecturer in education studies and is course leader for the M.A. in Teaching and Training Studies at the University. He was employed by Surrey and the London Borough of Hounslow as a primary school teacher after which he went on to undertake research at Lancaster University, publishing several articles on various aspects of primary education. More recently, his research interests have focused on the potential for parental partnerships with primary schools and he has received funding from the European Commission to undertake and co-ordinate an international study in this field. He lives in Heptonsall near Hebden Bridge with his wife and young son, Edward.

Alan Hurst is a professor in the Department of Education Studies and is also one of the University's advisers for students with disabilities and learning difficulties. Currently he convenes the higher education working party of Skill: The National Bureau for Students with Disabilities and he is senior vice-chair of the organization. His research interests are disability in post-compulsory education about which he has published a number of items and presented conference papers at many events both in the United Kingdom and abroad. He is working on the compilation of a book about policies and provision for disabled people in higher education throughout the world.

Paul Trowler is senior lecturer in education at the University, having previously worked in further education, teaching sociology and doing teacher training. He has written several books on sociology for A level and above and has been published in academic journals. He is currently course leader of the B.A. in Teaching and Training Studies at the University. Presently he is writing second editions of two previous books and completing his PhD on the phenomenology of change in higher education. He is married with a small son, Oliver, and lives in Lancaster.

Preface and how to use this book

Reading the chapter on 'the sociology of education' in most standard textbooks for 'A' level might lead you to think that research in this area stopped in the mid 1970s when Paul Willis' *Learning to Labour* and Bowles and Gintis' *Schooling in Capitalist America* were published. You might also come to believe that educational policy making stopped at around the same time. You would, of course, be wrong on both counts. Educational research and development has been vigorous since then and policy making in the area of education and (perhaps especially) training has undergone a revolution in both scale and substance.

This book brings these developments to the attention of the non-specialists and those just beginning the study of the sociology of education and training. The landscape of this area is large and complex, and to paint an accessible picture of it, we have needed to use a broad brush. Specialists will forgive us for this.

The book uses a number of features which may need explanation. They are:

Suggestions for further reading: This section, at the end of each chapter, gives you the information you need to enable you to continue independent investigation of the particular aspect of education and training covered. It may include addresses of organizations, sources of further information, and particularly useful books.

Bibliography: To increase clarity, only minimal references to the names and dates of books and studies are made in the text. However full details are given in the bibliography at the end of the book.

Task icons: Indicate whether a task is designed for

 an individual ,

pairs, small group or whole class.

These are suggestions only.

Definitions: There are also definitions of important ideas and, sometimes, theories at or near the location in the text where they appear.

The content of the book and the tasks around it put into practice a set of carefully researched educational principles based on findings from research on student learning. Authors such as N. Entwistle, P. Ramsden, R. Saljo, F. Marton and D. Laurillard are among those best known for this work, which was centred around universities in Sweden, Lancaster and Edinburgh. More recently the CNAA's Improving Student Learning Project, based at the Centre for Staff Development at Oxford Polytechnic, has worked on clearly identifying and spreading good practice in teaching and learning based on that earlier work. (Its final report was published in 1994.)

The research identified a number of different ways in which students went about the learning process. Some students were found to be effective learners in that their approach helped them develop a broad, structured and long-lasting, understanding of the material at hand and an ability to link it to other material. Other students adopted learning strategies which were less effective, resulting only in a relatively short-term memorizing of facts in an unstructured and unconnected way. A number of learning pathologies were also identified (traps into which the unwary student could fall). Among these are the inappropriate use of operation learning (learning in a serialist, stepwise way rather than a more holistic way known as comprehension learning), and improvidence (the failure to use common principles or to give sufficient detail in explanation).

Underlying all of this work are the concepts of deep and surface learning. Gibbs characterizes the surface approach as follows:

> The student reduces what is to be learnt to the status of unconnected facts to be memorized. The learning task is to reproduce the subject matter at a later date (e.g. in an exam).

(Gibbs 1990)

In taking a deep approach, on the other hand:

> The student attempts to make sense of what is to be learnt, which consists of ideas and concepts. This involves thinking, seeking integration between components and between tasks, and 'playing' with ideas.

(Gibbs 1990)

The crucial point about the findings on students' different approaches to learning is that they are not fixed characteristics of the students themselves, but strategies which tend to result from the organization of the curriculum, of assessment techniques, and of the way material is presented. In other words, individual students do not naturally or inevitably engage in poor (or good) learning strategies because of some basic feature they have as people. The same student may adopt surface approaches to learning in one subject and deep approaches to another. It is predominantly pedagogy, including the materials that support classroom practice, not psychology, that conditions learning strategy.

The content and tasks in this book, then, apply some of the principles identified by this research for facilitating a deep approach to learning. Those principles, as identified by the Improving Student Learning Project are as follows:

1. Motivational context

Deep learning is more likely when students' motivation is intrinsic and when the student experiences a need to know something. ...[they] learn best what they need to learn in order to carry out tasks which matter to them...

2. Learner activity

Students need to be active rather than passive. Deep learning is associated with doing. If the learner is actively involved, then more connections will be made both with past learning and between new concepts. Doing is not sufficient for learning, however. Learning activity must be planned, reflected upon and processed, and related to abstract concepts.

3. Interaction with others

It is often easier to negotiate meaning and to manipulate ideas with others than alone. The importance of discussion [or 'exploratory talk'] for learning is not a new idea...and autonomous student groups and peer tutoring can be very effective...

4. A well structured knowledge base

Without existing concepts it is impossible to make sense of new concepts. It is vital that students' existing knowledge and experience be brought to bear in learning. The subject matter being learnt must also be well structured and integrated...

(Gibbs 1990)

References:

Bowles, S. and Gintis, H. (1976) *Schooling in Capitalist America*, London: RKP.

Gibbs, G. (1990) *Improving Student Learning Project Briefing Paper*, Oxford: Oxford Centre for Staff Development.

Gibbs, G. (ed.) (1994) *Improving Student Learning: Theory and Practice*, Oxford: Oxford Centre for Staff Development.

Willis, P. (1977) *Learning to Labour*, Farnborough: Saxon House.

Perspectives on education policy

Gary Heywood-Everett

THE GOVERNMENT'S PLANS FOR EDUCATION.

If you don't like what the Government is doing to your public services, use your vote on May 5th.

UNISON

In this chapter we first examine the nature of educational policy. We then move on to consider various ideologies and political perspectives on education, and how these are translated into legislation. Finally we look at sociological and educational perspectives which relate to educational policy. Perspectives on particular aspects of educational policy, such as gender and ethnicity, are not discussed here, but in the chapters that deal specifically with those subjects.

Educational policy

Make a list of as many government policies on education as you can think of. Compare your list with that of another member of the group.

There have been two major trends in educational policy since the 1960s:

1 it has become more party political and controversial;

2 there has been much more policy making.

Before the mid 1970s, educational policy was often made over a leisurely lunch at the National Liberal Club. According to the historian Bogdanor, the hungry policy makers would usually consist of 'Sir William Alexander, Secretary of the Association of Education Committees, Sir Ronald Gould, the General Secretary of the NUT and the Permanent Secretary at the Department of Education'. There was usually little disagreement among these diners.

The marked increase in the amount of policy making was partly because of social and economic change. For instance, pressures on the school system were caused by less stable family structures and a shifting population as people moved about the country to find work. People were also being educated for longer. New technologies increased the amount and type of information that had to be absorbed into the curriculum. Above all, mounting unemployment and the economic crisis were critical in causing a fundamental rethink in social policy, including education. Decisions about health, education, social and local services were seen to be more important than before – too important (and expensive) to leave to those informal meetings at the Liberal Club. Instead, services were called to account for their spending and professionals such as teachers had to justify their practices.

Politicians of both the left and the right, like James Callaghan, the Labour Prime Minister, in his Ruskin College Speech of 1976 (see pp. 69–70), and Sir Keith Joseph, on the right of the Conservative Party and later Secretary of State for Education, began to propose radical changes in direction for education policy.

Figure 1.2
Sir Keith Joseph

The Conservative Cabinet Minister Sir Keith Joseph raised the political stakes in education by describing previous educational policy as a 'left-wing racket'. He felt that the middle ground was 'fixed in relation to the Labour left and the Conservative centre' (1976) and began a right-wing 'back to basics' crusade to change the shape of the educational curriculum. For him the future of British industry – and even British society – depended on a workforce and population effectively schooled in the 'three Rs' or (in today's language) literacy and numeracy.

Throughout the 1980s, with large Conservative majorities in the House of Commons and a largely ineffective opposition, the development of education into a party political issue continued. Initiatives such as the National Curriculum and Records of Achievement, which began as socialist ideas, were translated into Conservative terms and thereby 'claimed' by the Tories, who used a conflicting and powerful ideology.

Choose five contentious issues in education or training and draw up a list of arguments in favour of and against each one.
(Examples might be issues such as 'the wearing of school uniform' or 'publishing league tables of school results'.)

Politics, ideology and policy

A political party such as the Labour or Conservative Party is in reality a loose alliance of groups with different (sometimes very different) ideologies. This is at odds with the image the parties like to portray, of being a united group in agreement on almost all issues. Actually socialism and conservatism have now split repeatedly from their originally 'pure' forms so that the relevant parties contain many factions. As a result, there seems to be a general measure of policy agreement over some issues between the opposing parties across the floor of the House of Commons. It is helpful, therefore, for us to concentrate on the ideologies behind policy and practice – not the political parties themselves – in order to see more clearly how educational policy decisions are reached.

Ideology

An ideology is a combination of theories which makes up a statement of belief or 'world view' about the nature of social affairs; this is then used in order to determine social action.

There are only a finite number of possible ideological positions – they are limited by the nature of political and social interaction. However, there are basic distinctions between the theories which make up the differing major ideologies. We will now investigate each of these theories in turn.

 Look quickly ahead at the section on Marxist ideology (p.12). Make a list of five theories or basic beliefs which make up Marxism as an ideology.

The New Right and education and training

New Right thinking (see p.72 and p.111) has informed government policy since 1979 when the Conservatives were elected to power. Although some people consider New Right ideology and Thatcherism to be the same thing, Margaret Thatcher's ideology represents only one aspect of the New Right, as we will see in the following sections. The fundamental ideas behind New Right thinking can be summed up in five key points.

Key aspects of New Right thinking

1 Market forces raise standards: individuals, companies, schools and colleges which have to strive for success in a competitive environment either fight to become the best or go under.

2 Freedom of choice for the consumer is central: if consumers are free to make decisions in a crowded market, then this makes that market truly competitive. Interference in that choice by government or anyone else is counterproductive.

3 State intervention restricts individual freedom: people need to be left to make their own decisions. When state bureaucracies become involved, they start operating in their own interests and against those of the people.

4 Information is paramount for consumers to be able to make choices: without information on which to base choices the market is not really 'free'.

5 Individual rather than collective freedoms should be encouraged: individuals, especially enterprising individuals, are crucial to the future of the nation.

The idea of 'the market' has been promoted above all others in recent years as part of a New Right programme to make individuals and schools more accountable. Education, in this view, becomes a commodity like any other, to be bought and sold. The idea is

Figure 1.3
Old and new 'Rights'

Complete the balloons.

that consumer demand determines what is provided in education and training and as a consequence standards are raised by effective organizations (schools, training agencies, courses of study, etc.) succeeding at the expense of the ineffective. The theory is that, if it's good for the commercial world, then it's also good for education.

The power of the market is therefore invoked to determine effective schooling and training.

It is clear that from this viewpoint there should be no interference from local authorities, health authorities, trades unions or other pressure groups. Rather, individuals are granted power to satisfy their own needs through enhanced citizenship and charters such as the Parent's Charter, the Passenger's Charter and, more generally, the Citizen's Charter. Consumerocracy, however, can only work where there is freedom from state interference.

Figure 1.4
Charter Fever!

On this point there is some disagreement within the New Right between neo-liberal free-marketeers and neo-conservatives. (Neo simply means 'new'.) The ideas we have just discussed are neo-liberal ones: they stress *freedoms* (hence the word liberal, as in 'liberate'). However, neo-conservatives within the New Right stress constraint and the need for the state to intervene in the market. They distrust individuals and believe that they need to be watched and controlled.

A good example of the contrast between neo-liberals and neo-conservatives is seen in their respective policies regarding television. While neo-liberals stress deregulation and choice for the viewer, neo-conservatives worry about pornography and other 'evils' that choice can bring and so favour government restrictions on viewing.

The neo-conservative aspect of the New Right was dominant among the Black Paper group writing in the late 1960s. This group was led by Brian Cox, now professor of English at Manchester University, and Rhodes Boyson, a Conservative MP. They were highly critical of some of the practices in schools during the 1950s and 1960s. They called for a return to very traditional teaching methods: whole class teaching to large groups from the front, assessment by examination, and a traditional curriculum with a heavy emphasis on literacy, numeracy and the learning of facts.

It is interesting that even Brian Cox now thinks that education policy has gone too far in the direction he once argued for, and said so publicly in his own television programme in 1993. He now argues that some aspects of the National Curriculum and its testing – such as the rigid guidelines set down for teachers and pupils and excessive control over what is taught – threatens to destroy what is valuable in education.

Critics of the neo-liberal strand of New Right policy believe that education is fundamentally different from industry and commerce and that to try to apply the

Table 1.1   Neo-liberal and neo-conservative views of education

Neo-liberalism	Neo-conservatism
Market forces raise standards; schools compete with each other to improve their placing in published 'league tables' of examination results.	Standards raised by competition within schools to achieve clear goals (e.g. exam passes) and by firm discipline
Freedom for the consumer: parents should be able to choose any school they want for their child.	Restrictions on freedom where necessary; for example in choosing what to study (the three Rs must be studied)
No state intervention; schools are able to 'opt out' of LEA control if they and the parents want to.	Strong state is necessary to ensure effective schooling
Information is paramount; schools have to publish their examination results and other information each year	Effective provision is paramount; the state must ensure that teachers are well trained, do their jobs properly and teach a useful curriculum
Individual freedoms stressed; there should be many different types of schools available with different 'missions' to give maximum choice.	The nation is stressed; individuals should work not only for their own benefit but to make Britain more competitive and a better place

rigours of 'the market' to education at any level is to misunderstand what education is about. They argue that:

- Seeing parents as 'consumers' and university students as 'clients' gives 'an image of a cold and demanding face on the other side of a metal grille' according to Joan Sallis, a researcher with a special interest in parents and schools. Ted Wragg agrees that this sort of language 'fits easily into transactions of commerce but sounds mechanical and insensitive when applied to education'.

- Parents are not just consumers: they play a vital role in the educative process through their influence on children in the home.

- Consumers can get a refund or redress if things go wrong; parents cannot.

- Consumers' choices don't affect the product; choices about schools do change the nature of those schools. A study by Adler and others in Scotland concluded that: 'All in all the evidence in Edinburgh and Dundee suggests that [parental choice] is leading to the emergence of a number of "magnet" and "sink" schools and thus to increased inequalities in educational provision.'

- Consumers can choose not to buy. In contrast, education is compulsory to the age of 16 years.

- Many parents cannot shop around effectively: they are limited by transport and time. Adler's study showed that *distance* from the school was the most important factor determining choice, especially for the working class.

- The market is not really 'free'. The government has loaded the dice in favour of city technology colleges (CTCs) and some other types of schools by giving them more resources.

 Where do the following recent educational initiatives find their origins in the two strains of the New Right above? Do they fit into the neo-liberal or neo-conservative perspective?

- *A National Curriculum for all citizens in the UK.*
- *Local management whereby schools can run their own institution much as a business is run.*
- *Further education (FE) 'incorporation' whereby colleges compete with other colleges over student intake and have the freedom to organize their own affairs.*
- *The boom in the school prospectus industry whereby brochures are becoming more and more glossy.*
- *National Vocational Qualifications (NVQs) – the reorganization of national awards (see p. 95).*
- *'Vouchers' for students to 'cash in' against the training of their choice (see p. 93).*
- *Parental choice of a school for their child.*

Social democracy and education and training

In contrast to the New Right, social democracy encourages more state intervention in policy making. It puts an emphasis on equality of opportunity and the provision of welfare. Social democracy also stresses the importance of the community – an attitude criticized by the former Prime Minister Margaret Thatcher when she declared that 'there is no such thing as society'.

Social democracy recognizes that not all individuals or groups begin from the same social standing, nor is there always a 'level-playing field' for all. The importance of the state in 'levelling' the playing field becomes a dominant theme in this ideology, particularly in equalizing opportunities to succeed. In order for this to happen, support structures need to be in place so that inequalities are deliberately levelled, often through positive discrimination. Government, from this perspective, becomes highly interventionist.

Key aspects of social democracy

- Individuals should be given equality of opportunity wherever possible.

- There should be state control and regulation to protect individual freedom.

- Interest groups should have their rights protected by law.

It is clear that a major focus of concern in social democracy is the role of education and training as a means of achieving equality. Social democrats see the role of teachers and trainers as crucial. They understand the complexities of social situations and are sensitive to individual needs and interests. Social democracy has also supported the view that school activities and curricula must be relevant to the particular student group for which it is intended.

Individual rights within education, therefore, have to be protected and maintained. This was the clear foundation upon which such major reports as Plowden (1967) and Warnock (1978) built their views, so that they could be carried out in practice in schools to the educational advancement of individuals, groups, and eventually society at large.

Social democrats also recognize that the importance of the group does not necessarily clash with its support for *individual* interests and needs. Policy making, for the social democrats, must be taken at a level which is in tune with individual needs and should not be politically centralized causing individuals to be marginalized. They therefore support decision-making at a level close to institutional and individual action (local authorities, trades unions, pressure and interest groups, etc.)and are unhappy about, for example, the reduced role of local education authorities (LEAs) in educational policy-making.

Liberalism and education and training

The liberal explanation of education and training rests on the assumption that individuals should be free to determine their own destiny. Such a view has its roots in various differing writers such as Rousseau and Locke, the political propaganda of Tom Paine and the economic writings of Adam Smith.

Liberalism, with its appeal to individual freedom, has been transformed into such diverse educational initiatives as the child-centred movement of the 1960s (see the humanistic school, p. 19), the local management of schools, and the neo-liberalism of market force theory in the 1980s (see p. 6).

An important aspect of liberalism is its insistence upon incremental and gradual (non-revolutionary) change within social institutions such as schools, which comes about as a response to individual reactions to social and technological developments. The rational way that this can be done – and liberals place great emphasis on rationality – is through the democratic processes: through the ballot box along with an independent judicial system. By this means, reform equates with social change. Reform is a central belief within liberalism. This distinguishes liberalism from neo-liberalism because of the emphasis the latter places upon the market, not democratic reform, as an intermediary between the individual and social change.

The critics of liberalism would suggest that ballot box democracy, whilst maintaining a humanist and fair-minded position, does not necessarily lead to independent representatives in Parliament formulating healthy policies. Critics such as Chitty (1992) and Lawton (1989) have also suggested that the liberal mission has been hijacked by party political interests which, at the same time as using the sentiments of individual freedom, have in fact, curtailed them.

The true liberal perspective would be one where individuals really did determine their own freedom within a free society. Perhaps, however, this is unrealistic given the fact that ours is not a completely free society. Our freedoms are necessarily restricted by others' freedoms: by community sanction (the agreement of others) and by a legal framework intended to protect society at large.

A fine balance needs to be struck between the rights of individuals and fairness for all on the one hand, and social and economic progress on the other. Too great a concentration on the latter may lead to an over-centralized system dominated by political decisions and individuals who are puppets of state policy. When educational correspondents of national newspapers (*Observer* 2 August 1992) claim that the UK has 'the most centralized, undemocratic and bureaucratic education system in the Western world', we can perhaps see how liberalism and its ideals may have already been used in the determination and manipulation of people's lives.

Working as a small group, draw up a list of educational changes which you think are the result of public pressure on politicians.
Discuss your list with another small group.

Ideology into legislation

The following Education Acts inevitably reflect different aspects of ideology. Increasingly the commitment to a single ideological view has characterized government policy, recommendations and statutes (laws). Although it is possible to outline features of these acts, it is important to recognize that only a close reading or commentary would reveal all such aspects.

Table 1.2   Recent educational legislation.

Concern	*Legislation Established*
1944 Education Act	
Access to secondary education	Secondary education for all
Progression through schooling	Schooling should be a continuous process: primary-secondary-FE/HE
Relevance of subjects taught	Tripartite system: Grammar, Technical and Secondary Modern Schools
1979 White Paper	Secondary organization LEAs no longer required to organize on comprehensive lines
1980 Education Act	
School governance	Committee of Enquiry on school governors in order to make schools more accountable to the public they serve
Individual freedom	Parents to have rights to express a preference about their child's school
1988 Education Reform Act	
Standards	Setting up a national inspection body to replace HMI
	A National Curriculum and Assessment programme
	Setting up national Teacher Appraisal schemes
Freedom	Schools able to 'opt out' of LEA control and go for grant-maintained status
Choice	Schools to manage their own funds through local management formulas
	Parents given extended rights to choose a school for their child
	Extending choice of schools by setting up the City Technology Colleges (see page 91)
1992 Education (Schools) Act	Standards Removal of Powers of inspection/advice from LEAs
1992 White Paper	
Quality	Government-appointed advisors to identify and remedy underachieving schools
	Schools to specialise in 'strong subject areas'
Freedom	'Opting out' process to be streamlined
Choice	Extending choice of school with the Technical Schools initiative

Discuss the changes in concerns between those of the 1944 Education Act and all other concerns from 1979 to the present day. Is a significant change in emphasis detectable?

Sociological perspectives

On a more theoretical level, it is important to analyse developments in education by peering beneath the ideology at how such changes are explained by sociology.

At a simple level, we may wish to say that there is a basic distinction between conflict theories and consensus theories – conflict theories see opposition as inevitable while consensus theories are based on the idea of a general agreement between people and groups holding differing views of society. However, some theorists see this definition as being too simplistic.

 Consider either how our outline of the market and its effects or the views of those defending social democracy relate to conflict or consensus perspectives.

Functionalism

Functionalism is based on the notion of social consensus. It sees social organization as possessing many similarities to the physical make-up of an animal's body. Both an animal's body and society consist of distinguishable parts (legs, eyes, etc. for the one, the church, family, etc. for the other). In both animals and society all parts play some clear role – that is, they fulfil a function (on one hand movement, sight, etc., and on the other social integration, human reproduction, etc.). In both a body and society, too, the different parts act together to form a system which (usually) operates smoothly to fulfil the goals of the whole.

Key aspects of functionalism

The functionalists maintain that:

- societies are made up of social institutions (the parts);
- which perform identifiable functions;
- and together make up the social system (the interacting whole).

So functionalism, at least in its early days (the end of the last century and the first half of this one), tended to see everything which existed in society as fulfilling some sort of function. As in the animal kingdom, there was no room for dead weight – anything which was of no use was eliminated by natural selection.

As applied to the study of education, functionalism takes the view that the education system performs the important function of socialization. The curriculum, particularly at school, should reflect and propagate the common culture to ensure that all members of society act out their particular roles in society's interests. The job of the teacher is to transmit this common culture:

> The teacher must therefore be committed to presenting [the rule], not as his own personal doing, but as a moral power superior to him, and of which he is an instrument, not the author. He must make the student understand that it imposes itself on him as it does on them; that he cannot remove or modify it; that he is constrained to apply it and that it dominates him and obliges him as it obliges them.
>
> (Durkheim 1956)

In all this the child is an empty vessel: a 'mug' waiting to be filled by the teacher's 'jug'.

Society finds itself with each new generation, faced with a *tabula rasa* [clean slate], very nearly, on which it must build anew. To the egoistic and asocial being that has just been born it must, as rapidly as possible, add another, capable of leading a moral and social life. Such is the work of education.

(Durkheim 1956)

Teachers, in other words, are strictly in charge and should treat their classes as whole items, rather than deal with the individuals in them.

Since Durkheim's death, modern functionalists such as Talcott Parsons have built on his ideas. Parsons agrees that the education system is important in providing a basis for socialization. He also stresses the function it performs in allocating individuals to their social roles. According to Parsons, through the examination system which awards qualifications according to merit, individuals are filtered so that they can then be allocated to the most appropriate jobs for them. This is the function of placement. The education system also provides the skills, values and attitudes that individuals will need to do their jobs properly and contribute as much as possible to the economy.

Carr and Kemmis (1986) felt that until the end of the 1960s it was generally agreed that functionalism provided the clearest and most appropriate framework for the study of education: it seemed to make particular sense to the academic community of theorists and educational analysts at that time. Nowadays it is no longer so widely accepted. However, although many policy makers are probably not aware of the academic work on functionalism as such, much of what they do was and is often informed by ideas close to functionalist ones. For example, the Robbins Report of 1963 on the future of higher education (HE) in Britain began by saying that it had four functions:

- instruction in occupational skills (to develop the nation's economy);

- the promotion of the powers of the mind (to develop the intellect of the person);

- the advancement of learning (to develop knowledge);

- the transmission of a common culture and common standards of citizenship (to develop society).

More recently policy makers have been keen that the education system should transmit a particular set of norms and values such as independence, hard work, and achievement. The Enterprise in Higher Education initiative (see p. 93) is a good example of this school of thought.

Policy makers also want the education system to reward individuals who operate according to these norms. The examination system is one way in which it does this. As 'gate-keepers' to employment and HE, the examination boards provide guidelines not only to the intellectual levels of achievement, but also to the form examinations should take. Therefore, the examination boards define and recognize acceptable performance. They are important in determining exactly how the placement function operates.

Particular forms of testing and examinations are popular among Conservative policy makers especially. Which ones and why?

The National Curriculum provides a good example of functionalist ideas being translated into policy. The 1988 Education Act in which it was introduced says:

> It shall be the duty of the Secretary of State, of every LEA, and of every governing body or head teacher of a maintained school, to exercise their functions. . . with a view to securing that the curriculum satisfies these requirements: that it should be a balanced and broadly based curriculum which promotes the spiritual, moral, cultural, mental and physical development of pupils at the school and of society, and prepares such pupils for the opportunities, responsibilities and experiences of adult life.

> (National Curriculum Council 1989)

Again we see in this the functionalist idea that the education system should transmit a common set of norms and values, and should fulfil a placement function.

 What criticisms do you have of this aim of the National Curriculum? Is a national curriculum the best way to achieve this aim?

Marxism

> **Marxism** sees society as inevitably divided into competitive classes, one which owns the means of production (land, factories, etc.) and the other which does not. Human history is largely driven by the clash between these opposing classes. Both they and the nature of the economy and society change over time after periods of crisis and revolution, but class conflict is constant until the dawning of communist society.

Marxists point to the inadequacy of liberalism as an explanation of society in that it sets too great a store by 'reform', whilst ignoring the political and ideological dynamics which constitute 'the struggle' between capitalism and interests located within social institutions such as schools and colleges. Equally, Marxists claim that the liberal idea that individuals are born free and can make rational decisions does not recognize that most people have never been free from the decisions of certain dominant groups.

For Marxists, all of the social life of individuals within capitalism is coloured by their relationship to the industrial and economic production process, be they machine-hands, office workers, teachers, housewives or the children of any of these groups.

Like the functionalists, Marxists agree that education is functional in that it maintains the dominance of certain powerful groups in society. Unlike the functionalists, however, Marxists do not believe that it works for the benefit of all. Instead they argue that the education system sustains one small group's ideas about appropriate forms of schooling and assumptions about what knowledge is. The system also maintains different levels of access to knowledge for different groups and thereby prohibits the widespread dissemination of knowledge to everyone (which could be dangerous for the dominant group).

> Assume a particular state of development in the production faculties of man and you will get a corresponding form of commerce and consumption. Assume particular degrees of development of production, commerce

and consumption and you will have a corresponding form of social constitution, a corresponding organization of the family, of orders or of classes, in a word, a corresponding civil society.

(Marx and Engels 1970)

In order for us to clarify this quotation, it might be useful to break it down into constituent parts and to provide an interpretation for each part.

Table 1.3	A Marxist Interpretation
Marx	*Interpretation*
. . . a particular state of development	For example: Capitalism
. . . corresponding form of commerce and consumption	Sub-division of society into social classes
. . . corresponding civil society	Institutions in society organized to cater for the needs of differing social classes (e.g. education

The form and content of educational transmission embody class ideologies.

(Bernstein 1975)

Think back to your own educational life in infant, primary and secondary school. Underneath two headings – 'Form' and 'Content' – recollect instances where the way you were taught (Form) and what you were taught (Content) reflect a social class bias in any way. Did this bias change from school to school in your experience?

Compare your recollections in terms of social class.

Although both the previous perspectives are functionalist to a degree, Marxists and functionalists have a different starting point for their principles. Whereas the functionalists begin with the expectation of social order through consensus, Marxists begin with the express purpose of liberating individuals through conflict.

One of Marxism's most important contributions has been to highlight the fact that knowledge itself is not 'disinterested': it is linked to the interests of those who produce and disseminate it – the dominant social class in society. Schools, therefore, form part of the socialization process which attempts to ensure conformity to an ideology which serves to deflect attention away from the reality of exploitation practised by the dominant classes. Marx refers to this as false consciousness.

In the twentieth century many neo-Marxist educationalists have reconstructed the original works of Marx in the light of social change. For example, Basil Bernstein's work on social class and education has argued that children are socialized at an early age to view knowledge itself as property or commodity to be stored, saved and privately invested.

- *horror films;*
- *popular romantic novels;*
- *the climate of the USA;*
- *pop music;*
- *computer games;*
- *fossil remains;*
- *stamps of the world;*
- *teddy bears.*

Compare your scores with those of others. How close were they?

For Young it is not just the *type* of knowledge, but the *way it is thought about* that is important. For example, popular romantic novels could be memorized or studied from sociological or literary points of view.

 How could your low scorers be transformed into high scorers and vice versa?

The critics of this new sociology of education seized on what they saw as its fundamental drawback: its implications for educational policy. If, as Young seemed to be arguing, all knowledge was as good as all other knowledge, then what should teachers teach, if anything? Those teachers who were convinced by these arguments during their training were reluctant to impose alien knowledge on students. They wanted to draw on and value the interests and experiences of students themselves and the cultures they came from.

From the critics' point of view this has at least two drawbacks.

1 It seriously disadvantages the students because they need to gain qualifications which are awarded on the basis of high-status knowledge and will suffer if they do not.

2 The nation as a whole will be disadvantaged because the education system would no longer be transmitting the important knowledge and skills that the nation needs.

One area in particular has generated considerable heated discussion in the early 1990s – the teaching of English. The argument was over the relative status of standard English, i.e. the form of English used by the Queen, newscasters and on Radio 4, compared to non-standard varieties which use grammatical forms and vocabulary that would be considered 'wrong' in standard English. From a relativist point of view such as Young's, both forms of English should be given equal status. From a more traditional perspective, and from the government's, only standard English should be taught to and accepted from pupils in schools.

> **Relativism** is the idea that there are no absolute standards of 'truth' or 'correctness'. Knowledge and ideas of right and wrong are generated by different social groups and all are of equal value.

Symbolic interactionism

As sociological theories, functionalism and Marxism address society-wide implications of individual human activity and build large-scale (macro) themes from them. An alternative theory which focuses exclusively upon individual activity within a specific context is symbolic interactionism.

> **Symbolic interactionism** is a theory which argues that social meaning is developed through language or alternative interaction with others, as a consequence of which individual roles are learned and reinforced.

To the symbolic interactionist, meanings are developed within the individual but have their beginnings in social relations and interactions between people. George Herbert Mead, the American founding father of symbolic interactionism, argued that the mind of the individual functions as the internalization of the social process through which meaning emerges.

It is not surprising to learn that symbolic interactionism emerged in the USA (and developed in Chicago) where individualist thinking is valued above class/group-based theories which have traditionally had their roots in European thought. Mead's famous maxim summarizes this: 'to exist or to be, is to know that one is in interaction' (Mead 1934).

The development of roles in society goes on, for the symbolic interactionist, at all ages and in all institutions. In schools through play, language and social interaction, children develop attitudes and social mores (normal patterns of behaviour). These are determined by the individual's realization that other points of view exist outside of his or her own. This development has much in common with developmental aspects of the work of the child psychologist Piaget (see p. 27) in that an individual has a particular point of view, but contrasts it with another's point of view in order to grow and develop.

Some individuals have special importance in the shaping of our lives. Mead called these 'significant others' and it is these people who provide ways of perceiving and defining the world. We borrow from their standards and judgements, and their views of what is real. We do this most effectively through language. Language is an important dimension in the formation of 'the self'.

However, 'the self' is also an amalgamation of all those experiences a person has had in the past. When someone takes on a role, then, that role is filtered through the recipient's self-concept and is a continuing process. From this perspective, individuals are viewed as active participants in the social world, not passively accepting a supposed consensus (as in functionalism, see p. 10), or viewing themselves as individuals subject to uncontrollable social forces.

By developing a role through interaction with others, the children and adults increasingly develop the ability to see themselves as social beings. Mead, therefore, distinguishes between the I (the response of the individual to the attitudes of others) and the me (the organized set of attitudes which make up a social identity).

Key aspects of symbolic interactionism

Symbolic interactionism focuses on:

- the individual use and interpretation of symbols, suggesting that people consciously construct social life by generating meanings and making interpretations within social groups;

- a concern with the ways in which individuals make sense of, analyse or interpret any given situation;

- subjectivity;

- the processes, not the structures, in social life.

The implications of symbolic interactionism for education have been to re-emphasize the importance of the micro (the smaller scale) and, in particular, the processes and interactions which take place in the formation of the social reality of education. For example, the student will learn not only through student–teacher contact within the teaching lesson, but also through interaction with other students about how to *be* a student, how to view teachers, how to interpret 'learning', 'failure', 'achievement' and many other aspects of education processes.

The experience of being educated (in a very wide sense) is a result of interactions which become symbolic of a view of society and its institutions. The individual person may or may not subscribe to these views and constantly (but usually unconsciously) works at his or her definition of the situation.

The formation of subcultures within schools and colleges, of group identities (including that of the teaching staff) and of ways of coping with symbolic hierarchies (swots, dossers, etc.) are all a result of interaction. These processes determine much that goes on in schools and colleges, especially the educational opportunities of students in them.

List a number of ways in which you:
1) negatively and
2) positively

interact with others at your school. (This may include all adults.)

Compare your answers from the pairs exercise and then discuss the roles that are developed in your school by addressing the following questions.
1) Is there more than a single definition of a student's role?
2) How do such roles determine your place in the process of learning and success at school?
3) How are roles played by school girls different to those played by school boys?
4) Does your role 'fit' with the role of all your teachers?

Educational perspectives

It should be clear that the ideology of those who make decisions in society strongly influences educational policy and practice and thereby the experiences of those participating in teaching and learning. This is as true for the classroom as it is for the school or the education system as a whole. Also, as theorists from functionalist and Marxist traditions would agree, the very activity of learning itself is influenced by the approach to learning which the child and the teacher decide (or are forced to decide) to make.

There are various learning theories which come out of the different perspectives and which represent various assumptions about the child, the learning process, the curriculum, and appropriate social action. What is more, policy can never be completely dissociated from learning theory: each Education Act contains within its legislation a theory about what a pupil or student is entitled to expect from the education system. There are also assumptions about appropriate experiences they should have within school and college life, as well as what and how they should learn and for what purposes. These are, in short, assumptions about who or what is at the heart of education. However, even the policy makers may disagree:

> The child is at the heart of education.
>
> (Plowden Report 1967)

> The curriculum lies at the heart of education.
>
> (National Curriculum Council 1992)

> At the heart of the education process lies assessment.
>
> (DES 1988)

Discuss the following questions.
1) Can all of the quotations above be correct?
2) What would you say was at the heart of primary school education?
3) What would you say was at the heart of secondary school education?
4) What would you say is at the heart of vocational education and training?

In the same way as most recent educational decisions have been politicized, the focus on learning itself has been subject to policy attention. This was clearly so in debates in the past about children with differing, 'natural' learning orientations (Spens Report 1939), but was more recently politicized as a part of the 'back to basics' Conservative campaign of 1994, which called for a return to traditional values in teaching and learning. The following extract from a newspaper article makes this clear:

> Yet another policy shake-up is promised. A confidential Downing Street strategy document – leaked in yesterday's *Sunday Times* – calls on ministers to frame new 'back to basics' policies based on 'traditional values, common sense and a concern for the citizen'. This new approach is meant to challenge 'a number of the social orthodoxies that took root in the 1960s. . .' particularly 'those areas of social policy where theorists dragged professionals and administrators furthest from common sense'. Law and order, education, welfare and social work will all be included.
>
> (*Guardian* 8 November 1993)

Schools of psychology with different perspectives approach such debates in contrasting ways.

The humanistic school

The humanistic approach includes a number of theories which share a common emphasis on the individual's potential for self-direction and freedom of choice. They

Figure 1.5

The student centred school

are concerned with the 'self' and share a positive perception of the individual's natural tendency towards growth and self-actualization.

Key aspects of the humanistic school

- A concentration on the development of the 'self'.

- Individuals have the greatest understanding of their own development.

- Self-knowledge is the basis of personality and growth.

- Positive self-regard promotes learning.

This perspective places great value on an individual's right to interpret the world as he or she sees fit, and although originally based on the study of personality, humanistic theories have many implications for education and teaching.

Psychologists from different schools have conflicting views on how motives for action originate and operate. The humanistic psychologists, and Abraham Maslow in particular, argue that human beings are naturally inclined to seek beauty, truth and the fullest possible development of their own potential. Self-actualization represents this self-fulfilment and is achieved through positive self-regard, motivation and the individual freedom to learn.

Maslow felt that the individual had to satisfy a hierarchy of needs in order to self-actualize. These needs included those of education. However, it is important to recognize that needs that are low in the hierarchy must be at least partially satisfied before the higher ones can be.

This has important implications for the teacher, such as:

- Is the learner physiologically ready (or instead is the learner hungry? tired? disabled?)

- Is the learning environment adequate and reassuring?

- Is the learner emotionally stable?

- Is the learner valued intellectually by the teacher and by peers?

Figure 1.6

Maslow's hierarchy of needs

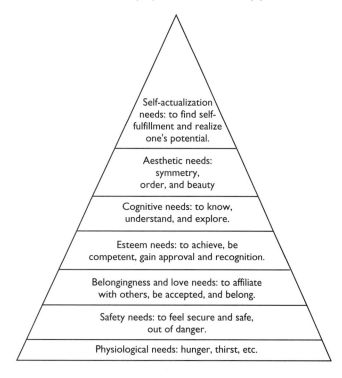

Maslow (1954, 1967) was able to outline certain features which characterize the self-actualizer. He or she:

- perceives reality efficiently and is able to tolerate uncertainty;

- is spontaneous in thought and behaviour;

- is problem-centred rather than self-centred;

- is highly creative;

- is capable of deep appreciation of the basic experiences of life;

- is able to look at life from an objective viewpoint.

Characteristics such as these provide the foundations for a child-centred view of learning in school which reached a highwater mark with the Plowden Report (1967) which stressed that the focus in education should be upon the child, and not upon the curriculum or the teacher:

> All learning calls for organization of material or of behaviour on the part of the learner and the learner has to adapt himself and is altered by this process. . . each new experience re-organizes, however slightly, the structure of the mind and contributes to the child's world picture.
>
> (Plowden Report: Section 521)

The child is the agent of his own learning.

(Plowden Report: Section 529)

The other main theorist of the humanistic school was Carl Rogers who developed psychological treatments within a client-centred therapy. The non-threatening relationship envisaged between therapist and patient creates freedom for the individual to express feelings, develop ideas and grow intellectually.

In the same way, child-centred philosophies of learning in the classroom (developed, for example, by the French philosopher Jean-Jacques Rousseau and the American educationalist John Dewey) attempt to develop independence, problem-solving and creativity. Motivation should come from within the child and not from external rewards (see behaviourism, below). There should be a high regard for the child, not as inferior to the teacher or a blank slate upon which to write another's life, but as 'a person of unconditional self-worth; of value no matter what his condition, his behaviour or his feelings' (Rogers 1951). This contrasts markedly with the functionalist viewpoint.

While Education Acts are not formulated to include psychological theories like Maslow's or Rogers', commissioned reports such as Plowden or Warnock take account of such theories in making their recommendations. In turn, these ideas find their way into the classroom (particularly those of infant and primary education) and profoundly influence the relationships between teacher and child, changing them from one where the child is a passive recipient of knowledge to a relationship where the teacher becomes the facilitator of the child's active learning.

From the government's perspective, these ideas have become too pervasive. It went to the lengths of commissioning a report from the so-called 'three wise men' in 1991. It seems that the intention was to attack education practices in schools, rather than to conduct a serious study. The three wise men were carefully selected so that this would be the result and they were given only a few months to write the report. The DES press release that was issued with the report when it was published claimed that it did attack current education practices. Unfortunately for the government, the authors disagreed with this assessment.

This activity should be carried out in pairs. Think about your own school careers. Have you always experienced 'unconditional self-worth' in your relationships with teachers or others?

Tell each other about:

1) one incident when you did experience unconditional self-worth and

2) one when you did not.

Did being treated positively help you to learn?

Behaviourism

Mind, consciousness, souls and ghosts were all the same to John B. Watson, one of the founding fathers of behaviourism – none of them had any place in natural science. Psychology, he felt, should only be the study of objective behaviour in order to predict or explain it. Human beings, in this way, are no different from any other observable living animal.

Learning, for behaviourists, involves a relatively permanent change in behaviour caused by the reorganization of skills, habits and tendencies which already exist. Learning must always be a response to an outside stimulus and can be subdivided into two types: classical and operant conditioning.

Classical conditioning

Whilst studying the relatively automatic reflexes associated with digestion, the psychologist Ivan Pavlov noticed that a dog salivated not just when food was in its mouth but also at the sight of food. The relationship between the sight of food and salivation, he felt, had been learned and thereby was a conditioned response. He then taught the dog to salivate at the sight (or sound) of other signals which were followed by the reward of meat (the conditioned stimulus). The dog then salivated at the signal alone. However, with the withdrawal of reward at the signal, the response gradually became extinct.

This process is known as classical conditioning.

Figure 1.7

Pavlov's dog – an example of classical conditioning

Operant conditioning

In classical conditioning there is a natural relationship between stimulus (meat/signal) and response (salivation). In operant conditioning no such 'natural' relationship exists. However, learning can still take place and animals can be taught to perform activities not normally associated with the reward. To describe this kind of learning, the famous psychologist B.F. Skinner introduced the concept of operant conditioning because the subject 'operates' on the environment to produce some effect.

In experiments, hungry rats accidentally trigger the reward of a food supply in an otherwise empty box. This reward reinforces repeated triggering of the response. This is the Law of Effect (Thorndike 1911) whereby acts which are rewarded (reinforced) tend to be repeated and acts which are not reinforced tend to die out. Behaviour, in this way, can be modified or 'shaped' by external control.

The implications of the behaviourist view for education are immediately clear as demonstrated in repeated classroom exercises, drills and practices, rewards and punishments. We can summarize what behaviourism means for teaching in the following series of steps teachers should follow:

1 Define the objectives: what do you want students to be able to *do* after they have been taught? (Stick to observable behaviour only.)

2 Identify effective reinforcers: what rewards will be attractive to students so that they will do what you want?

3 Observe each student's initial behaviour. What can they do before you start teaching them?

4 Tell the student what to do in small steps; shape their behaviour gradually.

5 Immediately reinforce performances which are close to what you want. However, gradually make it more and more difficult to achieve a reward so the student has to try harder each time.

6 At the end, assess the student. Can she or he achieve the desired performance? If not, go back to the necessary stage again.

 What is your view of this model of teaching and learning?

Unfortunately for those teachers trying to apply behaviourism, the relationship between rewards and desired behaviour is not as simple as it may appear. The 'Peanuts' cartoon below illustrates one unfortunate consequence of dependence on reward, for example.

Figure 1.8

Learning is its own reward

Table 1.4	Behavioural teaching and learning style	
	Appropriate	*Inappropriate*
English grammar		
Music practice		
Music theory		
Art		
Mathematics		
History		
English Literature		
French		
Science		

 Use Table 1.4 to mark the school subjects as being appropriate or inappropriate to a behavioural teaching and learning style (i.e. drills and practices, correct responses, right answers, rewards and punishments).
Compare your conclusions with a partner.

Certainly reward works for the automatic correct stimulus (right answers). But do you think we should translate a reward system to activities which should, by their nature, be intrinsically rewarding? Is anything which you learn intrinsically rewarding ?

The Hungarian philosopher and novelist Arthur Koestler argued that behaviourism had reversed the anthropomorphic fallacy: 'ascribing to animals human faculties and sentiments. . . it has substituted the anthropomorphic view of the rat with a ratomorphic view of man'. Others have argued against the denial of a conscious experience which mediates between the senses, the mind and behaviour, and that to talk about 'mind' is not just to talk simply about 'behaviour' but involves something more.

Unlike the humanistic position, behaviourism has had policy implications, most clearly in government support for programmed learning in the 1950s, for testing (and reward) in the National Curriculum, and in the long-standing debate about corporal punishment in schools. In training, the growing competence movement of the 1990s has clear behavioural undertones.

This can be seen in the list of 'basic abilities' as specified in the City and Guilds Vocational Preparation Course:

On completion of the training programme, the trainee should be able to:

Health and safety

Maintain high safety standards for premises, equipment and stock, taking due regard for the safety of customers and fellow workers.

Hygiene

Observe and carry out health and hygiene regulations relating to self, equipment, goods and environment.

Distribution organisation

Indicate an understanding of the importance of the distributive industry nationally and locally and identify the diversities of the industry.

Stock

Deal correctly with procedures affecting stock receipt, issue, control and care.

Cash handling

Organise and handle personal cash, taking into account the short-term and long-term effects of saving and borrowing.

Cash payment methods

Follow set procedures, for receiving payments by cash, cheques, credit cards, giving change and receipts, recording payments and balancing totals.

Information technology

Operate and use applications of computer and information technology relevant to the distributive industry (see Core Skills Part II) and demonstrate an appreciation of the implications of new technology to the distributive industry.

Customer service

Act appropriately in situations involving customers and retain the good-will of customers.

Customer selling

Serve and sell to customers in order to create business and promote custom/success.

Security

Carry out the functions necessary for effective operation of security procedures.

Sales administration

Deal competently with the paperwork a sales assistant is likely to encounter.

Product categories – Commodity groups

Demonstrate a knowledge of commodity groups.

Product categories – Knowledge by sector

Demonstrate a sector knowledge of products identifying customer benefits and using information from a variety of sources.

Product categories – Display by sector

Display sector products effectively according to company policy.

Legislation – Consumer/retail

Observe and promote the relevant rights and obligations of manufacturers, distributors and customers.

Stock room

Deal correctly with procedures affecting stock checking, handling and storage for:

* retailing

* wholesaling.

Specific job skills

Carry out the functions necessary for effective performance in a specialised skill area, eg butchery, fresh produce.

Transportation/location

Operate systems and procedures necessary for the transportation of goods to identified locations on time for:

* retailing and/or

* wholesaling.

Consumer/competitor knowledge

Conduct a survey of consumers/competitors for a specific company.

Business viability

Demonstrate a working knowledge of the accountancy, book-keeping systems and procedures which enable a business performance to be analysed.

Distribution trends

Show an understanding of the trends in distribution.

Retailing and the economy

Show an understanding of the effect of retailing on the local and national economy, and its relationship with the local community.

Mutuality and self-help organisations

Show an understanding of the various voluntary, mutual and self-help organisations within the distribution sector.

Information gathering

Collect and collate oral and written information/instructions effectively

Communications – including working with others

Establish and maintain effective communications and working relationships with others.

Legislation – employment

Demonstrate a working knowledge and understanding of employment legislation.

Reproduced with the permission of the Controller of HMSO from: *Illustrative Scheme for the Distributive Industry*, MSC, 1986

This list of competences can be 'observed to be' accomplished (or not as the case may be). This is basically a behavioural process and is therefore subject to criticisms of tokenism, narrowness and training rather than education. Many of the NVQ programmes have been similarly criticized for being strong on practical behaviours but weak on knowledge and understanding. In the National Curriculum, too, the influence of behaviourism is clear. For example the Statements of Attainment, which specify what pupils should be able to do at different stages in school, are phrased in a behaviourist way. For example, the English syllabus on *Speaking and Listening* states that pupils should be able to:

Respond appropriately to simple instructions given by a teacher. . .

Convey accurately a simple message. . .

Listen attentively to stories and poems and talk about them. . .

Take an active part in group discussion, displaying sensitivity, listening critically and being self-critical. . .

 Discuss the hypothesis (the starting point for further investigation) that behaviourism is an appropriate teaching and learning approach for vocational training but not for general education.

The structural model

Jean Piaget attempted to trace the process of socialization within a child through various developmental discontinuities which had long been acknowledged. This has stimulated a great deal of research and 'has done the most to make a stage concept of development possible' (Hilgard 1975).

A stage of development usually defines a set of possible behaviours which occur together. As a group they differ appreciably from the quality of behaviours in earlier or later stages.

Piaget's stages are shown in Table 1.5

Table 1.5	Piaget's stages of development	
Stage	*Approx. age*	*Characterization*
1. Sensorimotor	Birth –2 years	Infant differentiates him/her self from objects, becomes aware of his actions and their affects
2. Preoperational	2–7 years	Uses language and represents objects by images and words. Is still egocentric. Classifies objects by single important features.
3. Concrete operational	7–12 years	Is capable of logical thought. Is able to understand number, mass and weight. Can classify objects and understand relational terms.
4. Formal operational	12 and up	Can think in abstract terms. can follow logical propositions and reason by hypothesis. Becomes concerned with ideological problems.

This psychological perspective has had an enormous influence upon policy in terms of the different ages at which children attend school and the age of transfer between schools. Furthermore the implications of Piaget's work have been critical in determining the nature of activities which children are considered able to perform at certain ages. This has stimulated much debate, and a great deal of curriculum design (and re-design) looked to the structural model for guidance and as a rationale for progression. Considerations such as these may have informed the National Curriculum working parties, for example, in their recommendations for progression through school subjects.

Conclusion

In this chapter we have outlined the nature of policy making, first through ideological and then through theoretical perspectives. It is clear that although no absolute lines can be drawn between them (for example between New Right thinking and functionalism), certain political tendencies since the mid 1970s have promoted some ideologies and theories whilst relegating others to insignificance.

In response to economic pressures, the New Right has presented education and training with an ideology which avoids the costs and compromises of social democracy. It also sets out an agenda to sustain professional and non-professional activities and processes. Market forces and individualism have combined to promote a certain aspect of New Right thinking (neo-liberalism) which has swept all before it by eliminating other tiers of decision-making which may have stood in its way.

In this sense, the ideology of the New Right has, to some degree, determined the parameters for education and training. It has also determined which theoretical perspectives are considered the most appropriate. For instance, it is more functional than interactive, and it has tended towards the behaviouristic rather than towards the humanistic. As such it has had effects on educational practice in all sectors from primary schools through to universities and still, largely, calls the tune.

Until an alternative and robust ideology emerges to influence the processes of education, or until individuals reject the notions of the market at the ballot box, aspects of New Right thinking will continue to have an effect on all our lives within education and training.

Match the quotes in the first list to the perspective in the second list. (The answers are given at the end of the chapter.)
1 'Children need to be themselves, to live with other children and with grown-ups, to learn from their environment, to enjoy the present, to get ready for the future, to create and to love, to learn to face adversity, to behave responsibly, in a word, to be human beings.'
2 'We believe all parents have the right to choice in education – not only those who can afford school fees. . . We believe that young people [after 16] should be free to choose between college, work-based training and sixth form studies.'
3 'Every society. . . must employ some systematic way of selecting individuals in accordance with their merits, potentialities or, sometimes (as in a customary division of labour between the sexes), their traditional status. This is necessary so that appropriate kinds of education, instruction and training can be given. . . '
4 'The educational system does not add to or subtract from the overall degree of inequality and repressive personal development. Rather, it is best understood as an institution which serves to perpetuate the social relationships of economic life through which these patterns are set by facilitating a smooth integration of youth into the labour force.'

5.

MATERIAL
FACTORS
ON SETTING

Gradualists
reform

SOCIAL STRUCTURE

AND HEGEMONY

Material constraint

School allocation patterns

CLASSROOM

Contradictory
roles

Dilemmas

Contradictory
roles

Dilemmas

TEACHER
ROLE
FACTORS

Social
interests
and
ideologies

Teacher
culture

TEACHER

CHILD

Child
culture

Social
interests
and
ideologies

CHILD
ROLE
FACTORS

Expectations

SELF

SELF

Expectations

Knowledge
perspectives

Knowledge
perspectives

INSTITUTIONAL BIAS

Social class
and cultural
resources

Social class
and cultural
resources

HISTORY

TEACHER
BIOGRAPHICAL
FACTORS

CHILD
BIOGRAPHICAL
FACTORS

a *New Right: The 1992 Conservative
   Election Manifesto*
b *Marxist: Bowles S. and Gintis H ;* Schooling in Capitalist America,
   Routledge, 1976
c *Social interactionist: Pollard A.;* A Social World in the Primary School,
   Holt Education, 1985
d *Humanistic: The Plowden Report*
e *Functionalist: Fletcher R.;* Education in Society, *Penguin, 1984*

Suggestions for further reading

Statham, J. *et al.* (1991) *The Education Fact File*, London: Hodder & Stoughton.
This is a very useful summary of legislation, official reports and information about the education system in general. It is an invaluable source of reference. Try to get the most recent edition for up-to-date information.
Paul Corrigan (1981) *Schooling the Smash Street Kids*, London: Macmillan, is a good example of the application of the 'new' sociology of education in a study of two schools. It is readable and interesting.
Donna Brandes (1986) *A Guide to Student-Centred Learning*, Oxford: Blackwell, gives a readable and interesting introduction to the humanistic view of education from a committed supporter of it.
The Centre for Policy Studies is a right-wing think tank on educational and other matters and has published a number of influential papers. A list is available from:

> Centre for Policy Studies
> 52 Rochester Row
> London
> SW1P 1JU
> (0171 828 1176).

For an interesting read about the politics behind the policy making on the National Curriculum see Graham (1993) *A Lesson for Us All?*, London: Routledge.
On the radical left the Hillcole group also publishes papers on education. These are available from:

> The Hillcole Group
> The Tufnell Press
> 47 Dalmeny Road
> London N7 0DY

Answers to the exercise on p. 29
1: d
2: a
3: e
4: b
5: c

2 Approaches to research in education

Paul Trowler

Figure 2.1

A valid educational research method?

 Write a list of as many methods as you can think of that could be used in educational research. When you have finished, compare your list with other students' answers and/or with Table 2.3 on p. 61. (There are fifteen methods listed there.)

Educational research is similar to research in other social sciences, particularly sociology, yet it does have some distinctive features. These concern the subjects it studies, the methods it uses and the way its results are used.

The subjects

Educational researchers tend to study formal educational institutions, despite the fact that, according to Alan Tough, around 80 per cent of adult education takes place in non-formal settings. Most attention is given to schools and little to further, adult or higher education (HE), vocational educational and training (VET) or education in commercial or medical settings. Educational research also tends to concentrate on teachers and teaching methods, on achievement and underachievement, and on gender and ethnicity. There is little research nowadays on class, student subcultures or alternative forms of education. Topics of research are often victims of fashion and political influence.

The methods

The methods of educational research used now tend to rely on qualitative rather than quantitative data: that is, on the researcher's interpretation of events rather than the statistical analysis of data about them. The contrast between older and newer approaches is seen in the differences between Bennett's and Skeggs' studies which we describe on the following pages.

Methodology

The suffix 'ology' means the study of something, so strictly speaking, methodology means 'the study of the use of methods'. However most people use it to mean both this and the actual methods themselves, so that 'methods' and 'methodology' are often used interchangeably. Other people, though, use 'methodology' to mean the general approach adopted by a researcher (e.g. an interpretive one or a positivist one) and 'method' to mean the research techniques they use (e.g. questionnaires or interviews).

Quantitative data are numerical, for example IQ test scores, the number (or percentage) of people who answered 'agree' to a statement, or the number of times the teacher asked a question in a class.

Qualitative data are, essentially, non-numerical. They could include verbal answers to interview questions, a picture drawn by a child, field notes written by an educational researcher, or a videotape of a lesson in a primary school.

Educational research often involves teachers as researchers so there is a direct involvement in the subject of study. Participant observation and, especially, action research, are very widely used in educational research. These frequently can have ethical, methodological and other consequences. Geoffrey Walford notes, for example, that researchers studying HE find it difficult to keep institutions anonymous (because there are comparatively few of them and they are very different) and that a researcher looking for promotion who is considering studying their own institution 'might think twice about the wisdom of such a research project'. In addition – more often than many other areas – educational research involves subjects who are not able to express themselves well and are in a position of low power and status compared to the researcher.

Action research is small-scale involvement in the world using research methods to study the effects of actions and making changes based on the results. An example is the *Improving Student Learning Project* described in the Preface.

The results

The results of educational research are often used politically. For example, Neville Bennett, at the time a researcher at Lancaster University, produced findings (see p. 37) which were given extensive publicity, including prime-time TV coverage, and were used to support the right-wing critique of 'progressivism'. However, when re-analysis of the data by Bennett himself and others undermined their findings, this was virtually ignored. More recently Professor Robin Alexander, one of the 'three wise men' commissioned by the government to report on primary school teaching, wrote an angry article in the *Guardian* in February 1992 complaining about 'political and media hype' surrounding the report, which had been misinterpreted as only critical of progressivism by both the DES and the media.

One reason why politicians and the media are interested in educational research findings is that they can be put into practice more easily than many other areas of social research and can have a real impact on both social policy and classroom practice. The reality, though, is that policy making is not a rational, step-by-step process with clear decision points which can be informed by research results. Policy making is a 'messy' process, and policy is more likely to be informed by ideology and politics than careful consideration of research output. This is the case even where large amounts of public money have been spent on research, as with the £10 million evaluation of Records of Achievement in schools exposed by James's study.

Obtaining the data

In this chapter we look at the methods of data collection used in educational research, concentrating our attention on the most characteristic ones. Before we analyse these in detail on pp. 41-61, we discuss some general considerations which researchers have to take into account when deciding upon a research method.

Data collection is concerned with methods of gathering primary data, for example through questionnaires or interviews.

Data analysis consists of *examining* the data collected, *reducing* it by categorizing, tabulating, or otherwise recombining it, *displaying* it in some more accessible form and finally *drawing conclusions* from it.

Sometimes a method (e.g. content analysis, which we discuss on p. 58) can be seen as both a way of data collection and data analysis.

Primary data means data which have been collected by the researcher specifically for the purposes of the research and which did not exist before, for example, answers to interview questions or responses to a questionnaire.

Secondary data are also used by the researcher, but they were already in existence, for example, the results of other studies, documents from the site of the research, or statistics collected by a government agency.

Qualitative secondary data are not in numerical form but consist of personal accounts, comments, stories and other sorts of material. These can be used to substantiate theories that the researcher is putting forward (e.g. by referring to historical accounts or quoting from autobiographies) or they can be worked on to provide evidence which is more substantial than anecdotal.

Positivist and interpretive perspectives

The methods a researcher chooses are largely a governed by three things:

1 the subject of study: the methods must be fit for the purpose or topic of research;

2 practical considerations like the resources available to the researcher;

3 the researcher's broad approach to the social world. To simplify this, researchers can be placed somewhere on a continuum:

Positivist————————Interpretive

The positivist approach

Positivists tend to see social behaviour as regular and patterned. People play social *roles* (e.g. 'teacher', 'daughter', 'consumer') which they learn in social institutions (e.g. schools, the family, the mass media). Consequently behaviour is quite predictable – at least when the behaviour of a large number of people is studied – and patterns can be determined. Because of this it is perfectly possible to use similar methods in the study of education to those used in a natural science like physics. Such methods may include experiments, searches for correlations between phenomena and the discovery of 'laws' of behaviour which are expressed in the form: 'if A happens in circumstances Z, then Y always follows'. To establish these laws the hypothetico-deductive model is often used.

The **hypothetico-deductive model** is a model of knowledge creation based on the methods supposedly used in the natural sciences. Here the scientist:

- observes the natural world;
- forms a hypothesis about its operation: a guess at the reasons for the observed phenomena;
- predicts an event which would happen if the hypothesis were true (which forms the basis of an experiment);
- tests the validity of the hypothesis by searching for the predicted event under carefully controlled conditions;
- develops a theory which can be subjected to further testing until it is proven to be true and becomes a 'law'.

Karl Popper, a philosopher of science, argues for a variant of this. He suggests that we can never prove anything to be universally true since at some point in the future we may discover contradictory evidence. Thus researchers following the hypothetico-deductive approach should aim to disprove their hypothesis rather than prove it – to test it to destruction. We know we can have more faith in hypotheses which can stand up to these tests than those which cannot, although universal 'laws' are impossible.

The interpretivist approach

Interpretivists, in contrast, see free will as more important than positivists do. They see social reality as much more in flux, with people interpreting 'what is going on' in different ways. These interpretations actually have an effect on the social world itself. From this perspective people's attitudes, beliefs and values are not just shaped by the social world (as positivists tend to believe) – they help shape it too.

For this reason interpretivists believe it is very important to study and understand these values and attitudes. The methods used to do this are different from those of the natural sciences, which do not need to study such things. In addition, the results of research cannot be expressed as 'laws'. Instead the aim of research is to illuminate social reality and to help us understand parts of it: often quite small and very specific parts. The grounded theory approach is often used to do this.

The **grounded theory** approach comes from the work of Glaser and Strauss and is the 'opposite' approach to the hypothetico-deductive model. Here the researcher goes in to the field without strong hypotheses to test. Instead the part of reality being observed (e.g. a single school) is examined in great detail and, as far as possible, without preconceptions. Ideas, themes and concepts are allowed to emerge from this observation and a theory is developed from these.

This approach is inductive rather than deductive, i.e. ideas and theory come from an open observation of reality rather than from an imposed preconception of reality. The researcher here is like an anthropologist studying a tribal society about which she or he has no prior knowledge – they try to understand it through what is seen and heard.

According to Fetterman, **ethnography**:

> is the art and science of describing a group or culture. The description may be of a small tribal group in some exotic land or a classroom in middle class suburbia.
>
> (Fetterman 1989)

Hitchcock and Hughes say it involves:

1 producing a description of the cultural knowledge of a group;

2 describing the activities of the group from its members' point of view;

3 describing the key characteristics defining membership of a group;

4 describing and analysing patterns of social interaction that the group experiences;

5 providing as far as possible 'insider accounts';

6 the development of theory (though some ethnographers limit themselves to description).

Ethnography is therefore a good example of an interpretivist approach.

The different ends of the positivist/interpretivist spectrum are best illustrated by examples. To do this we have chosen a study conducted by Neville Bennett (on the positivist side) and one by Bev Skeggs (on the interpretive side).

A positivist case study

Bennett *et al.*'s study started with the hypothesis that some teaching styles (e.g. formal/traditional or informal/progressive) are more effective than others. This was translated into two research questions:

1 Do differences in teaching styles make a difference to the rate of intellectual and social development of primary school pupils?

2 Do different types of primary school pupils perform better under certain teaching styles?

The fieldwork

The research was conducted in the following stages:

1 The researchers analysed the literature and developed descriptions of different

teaching styles (twelve were identified, ranging from very formal to very informal). They also developed a teaching-style questionnaire from these descriptions.

2 They sent a teaching-style questionnaire to a representative sample of teachers in 871 schools in Lancashire and Cumbria, and used the responses to group teachers into the twelve categories.

3 They then checked their allocation of groups by observing a sample of teachers from each category. This was done by researchers and LEA advisers. (There was an 80 per cent correspondence between their descriptions and the groupings from questionnaire.)

4 They selected thirty-seven teachers as ideal examples of each category. They pre-tested their pupils (1,100) on a wide range of abilities. After one school year they conducted a post-test.

5 Then they conducted a quantitative analysis (teachers' marking and content analysis) of pupils' writing for scores on imagination, description, punctuation and spelling.

6 The researchers then developed and administered a personality test for these pupils.

7 They used the responses to group pupils into eight personality types organized around attitudes to school, motivation, self-concept, sociability and conformism.

8 The researchers then checked their allocation of groups by observing the classroom behaviour of a 10 per cent sample of pupils.

9 Finally they tested for answers to questions using a statistical analysis of gains in pupil scores on tests of abilities.

Examples of the twelve categories of teaching styles are:

Type 1

These teachers favour integration of subject matter, and, unlike most other groups, allow pupils choice of work, whether undertaken individually or in groups. Most allow pupils choice of seating. Less than half curb movement and talk. Assessment in all its forms. . . appears to be discouraged. Intrinsic motivation is favoured.

(Bennett 1976)

Type 12

None favour an integrated approach. Subjects are taught separately by class teaching and individual work. None allow pupils choice of seating, and every teacher curbs movement and talk. These teachers are above average on [the use of]. . . assessment procedures, and extrinsic motivation predominates.

(Bennett 1976)

The results

The conclusions were that formal styles were more effective in reading, maths and English, especially for the higher achievers. However, low ability boys (but not girls) did not thrive in formal classrooms. Informal teaching tended to be effective where there were clear goals and curriculum structure and an emphasis on intellectual, not social, development.

There is little comment on the social or emotional progress of pupils under different teaching styles, despite the research showing that informal teachers rated this an important goal of education. A re-analysis of the data by Aitken and Bennett in 1981 threw doubt on these conclusions, as did a third analysis by Gray and Satterly in the same year. These sociologists found that:

- differences in teaching styles within the twelve categories were greater than differences between them;

- differences between these teaching styles were so small as to be 'overwhelmed' by the impact of other variables;

- the direction of differences between the teaching styles meant that they did not represent a continuum from formal to informal;

- the progress made by pupils varied considerably within teaching-style categories;

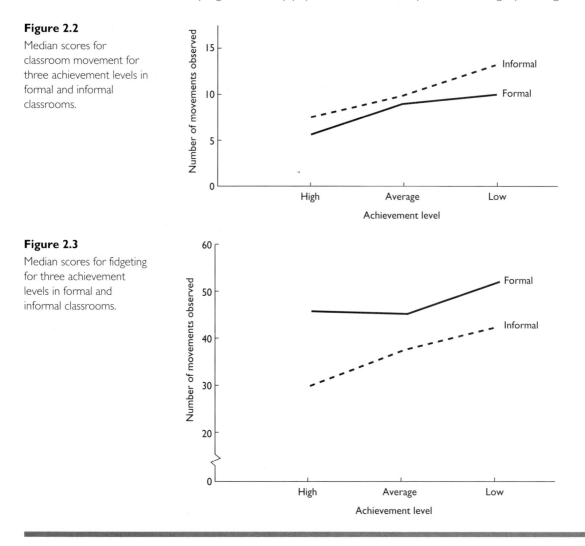

Figure 2.2

Median scores for classroom movement for three achievement levels in formal and informal classrooms.

Figure 2.3

Median scores for fidgeting for three achievement levels in formal and informal classrooms.

- there were examples of pupil progress which contradicted the overall findings so markedly as to be inexplicable.

1) What do these diagrams tell us?
2) In what ways could we explain these graphs?
3) Which of the above explanations seems most likely? How could it be verified?
4) What problems do you see with these sorts of data?
5) Compare your answers with other people's if possible.

1) What advantages did Bennett have in conducting this research?
2) What practical considerations might have been relevant to Bennett's research?
3) What ethical considerations are there in this sort of research?

An interpretivist case study

Figure 2.4

Bev Skeggs.

The fieldwork

In 1980 Bev Skeggs was a 21-year-old PhD student doing part-time sociology teaching on 'caring' courses in a northern FE college. She had come from a working-class background and had once signed up for a caring course at an FE college herself. She decided to study the young women on the courses she taught. She was interested in their attitudes and responses towards the various types of oppression they encountered. Some fifty-two of the women were subjects of intensive participant observation for three years.

She was given access to the lives of the women in different ways and established different types of relationship with them; sometimes very social, sometimes more individual and personal. These different types of relationships yielded different sorts of information.

As well as formal interviews and contact through teaching, the young women visited Skeggs' flat socially. Fieldwork even included parties and at first the women were suspicious of Skeggs' presence and her attitude. They were not used to teachers treating them as adults and 'flashing fags' as they put it. One said that she was 'gobstruck' by Skeggs' behaviour. However, trust and confidence were firmly established when Skeggs held her own party which the women thought was a 'riot'. Skeggs was especially popular with the women when they realized that her university contacts meant she knew 'loads of fit fellas'.

Skeggs taped the interviews, transcribing some but listening and re-listening to most. Some of the women asked if they could listen to the tapes too and these sessions turned into regular social events. These too were useful for the research as the women would engage with what they had said on tape, changing their minds and elaborating on or denying comments. Such was the intensity of this research that

Skeggs says she now finds it odd when people claim their work is 'ethnographic' although it is only based on a few weeks' work involving a small number of interviews.

The problems

The problems Skeggs faced in conducting this research were many. For example:

- the research took over her life and she found it difficult to maintain personal relationships outside of it;

- she wanted to share her research ideas with the women but found the language she used was not accessible to them;

- as a female researcher studying young women she was immediately labelled a feminist (she notes that male researchers are somehow considered gender-free). The women understood what feminism was but were not feminists. They used its ideas if they were of advantage to them;

- the research was jeopardized to some extent because interviews often turned into counselling sessions after disclosures of violence, child abuse or sexual harassment;

- being a young woman researcher meant limitations on access to space (e.g. streets at night, city centre pubs) and she was sometimes pestered by men. In one case the best friend of a student's boyfriend would not leave her alone;

- she felt a debt to the women she studied and was worried about using them for her own career advancement without helping them in return.

1) What advantages did Skeggs have in conducting this research?
2) What practical considerations might have been relevant to Skeggs' research?
3) What ethical considerations are there in this sort of research?

Ethics refers to the assessment of the way we behave and quality of the moral values we have. In educational research ethical questions are often raised about considerations of confidentiality and anonymity, the rights of the subjects of the research, how far researchers must be open about what they are doing, how far they can go in investigating their subjects and so on.

Would you agree or disagree with the following statements?
- *Skeggs' is an interpretivist study, Bennett's is a positivist one.*
- *Both studies use methods which were fit for the intended purpose.*
- *Skeggs' research uses grounded theory, Bennett's study employs the hypothetico-deductive model.*
- *There are more problems associated with Skeggs' research strategy than Bennett's.*

If you are working in a large group, compare your views on the statements.

Brainstorm as many differences as possible between the Skeggs and Bennett studies. Then for each point identified, discuss its pros and cons.

Research methods

This section looks at different types of research methods in the four categories of:

1 asking questions;

2 observing;

3 doing experiments;

4 using secondary data.

We give examples of studies to illustrate their use. In each category, methods yielding more quantitative data are examined first, then those yielding more qualitative data.

Asking questions

Closed-ended questionnaires

Alison Kelly used closed-ended questionnaires (with 'tick the box' answers) in a study of teachers' attitudes on gender issues to see how these related to subjects taught. She selected seventy secondary schools in England and Wales and within these schools, six main curriculum areas: maths, science, craft, English, modern languages and humanities.

Taking each of these areas in turn, she sent letters containing ten copies of the questionnaire to a head of department at each school with a request to distribute them appropriately within the school. In this way a semi-random sample of 700 teachers from across the country was eventually achieved. An additional sample of 200 teachers was drawn by sending the same letter to the head of science and head of technical craft at the ten schools involved with the *Girls into Science and Technology* project that Kelly was involved in.

On the returned questionnaire (which did allow space for teachers to make comments if they wanted) respondents were asked to give their sex, age group, type of school in which they worked, main and subsidiary subjects taught, teaching experience and qualifications. Additionally the school was classified according to its region and size of the town served. The final response rate was 43 per cent.

The study found a clear distinction between the (older) 'traditionalists' and (young) 'trendies'. It also found differences between men and women and between, for example, physics and English teachers. But many of the teachers disliked the form of the questionnaire:

> I don't like these type of questionnaires. They force you to make unreal decisions. The questions cannot take account of all opinions and are therefore biased. Results cannot be truly accurate. Written sentences are much better.
>
> (Kelly *et al.* 1987)

However, Kelly argues that:

> While it is undoubtedly true that written sentences (or indeed interviews) are better than closed questions at reflecting the views of any one individual, it does not follow that they are better for studying the teaching profession as a whole. The more they have to write the fewer people reply; what they do write is difficult to analyse. Despite the inadequacies of this questionnaire. . . some fascinating trends have emerged. . . This study aimed to map out the average teacher's attitude. . . and for this a closed questionnaire is most effective. It is of course quite valid for any individual teacher or pupil to say, 'that's not how it is for me'. But the task of mapping individual experiences belongs to the biographer. . .

(Kelly *et al.* 1987)

Reproduced here are some questions from the closed-ended questionnaire sent to the teachers in Kelly's study. It was used as a means to 'update and extend our knowledge of teachers' attitudes and the ways these varied between different groups'. On your own, complete the questionnaire. Then do the questions on p. 43.

Strongly agree   Agree   Unsure   Disagree   Strongly disagree

• Only people with a sense of vocation should teach

• Examinations are the most important part of education

• Education leads to greater equality of opportunity

• Education should not be a political issue

• Men are better teachers than women

• Coeducational schools produce better balanced children than single-sex schools

• Parents should have freedom of choice concerning the school their children attend

• Very little is learned in unstructured lessons

• Pupils should be involved in planning the curriculum

• Girls are naturally better than boys at art-based subjects

• Mixed ability groups hold clever children back

• It is important to find ways of encouraging girls to study physical science

• Children from deprived backgrounds can do well if they have special attention

• Teachers often allow boys to dominate in mixed classes

• Pupils should be encouraged to pursue any subject in which they show promise

• Girls should be encouraged to learn office skills

- School uniform is necessary to maintain discipline

- Science is less popular with girls because they receive less encouragement

- Children from ethnic minorities are less academic

- Lessons are geared to boys' interests rather than girls'.

1) How could you analyse, distil and portray the group's response?

2) What problems do you see with this battery of questions as a means of achieving the goal of updating and extending knowledge about teachers' attitudes?

3) What problems are there with individual questions?

4) Write and administer your own improved questionnaire to teachers in your institution.

Testing

Tests designed to measure intelligence quotient (IQ tests), aspects of the personality (psychometric tests) or achievement, usually rely on subjects giving answers to questions which can be analysed quantitatively. We saw on p. 37 how Bennett used achievement tests at the beginning and end of the school year to give information about pupil progress under different teaching styles. Rosenthal and Jacobson (see p. 55) used them to measure the influence of labelling by teachers. Bennett also used psychometric tests to measure aspects of students' personality.

The concept of intelligence quotient (IQ) was developed at Stanford University from the Stanford-Binet test, based on Alfred Binet's 1911 test of mental age. IQ is calculated thus:

IQ = (mental age divided by chronological age) × 100.

(Thus an average IQ for any age should be 100.)

The early Stanford-Binet test has since been revised four times, most recently in 1986, and is still widely used. A technical problem with IQ tests is that as children grow older the range and variability of mental ages increase so that IQ scores do not have the same meaning at every age. To cope with this the concept of deviation IQ was introduced; this tells us how far above or below the average a person scored compared to people in the same age group.

However, many researchers still feel that IQ tests are untrustworthy. They say these tests favour individuals who share the language and culture of the people who devise and administer them – usually white middle-class English speakers. Similarly the norms which are used to calculate deviation IQ are usually derived from a sample of people from this background, not minority ethnic groups, for example.

IQ, psychometric and achievement tests can all yield qualitative data, although analysis of these is more subjective. In psychology, projective techniques such as the Rorschach inkblot test may be used. This gives ambiguous stimuli which the subject must interpret or tell a story about. Tests like these are designed to reveal aspects of personality and thought processes.

Figure 2.5

A Wechsler Intelligence Scale test to assess spatial ability.

Figure 2.6

A Rorschach inkblot.

 What does this look like to you? Let your mind drift for a while as you look and think about the shape. Make up a story about it. What clues do the interpretation and the story give to your personality?

In education, qualitative testing of creative intelligence has been done by asking students to think of as many uses as possible for five objects: a barrel, a tin of shoe polish, a brick, a paper clip and a blanket.

 Try it – your creativity will be assessed not just by the number of uses you suggest for each object but the originality of the uses too.

With a partner discuss the problems which can arise with this type of test. Compare your answers with the rest of the class.

Sociometric analysis

Sociometric analysis is a method of measuring the emotional links within a group and the interaction patterns: it measures feelings of attraction, indifference or rejection between a group's members. Individuals are asked to write their own name on a sheet of paper. Then they are asked to put, in order of preference, the names of the other members with whom they would most like to work in a group. On the other side of the page they are asked to put the names of those they would least like to work with, starting with the least preferred name. They can write as many or as few names on both sides as they want.

Having collected the sheets of paper the researchers then draw a sociogram. They begin with the paper from the person who has been most chosen (C in Figure 2.7) and add symbols for anyone who both chose and was chosen by this person (A and B in Figure 2.7). The papers are worked through until a picture of the whole group is built up. Clearly it is important to keep this confidential, as a public airing of private preferences could be painful to those concerned.

Figure 2.7

An example of a sociogram for eight people.

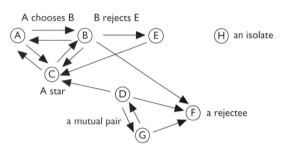

Apply this research technique to a group in your college or school. Do you consider the information it gives you to be reliable? What research purposes could you use the information for? (Think about issues of class, ethnicity, gender and educational underachievement.)

Semi-structured interviews

In *The Academic Life* Burton Clark, an American professor in California, used tape-recorded semi-structured interviews in his mid 1980s study of over 200 American academic staff. The interviewees came from a range of institutions (sixteen in total), varying from leading research universities to community colleges across the USA, and from different disciplines and various levels of seniority.

Clark says this about the interviewees:

> They provided rich. . . responses to questions about the nature of their work, their involvement in their disciplines and institutions, the beliefs they held about their own profession, their forms of authority and sense of power, their career patterns and opportunities, their participation in academic networks outside their own departments or professional schools and other related matters. Seeking fullness of response, the recorded interviews were guided rather than tightly pre-formed. . . Analysis based on recorded conversations gives respondents a fuller, more intensive role. I have quoted them extensively.

> (Clark 1987)

In *Just Like A Girl* Sue Sharpe comments on the relative merits of quantitative and qualitative data from interviews. She adopted semi-structured interviews because she was unhappy about the questionnaires she had tried first:

> 249 girls from the fourth forms of four schools in the London Borough of Ealing gave me information about themselves by filling up a question-

naire. . . By the time I had completed the research and was getting into the complex data analysis I had become increasingly alienated from the work. The warm and living nature of the feelings, ideas and hopes of the girls who had participated had been frozen somehow and lost within long computer sheets covered with endless statistics and calculations.

(Sharpe 1976)

Sharpe therefore abandoned the statistics and used the data from the interviews to write about the girls as 'separate individuals who share patterns of personality and experience through growing up in similar environments and having similar social positions and prospects'.

Develop as many criticisms as you can of Sharpe and Clark's arguments.

Imagine you wished to conduct a research project about the experiences of schooling that your fellow students have had.

Devise a schedule of questions for a semi-structured interview.

In turn, each person in the group should interview another using their schedule for about five minutes. The rest of the group should observe the interaction and take notes on the interviewer's approach.

After each interview, the interviewer and the interviewee should recount how they felt, what the difficulties were and so on. The rest of the group should then feed back their comments.

Focus group interviews: an exercise

A researcher is conducting an investigation of the use of Records of Achievement (RoAs) in schools and decides to use the focus group interview method. She chooses a sample of four different secondary schools and two colleges. With the permission of the head teachers she invites sixth formers and college students to a meeting with coffee and biscuits. She sets up a tape recorder and begins a discussion with the group on their feelings about RoAs.

• What might be the advantages and disadvantages of this approach?

• What methodological advice would you give her?

Set up a focus group interview about RoAs or anything else that interests you in the way described here. Then analyse the data obtained in any way that seems appropriate.

Autobiographies and case histories

Autobiographies are provided by the subjects themselves. Individual case histories are 'taken' by the researcher. Autobiographies and case histories both tend to focus retrospectively on what led up to a particular set of events, the contextual factors surrounding them, and the perceptions and attitudes of the person studied. These can then be viewed in relation to what happened in the end – the outcomes.

In this way an unusually detailed (if 'unrepresentative') exploration of possible causes and processes which may have contributed to the outcomes can be conducted. Alternatively a detailed picture with no attempt at analysis can be put together. Case histories and autobiographies can stand alone or be used to complement wider scale surveys.

Hilary De Lyon and Frances Migniuolo, who at the time were officers at the National Union of Teachers, have compiled accounts of some women teachers about their experiences. These give us an insight into the everyday realities of life from a certain social position, particularly that of individuals in minority groups. The following quote is from a gay woman teacher:

> It is impossible to be sanguine about the daily experience of a lesbian or gay teacher in school. . . I walk from my room to the staffroom and the boys are running, pushing, fighting, listening to music, lounging against the radiators, the top dogs are there, watching, tense to run and hit, tense to laugh as I pass – easy for them to call out. I prefer a big crowd to walk in; what's worse is a hall almost empty and their careless bodies calling out 'baggy trousers' – a mild remark. It scares me. That's three seconds to walk past and I'm a woman, a lesbian. They're practising'.

(Anon in De Lyon and Migniuolo 1989)

Table 2.1	A summary of the advantages and disadvantages of autobiographies and case histories

Advantages	Disadvantages
They can provide a very detailed account of one person's history, focusing on a specific personal characteristic or sequence of events they have experienced.	Information from a single individual is not representative.
They are most useful for studying small groups with distinctive sorts of experience	A personal account would at the very least need substantiation from a variety of other sources of evidence such as interviews with other people who have had contact with the subject, documentary sources and records etc.
When used to complement wider surveys they can paint the detail into the broader picture.	It is impossible to check all aspects of the kind of detailed account this method yields and so at least some of the data has to be taken at face value, which reduces reliability.
When used to complement wider surveys they can give balance to an account which if kept at the general level, might stress the importance of structural factors and not give sufficient weight to personal decisions, perceptions and influences.	The selection of the individual/s is also important, and here there is a danger that the researcher will consciously or unconsciously choose subjects who will confirm his or her ideas.

However, examples do not only come from individuals within minority or discriminated groups. Peter Woods uses the individual case history method with a recently retired teacher called 'Tom'.

> Tom and I talked. . . on a number of occasions for a total of some twelve hours, yielding over 500 pages of transcript. I had, too, my field notes and

interview transcripts from previous projects in which Tom had figured prominently.

(Woods 1990)

Woods began the work with the idea that teachers do not just accept social roles, rather they actively 'make' them and, furthermore, that they do not just accept the school curriculum, they help to 'make' it too. The individual case history method confirmed this but also showed that the teacher's early life was important in shaping how they respond to and can shape the curriculum.

Validity is the extent to which the research instruments used to actually collect data provide an accurate picture of what or who is being studied. The essential validity question is 'Is this method measuring what the researcher says it is measuring?'

Construct validity refers to whether the concepts used in a study have been clearly defined and are actually being measured by the instrument chosen.

Reliability is the extent to which the same results would be found if the research was to be repeated by someone else, perhaps using a different technique. The essential reliability question is 'Does the design and implementation of this study give us faith in its results?'

How could the validity and reliability of Woods' study be increased?

Phenomenography

Phenomenography is a method designed specifically to answer questions about thinking and learning. The word 'phenomenography' was coined in 1979 and was used in print for the first time in 1981 by Ference Marton from the University of Gothenburg, Sweden. In the UK it is associated with studies of higher education student learning by G. Gibbs, N. Entwistle, P. Ramsden, R. Saljo and D. Laurillard, centred around Lancaster, Oxford Brookes and Edinburgh universities.

The basic assumption of phenomenography is that people understand the same things in different ways but that there is only a limited number of ways in which people think about, or conceptualize, any given phenomenon. The method is designed to uncover these ways of thinking, to categorize them and then to identify what effects these different categories of thinking have on the world or the people that hold them.

The different ways people understand a concept are usually uncovered in phenomenography by asking a number of people questions about a single stimulus. This may be an experience they have all had, a question or something else. for example, Johansson, Marton and Svensson asked some university students: 'A car is driven at a high and constant speed on a straight road. What forces act on the car?'

The students answered in one of two ways. Some thought that the forces in the direction of movement are exactly equal to the forces in the reverse direction. Others thought that the forces in the direction of movement exceed the sum of the forces in the opposite direction ('. . . otherwise it wouldn't move forwards').

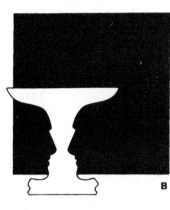
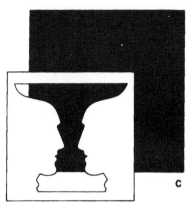

A   B   C

Figure 2.8

People understand the
same things in different
ways

1) *Which version do you subscribe to? (The answer is at the end of this chapter.)*
2) *Michael Prosser and Carolyn Webb use phenomenography to analyse sociology students' approaches to writing essays in an Australian university. Their results are summarized in 'Relating the process of undergraduate essay writing to the finished product' in Studies in Higher Education, vol. 19, no. 2 (1994) pp. 125–38. Obtain a copy of the article and try reproducing their methods with your fellow students. How far do your results match Prosser and Webb's?*

Repertory grid technique

Like phenomenography, repertory grid technique is a method for uncovering individuals' ways of thinking about a subject, or their personal constructs. It was originated by the psychologist G.A. Kelly in 1955 and is often called 'Kelly's repertory grid', although other versions have since been developed.

In the original version the person being studied is asked to nominate a certain number of people in his or her life (Kelly calls these elements). They could be people studying on the same course, friends or relatives. The names are written on cards. These are shuffled and then presented back to the person in threes. It is their task to say how two of them (any two) differ from the third. Responses might be that they differ according to attractiveness, flexibility or fear of criticism.

The words or phrases which result from this form a series of construct pairs. An example for one individual might be:

- attractive – unattractive;

- studious – lazy;

- intelligent – stupid;

- and so on.

This grid gives an insight into the different ways people view the same social situation and helps the researcher understand the way participants perceive what is going on. It is, therefore, a technique which is a useful supplement to other approaches.

In Kelly's original version both the list of elements and the constructs come from the person being studied. In some later versions one or both are developed by the researchers. For example, in a study of members' views about the ethics and values of the polytechnic they worked in, 250 staff and students were asked to complete the grid shown in Figure 2.10. Both the elements (top row) and the constructs (at the side) were developed by the researchers. They left elements 19 and 20 and constructs 13 and 14 blank so that respondents could add their own as well.

Two things are interesting about this version of the repertory grid.

1 The researchers could have derived the constructs and/or the elements from a sample of respondents by doing an initial pilot study but they did not do so.

2 The results from this version are quantitative: the numbers reply positively or negatively for any construct against any element. One of the findings of the study was that the further away from the self the element is, the more negative responses were given. This was paralleled by the fact that non-responses also increased the further away the element was perceived to be.

Figure 2.9

A version of Kelly's grid

Self	Peer Group Member Within Department/Service	Direct Line Manager	Head of Department/Service	Dean	Member of Recorate	Polytechnic Board member	Personnel Officer	Union Representative	Teaching Staff Member	APT&C Staff Member	Manual Staff Member	Formal Support/Guidance Person	Student	Peer Group Member in other Department/Service	Polytechnic Visitor	Friend Within Polytechnic	Spouse or Partner					Constructs. 0 = Positive X = Negative
1	2	3	4	5	6	7	8	9	10	11	12	13	14	15	16	17	18	19	20			
																					1	Open – Closed
																					2	Communicative – Non-Communicative
																					3	Collaborative – Non-Collaborative
																					4	Having Integrity – Unprincipled
																					5	Trustworthy – Untrustworthy
																					6	Responsible – Irresponsible
																					7	Respect – Disrespect
																					8	Aware – Unaware
																					9	Autonomous – Controlled
																					10	Assertive – Not Assertive
																					11	Valued – Not Valued
																					12	Moral – Immoral
																					13	
Source: University of Central Lancashire (1992) Report of the Ethics and Values Audit p. 108																					14	

Devise a similar grid to investigate attitudes towards an institution you are involved in. Decide whether you will define the elements and the constructs, or whether you will elicit them from respondents. Try using your grid.

Observing

Non-participant observation yielding quantitative data

The Flanders approach is possibly the most well known and (with modifications) most widely used example of non-participant observation yielding quantitative data. Others include the ORACLE studies (*Observational Research and Classroom Learning Evaluation Project*) reported in the books of Mauric Galton, an academic from Leicester University.

Flanders used time sample analysis to study classroom interaction. He identified ten types of classroom interaction.

Teacher:

1 Accepts feeling: accepts and clarifies the feeling tone of the students in a non-threatening manner. Feelings may be positive or negative. Predicting and recalling feelings are included.

2 Praises or encourages: praises or encourages student action or behaviour, jokes that release tension, not at the expense of another individual, nodding head or saying 'uh uh?' or 'go on' are included.

3 Accepts or uses ideas of student: clarifying, building or developing ideas or suggestions by a student. As teacher brings more of his [sic] own ideas into play, shift to category five.

4 Asks question: asking a question about content or procedure with the intent that a student answer.

5 Lectures: giving facts or opinions about content or procedure; expressing his own idea; asking rhetorical questions.

6 Gives directions: directions, commands or orders with which a student is expected to comply.

7 Criticizes or justifies authority: statements, intended to change student behaviour from non-acceptable to acceptable pattern, bawling someone out; stating why the teacher is doing what he is doing, extreme self-reference.

8 Student talk – response: talk by student in response to teacher. Teacher initiates the contact or solicits student's statement.

9 Student talk – initiation: talk by student which they initiate. If 'calling on' students is only to indicate who may talk next, observer must decide whether student wanted to talk. If he [sic] did, use this category.

10 Silence or confusion: pauses, short periods of silence and periods of confusion in which communication cannot be understood by the observer.

(Flanders 1970)

The researcher samples the activity going on in the classroom every three seconds and uses the categories to obtain a list of numbers: 5, 4, 4, 8, 3, 2, 8, etc., which indicate the activity going on at that time. These are then joined together like this:

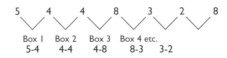

| Box 1 | Box 2 | Box 3 | Box 4 etc. | | |
| 5-4 | 4-4 | 4-8 | 8-3 | 3-2 | |

A dot is placed in the appropriate boxes of a grid made up like Figure 2.10.

Second number

First number

Trouble shooting: high scores in cell 4,8 and 8,4 but not in 8,8 would indicate too much drilling with little meaningful dialogue. High scores in the block of four cells in the 6's and 7's indicate potential discipline problems.

Use this scheme to categorize the interaction of a class in your school or college. (Get permission first.) Then analyse the results using Figure 2.12 for guidance.

What points does this experience raise about Flanders' grid as a way of categorizing classroom activity?

This type of method has been used more recently too, for example by Barbara Tizard in *Young Children at School in the Inner City*. In each of thirty-three London schools four children of mixed sex and ethnic origin were selected for observation. The aim was to get a numerical count of the prevalence of preselected categories of behaviour so that boys could be compared with girls, black with white children, and also associations with children's educational progress could be looked for. Tizard used a systematic observation schedule to provide a description of time spent by the children in five ways:

1   in different 'settings' (individual work, group work, play, etc.);

2   in different subjects (maths, language, etc.);

3   when in contact with teachers;

4   when in contact with other children;

5 when not interacting.

Each child was observed for six 5-minute periods each day, these periods being divided into thirty consecutive 10-second time intervals.

In a similar way, J.P. Powell recorded groups of tutors and students at the University of Papua New Guinea in weekly meetings of around 50 minutes duration. Records were kept of seating positions and at the final gathering of each group participants were given a sociometric test and a questionnaire. Powell arranged for some of the meetings to go ahead without the tutor present. The participation rate for each member was obtained from the tape recording like this:

> Each group member is assigned a code-letter and the appropriate type-writer key is struck at one second intervals according to who is speaking. Blanks are left for periods of silence. In this way the verbal interaction of an entire tutorial can be sequentially displayed on a single sheet of foolscap paper. Each member's participation score can then be calculated as a percentage of the total amount of speech. . . The content of what was said in tutorials was analysed in terms of a category system. . . devised to take account of the major forms of cognitive activity which might be thought to possess educational significance at the undergraduate level.
>
> (Powell 1986)

The 'category system' included:

- giving an opinion;
- giving information;
- arguing;
- asking for information;
- clarifying;
- formulating problems;
- group processes.

Some of the findings were that:

- tutors spoke on average for 58 per cent of the time;
- students increased their participation score considerably when the tutor was absent; in some cases they said nearly five times as much;
- some students who said nothing in any of a series of meetings with a tutor participated strongly in meetings without the tutor;
- differences between the cognitive content of the discussion were noted for different subject areas.

 Try using this technique in a classroom you are involved in or can get permission to enter. What results are obtained and how do they compare with Powell's?

Non-participant observation yielding qualitative data

Tizard and Hughes studied the language used by fifteen middle-class and fifteen working-class mothers and their daughters attending nursery school. They pinned radio-microphones to the girls' dresses; a receiver picked up the conversations which were then recorded. The girls' interactions were recorded during one afternoon at home and two mornings at their school. An observer was also present who followed the girls closely to add context to the audio-recording and to clarify where necessary. Girls were chosen because:

> in preschool years they are likely to talk more, and more clearly, than boys. In addition, we felt that in a society still dominated by men, there was some merit in focusing on girls, and on mother-daughter interaction.
>
> (Tizard and Hughes 1986)

The analysis of the data took the researchers 4,000 hours in total. The results are summarized in Chapter 5, pp. 151-2.

The Hawthorne effect refers to the effect that the presence of a researcher or observer can have on the behaviour of the people being observed. This is a problem because it means that the behaviour of people being researched is different from normal and so results are unreliable.

 Tizard and Hughes' research raises questions about the Hawthorne effect. Do you think this would have a significant effect here? What other potential problems are there with their methodology?

 Divide into two groups. Imagine each group is applying for a grant for research into the effectiveness of different styles of teaching.

Group A should prepare a case for using non-participant observation yielding qualitative data.

Group B should prepare a case for using non-participant observation yielding quantitative data.

Each should argue their case and then a decision should be made about which group is to receive the grant.

Participant observation

Martin Mac an Ghaill, who at the time worked in a state school, comments that participant observation:

> is not a single method but rather a characteristic style of research which makes use of a number of methods and techniques – observation, informant interviewing, document analysis, respondent interviewing and participation in self analysis.
>
> (Mac an Ghaill 1988)

Variants include the rather less intensive observant participation or reflective observation. This involves insider research with the careful writing up of notes and their use as data for later analysis.

It is, of course, difficult for the (adult) researcher to try participant observation with school pupils, but it has been attempted. Mandy Llewellyn, then a research student, explored the commitment to school of adolescent girls in two secondary schools:

> I wanted to enter the field as 'one of the girls'. . . I spent five days a week. . . for the entire school year September 1975 to July 1976 and two or three days a week regularly throughout the subsequent academic year. I was involved in every aspect of school life with the girls from quick fags in the lavvies to inter-form hockey tournaments and being humiliated in French lessons for only getting three out of twenty for my test. Although the girls were aware that I was undertaking some sort of project on girls in school, I spent so much time with them that they tended to forget this.
>
> (Llewellyn 1980)

 Would you describe Skeggs' study (see p.39) as being based on participant observation?

Doing experiments

Controlled experiments

Controlled experiments try to keep all important conditions constant and usually have two identical groups to test: the experimental and, for comparison, the control. One variable is introduced or changed in the experimental group but not in the control. Any subsequent differences between the two should therefore be the result of that change.

For example, in tests of the effectiveness of a medicine, it is administered to the experimental group. The control group, who are usually matched in terms of age, health, etc., get a placebo, that is, some 'treatment' which is known to be ineffective. The point in doing this is that receiving treatment of any kind can sometimes have an effect on the patient. Administering a placebo means both are receiving some 'treatment'. It is best if the experiment is a double blind one – that is, neither those conducting the experiment nor those being experimented on know who is receiving the medicine and who the placebo.

One of the best-known controlled experiments in the sociology of education is the study of the American psychologists, Rosenthal and Jacobson, *Pygmalion in the Classroom.*

The hypothesis being tested was that children could benefit from the effect of expectancy advantages, that is advantages at school gained from the teacher's expectation of an improvement in academic attainment. The researchers asked: 'If the teacher expects a child to do well, will that very expectation improve the chances of this actually happening?' In other words, will there be a self-fulfilling prophecy?

Rosenthal and Jacobson conducted their experiment on the pupils and teachers of 'Oak School', a public elementary school in a lower class community of a medium-sized city in the USA. About 17 per cent of the school's population were Mexican, an underachieving ethnic minority group. Each of Oak school's six year grades was banded into three ability levels, with the Mexican children heavily over-represented in the lowest band.

All of the children of Oak school were pre-tested with a standard test of intelligence.

However, the teachers were told that this was not a standard test, but one which would predict intellectual 'blooming' or 'spurting'. After this the eighteen teachers of Years One to Six were given the names of those children they taught who would show dramatic intellectual growth in the next twelve months.

Although these predictions were allegedly made on the basis of the 'imminent spurt detection test', actually the names were chosen at random. They consisted of about 20 per cent of Oak School's student population and this was the experimental group. Another 20 per cent were chosen also at random for comparison, the teachers being told nothing about these. This was the control group. The progress of the remaining 60 per cent was ignored by the researchers.

All the children of Oak School were re-tested (with the same IQ test as before) after one semester (roughly six months), after one academic year, and after two academic years. For the first two of these re-tests the children were still with the teacher who had been given the favourable expectations of some of them. For the final re-test the children had all been moved up a grade (age cohort) and so were with a new teacher, who had not been given any special expectation.

What ethical issues are raised by this study?
In a small group, discuss how you react to them.

The results of the experimental group were as follows:

- the youngest children benefited most, but only during the time they were with the teacher who had been given their names. In the second year their performance fell back almost to the norm;

- even the older children in the experimental group improved in performance compared to the control group, and they managed to sustain this in the second year (with a change of teacher);

- the children in the experimental group who were in the middle stream benefited more than those in the lower or upper streams (who, presumably, already had a strong label attached which it was more difficult to dislodge with the expectancy advantage);

- the Mexicans in the experimental group seemed to do better than the non-Mexicans. In fact, the more 'Mexican' a pupil looked, the more advantage they got from being positively labelled;

- there seemed to be little difference in the expectancy advantage enjoyed by girls compared to boys, though each sex in the experimental group improved most in that area at which it was strongest in the initial pre-test. Interestingly, this was in 'reasoning IQ' for girls and 'verbal IQ' for boys (the reverse of what is considered to be the normal sex distribution of abilities).

One of the problems with controlled experiments in the field of education is that, while they can throw up interesting results, the reasons for these results often have to be guessed at.

Rosenthal and Jacobson explain their results in the following way:

Teachers may have treated their children in a more pleasant, friendly, and encouraging fashion. . . .Teachers probably watched their special children more closely. . . Teachers may also have become more reflective in their evaluation of the special children's intellectual performance. . . To summarize. . . by what she said, by how and when she said it, by her facial expressions, postures, and perhaps by her touch, the teacher may have communicated to the children of the experimental group that she expected improved intellectual performance. Such communications together with possible changes in teaching techniques may have helped the child learn by changing his [sic] self concept, his expectations of his own behaviour, and his motivation.

(Rosenthal and Jacobson 1968)

1) *What comments do you have about this explanation and about the explanatory power of the experimental method used in this way?*
2) *Devise a research project which would better explain the results Rosenthal and Jacobson found.*

Quasi experiments

Quasi experiments are uncontrolled in the sense that not all conditions are kept constant. No proper control group is chosen and/or the influences on the outcome of the experiment are not properly kept under control. There are, in other words, sources of internal and/or external 'contamination' to the research which positivists would say put its findings in doubt.

In 1973 the New Zealand Council for Educational Research began work on a research project designed to measure the effects of a 'book flood' on the reading habits, tastes and abilities of school children. Two primary schools (5–11 years) took part in the study. Over half their intake were Maori children, many of whom had limited access to books. Large numbers of suitable books were introduced into the school over a period of two terms.

To assess the impact of this book flood a series of assessments of reading skills and attitudes was made between March and May 1976 before the books arrived, and then again six months after the book flood had begun.

The tests included reading comprehension, vocabulary and listening, and scales to assess children's interest in books, their attitudes to school, to reading and to themselves. The amount of reading undertaken in a two week period was recorded by the children themselves and the teachers' ratings of their interest in reading was obtained. Case studies were made of five children in each class and information was obtained about the books the children owned and had read, their home background, parental interest, library borrowing and TV viewing. Finally informal reading inventories were used to study the children's reading behaviour.

The result of the book flood was a significant change in the children's voluntary reading, and improvements in their reading abilities, attitudes and interests.

What are the problems with this research and how could it have been improved?

Devise and carry out a similar quasi-experiment. (Get permission first.) An example might be conducting two (or more) of your class meetings under different conditions and comparing the results in terms of learning. Differences might involve teaching method, environmental conditions or breaks taken.

Using secondary data

Content analysis of qualitative data

One way of dealing with qualitative secondary data in a systematic way is to use content analysis. This means subjecting the data to careful categorization, for example, counting the number of references to items in which one has an interest.

Glenys Lobban analysed six popular British reading schemes looking for evidence of gender stereotyping. She chose two schemes published before 1960 (Janet and John and Happy Venture), two published in the 1960s (Ready to Read and Ladybird), and two published in the 1970s (Nipper and Breakthrough to Literacy). She coded the content of 250 stories in all, dividing them into various categories such as adult roles presented, activities occurring, and the sex of the children taking the lead in various sorts of activities.

Not surprisingly she concluded:

> The female world was almost entirely oriented around domestic activity and childcare. . . the male world the schemes described did not include toys or activities that allowed expressive or nurturant behaviour.
>
> (Lobban 1987)

D. Smith and colleagues used content analysis on the 118 mission statements and seventy-six strategic plans from British universities. Mission statements describe the purposes and distinctive character of an institution. Strategic plans detail how these purposes are intended to be achieved over the next five years. The researchers were interested in what these documents had to say about access for non-traditional students. They faced some problems because the strategic plans in particular were very different from each other in their structure and content. Smith *et al.* coped with this by:

- developing a list of access issues that could appear in plans or mission statements;

- counting the number of times these appeared in each institution's documents;

- recording the researchers' subjective impressions about the degree of commitment to any item in the list.

The list was as follows:

- expansion of student numbers;

- expansion of course provision;

- widening of access, particularly for:

mature students;

part-time students;

those with non-traditional qualifications;

students with non-traditional or disadvantaged backgrounds (class, ethnicity or gender);

- students recruited from the immediate locality or region;

- students given access on the basis of study or experience elsewhere;

- modularization of course structure;

- access through franchise arrangements with other institutions.

The authors conclude:

> Taken as a whole the results of the analysis suggest that access and widening participation have emerged as major issues across a broad spectrum of institutions. The prominence of access is reflected in the majority of mission statements and strategic. . . plans. . .

> (Smith *et al.* 1993)

This is indicated in Figure 2.11. However the authors do note that the qualitative comments of the researchers suggest that in many cases access was being treated as a 'bolt-on' extra rather than being integral to the institution's values.

Figure 2.11

Institutional commitment to access and expansion

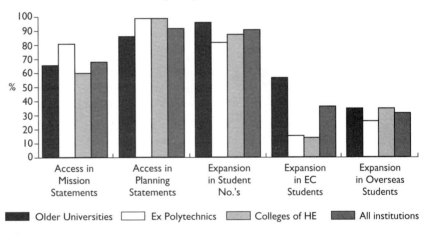

The authors are aware of a number of deficiencies in it. What would you say they are?
What are the strengths of this research?

Discourse analysis

Today content analysis has gone out of fashion as a research method in education. It has been replaced by discourse analysis. This has a number of different meanings and is conducted in different ways in different disciplines. A book on the subject in linguistics may have virtually no similarity to a discourse analysis book in another discipline like sociology or media studies. In educational research, though, it has three key characteristics.

1 It studies discourse: that is spoken language, written text, non-verbal or other forms of communication. The word used to cover all forms of discourse is 'text'.

2 Discourse is considered important because forms of communication don't just give information about the world, they affect it in important ways.

3 Discourse can only be studied by an interpretive process which analyses in depth the hidden processes which underlie communication.

An example of discourse analysis in action is given in the gender chapter (pp. 194-5). Read that section now.

With regard to point one above, note that French and French are interested in a number of aspects of discourse in the classroom. Looking at the spoken discourse they comment not only on what is said, but for how long and by whom. They also take an interest in non-verbal communication (e.g. hand-raising strategies to structure turn-taking) and for this reason French and French use videotape recordings of the lessons.

Note also (point two above) that French and French are not interested in discourse for its own sake, but for the ways in which it is used to influence the world. In this case it helps structure who gets most attention and who slips into the background, and they point out the importance of gender in this respect. In the long term this kind of discourse will make inequalities in education between boys and girls continue.

Finally, as in point three above, French and French are placing an interpretation on what is going on in the classroom. They base this on some quantitative data, but their analysis of turn-taking mechanisms is interpretive. Many studies of discourse are much more interpretive than this.

 For an example of discourse analysis used amusingly in fiction, read Nice Work *by David Lodge, especially pp. 154–7 in which Robin does discourse analysis on a Silk Cut poster for Gus.*

Burman and Parker (1993) note many of the advantages and disadvantages of discourse analysis as a research technique. Some of these are summarized in Table 2.2.

Table 2.2 A summary of the advantages and disadvantages of discourse analysis	
Advantages of discourse analysis	*Disadvantages of discourse analysis*
Explores subtleties of meaning; for example, by uncovering the loaded nature of words (e.g. 'community care', 'educational reform')	It is very labour intensive; considerable time and effort is often expended on analysing a small amount of text
Incorporates an interpretativist approach; the use of language both affects and is affected by the social reality in which it is used.	Changes in context can radically alter the meaning of the same text, so that an analysis will only be good for one context. This means that:

Can develop useful categorizations of viewpoints and approaches held by people being researched. These are accessed through the type of language they use.

In order to understand and evaluate a piece of discourse analysis, the reader must be culturally competent – i.e. be able to understand the references and hidden meanings. This excludes some groups from access to the method, its results or its evaluation.

Gives an extremely in-depth analysis of small aspects of social reality. For example there are whole books and at least one PhD thesis about fragments of speech which last for just a few minutes.

The focus of discourse analysis is at the very microscopic level (e.g. a few minutes' interaction in one classroom). This means that macroscopic structures and political processes are missed (e.g. the influence on educational inequality of the national curriculum).

Most people can begin discourse analysis quite quickly. Reading a few examples and perhaps Fairclough's 1989 text gives clear ideas for beginners.

The methodology is highly personal and lacks rigour. Results cannot be validated and they are unreliable. Interpretations of a particular text cannot be generalized.

Quantitative and qualitative approaches: irreconcilable opposites?

Table 2.3 summarizes the methods we have examined. They represent those that are most popular in educational research. It also separates them according to whether the data they give are more qualitative or quantitative.

Table 2.3	Educational research methods: a summary
Asking questions	
More quantitative	*More qualititative*
Closed-Ended Questionnaires	Semi-Structured or Unstructured Interviews
Testing I.Q., psychometric and achievement tests	Focus Group Interviews
Sociometric analysis	Autobiographies and Case Histories
	Phenomenography
	Repertory Grid Technique
Observing	
More quantitative	*More qualititative*
Non-Participant Observation yielding quantitative data	Non-Participant Observation yielding qualititative data
	Participant Observation

	Doing experiments	
More quantitative		*More qualititative*
Controlled Experiments		Uncontrolled Experiments (quasi experiments)
	Analysing secondary data	
More quantitative		*More qualititative*
Content Analysis of Qualititative Data		Discourse Analysis

The problem with this sort of table is that it suggests that quantitative and qualitative approaches are distinct and antagonistic. In the final section of this chapter we address this issue.

Triangulation

An example of an approach to using qualitative and quantitative techniques in one study to substantiate conclusions comes from a paper by Andy Pollard. Pollard gives an in-depth account of the classrooms of two teachers: Mrs Rothwell, whose classroom is run along very traditional lines, and Mr Harman, whom Pollard identifies as a 'progressive'. Pollard describes his methodological technique as follows:

> In the study of these classrooms I adopted the principle of methodological triangulation. . . and used a variety of data collection methods. The main one was the classic ethnographic method of observation and field notes but this was supplemented with sociometric analysis of the children's friendship groups, interviews with the teachers, systematic observation of child-teacher contacts, cassette recordings of verbal interaction and the study of non-reactive documents.

> (Pollard 1986)

Triangulation is one way of attempting to ensure that a study is reliable. It uses not one but two or more ways of approaching a research problem so that the results obtained can be compared against each other.

Methodological triangulation uses different methods to study the same issue.

Respondent triangulation asks the same questions of different types of people so that their responses can be checked.

Using these techniques Pollard concludes that:

- teachers and pupils arrive at a negotiated way of running a classroom, though the teacher (having more power) has the greater say. They achieve what Pollard calls a 'working consensus';

- pupils are differentiated into groups within the classroom (especially the more able and the less able);

- differentiation between pupils results from this negotiated consensus between pupils and teacher, not just from the teacher's definitions (as Rosenthal and Jacobson believed);

- some forms of this working consensus give rise to a multiplier effect, in other words a process of amplification, both of deviance and of success;

- within the groups differentiated in a traditional classroom regime, academic success and social class background will be linked more closely than those in a progressive regime.

There were several quantitative aspects to this study. One was a sociogram (which, among other things, tells us how many children have or want contact with any specific child and how far this is reciprocated). Another was the number (and therefore level) of the reading scheme each child had reached. A third was the number of child–teacher contacts of different sorts there were and who initiated them.

Pollard says:

> Contrasts between the two classrooms were clear by whatever type of data was studied. For instance, the very simple classification system which I adopted for collecting data on child-teacher contacts indicated differences particularly with regard to the direction of contacts initiated and the number of 'advisory' (managerial and disciplinary) contacts made.

(Pollard 1986)

Figure 2.12

Child-teacher contacts in two classes who initiated them

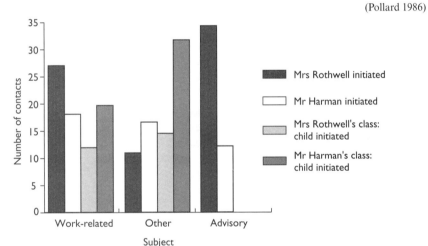

Figure 2.13 Generalized research stages

'Reality'	Selection of reality recorded by researcher	Researcher's account	Researcher's explanations

The research stages as exemplified in Pollard's study

Mrs Rothwell's and Mr Hartman's classrooms	Data collected in form of field notes etc.	Pollard's account of events	Pollard's concepts and explanations like 'working consensus', 'multiplier effect'

What does this quantitative data tell us about the two classrooms?

In *Classroom Ethnography* Martin Hammersley expresses serious reservations about his own earlier qualitative ethnographic methodology and moves towards a more quantitative approach to classroom interaction. Research reported in that book sought to discover the relationship between teaching styles (specifically knowledge transmission) and assessment techniques:

> Whereas the Downtown research [conduced for his PhD] was guided by a fairly traditional concept of ethnographic method aimed at producing a theoretical description of various aspects of social interaction within the school, this later research was explicitly concerned with developing and testing a theory. And, as part of this, there was an attempt to measure variations in transmission teaching. As a result, much of the emphasis came to be placed on quantitative data.
>
> (Hammersley 1990)

Hammersley also notes the following problems in much qualitative research, particularly ethnographic studies.

1　They rarely say how far the study is representative of other cases.

2　They often ask theoretical questions, claim to address them but actually do not.

3　The very nature of 'explanation' is thrown into doubt when studies adopt a relativist approach, i.e. say that there are no 'truths' valid for all of society.

Hammersley's move towards a positivist perspective can also be illustrated by his critique of Pollard's study. In this he raises concerns about the linkages shown in Figure 2.12.

Hammersley's argument is that, despite being a good example of mixed methodology research, Pollard's study is still too 'sloppy' in making these linkages. Hammersley makes the following points about Pollard's research.

1　Pollard's description is inaccurate.

Hammersley is happy about recordings and even field notes, but is unhappy about non-verbal elements of action which require interpretation on the part of the researcher. For example, Pollard tells us that 'Mrs Rothwell felt a sincere caring duty towards the children in her class whom she believed came from generally poor and unstable home backgrounds.' Pollard gives us no reference to any data collected to support this part of his description. Words such as 'sincere', 'caring' and 'she believed' come from interpretations of what respondents say and the way they say them. So, while qualitative researchers may criticize quantitative studies for using indicators which are not really related to the concepts presented, the same is true here.

2　Pollard doesn't define concepts.

Pollard does not tell us what he means by pupil 'collaboration', for example. So in his account we have to accept his presumably intuitive understanding of when it is and is not occurring.

3　Pollard uses participants' accounts uncritically.

These may be inaccurate or deliberately misleading for a number of reasons, yet they are used as a form of evidence. Even multiple accounts (another form of triangulation) have their problems.

4 Pollard's descriptions are specific to the one school; they cannot be generalized.

Ethnographers like Pollard make statements about behaviour which they portray as 'typical'. They don't usually specify time limits or contexts or give any evidence for these generalizations. Though Pollard, unusually, does give us a description of frequency in Figure 2.13, we are not told:

- over what period the observations were carried out;

- whether the observations were continuous;

- how rigorously the teacher–child contacts were identified (e.g. the definitions of types of behaviour);

- how the measurement was done (live coding, video or audio recording?).

5 There is limited construct validity (see p. 47).

This refers to how far an indicator actually measures the concept or construct it is supposed to measure. For example, a teacher's use of recitation of times tables might indicate that she or he is a traditionalist. But if this is being done only because a SAT test is imminent, it might not be a reliable indicator. One way of getting round this problem is to ask another observer, or the respondents to also make an interpretation. Another issue related to this problem is how far Pollard's documentation of the teachers' perspectives represents all the components of his definition of traditionalism/progressivism. There is no definition of either concept in Pollard's work.

To conclude, Hammersley says it is useful to keep three things distinct when evaluating any study:

1 Whether the description and explanations provided are correct.

2 Whether the researcher has taken the best precautions and made the best checks so as to maximize the chance of the validity of descriptive and explanatory claims, given the available methodology.

3 Whether the researcher provides the reader with the necessary information about the precautions taken and the checks made for an assessment to be made of their effectiveness.

(Hammersley 1990)

For Hammersley, then, it is possible to combine qualitative and quantitative approaches; indeed doing this adds strength to a study. In the past, qualitative researchers may have used their critique of the spurious rigour of positivism as an excuse for approaching research in a casual way. This needs to be tightened up so that concepts are clearly defined, the methods of data collection and analysis are transparent, reliability and validity are ensured wherever possible, and claims for the study are made explicit.

 Sort these statements according to the research methods they apply to. Compare your answers with those of other people when you have finished.

Table 2.4   Advantages and disadvantages of qualitative and quantitative research approaches

Advantages	Disadvantages
Large numbers of replies can be collected	They pre-structure the responses too much – respondents do not have a chance to express views or raise issues that are not included in the questionnaire's schedule
They are easy and quick to complete, so the likelihood is that more will be returned (i.e. the non-response rate will be lower)	They assume that responses will be accurate and consistent. However, questionnaires may be completed with little attention, and views on issues that have been given little consideration in the past are likely to be fluid, so that answers given today may be different from tomorrow's answers
They allow for easy collation and subsequent statistical manipulation	Gives detailed results, but these cannot be generalized to other cases
Cheap to get and readily available (usually)	Results are too influenced by the opinions of the researcher – they are not reliable
Can provide data about large numbers of people	The Hawthorne effect has too much influence here
Can enable the researcher to use the comparative method, e.g. comparison of different countries' statistics to identify the importance of factors which differ between them	Too dependent on the personal interpretation of the researcher. Different researchers would almost certainly get different results
All variables are carefully controlled to isolate the importance of the one the researcher is interested in	Has very serious ethical problems attached to it
Easy to replicate studies using this method – i.e. to check the results by repeating the study in another, similar, context	Often has serious practical problems attached to it
Is excellent for allowing the researcher to really understand another person's 'reality' and social world	Can be very dificult to analyse the results

Which methodological techniques would you choose, and why, for educational research projects with the following aims? What would your overall research design be?

Project 1. To discover how successful the implementation of a government scheme to introduce computers into primary schools has been.

Project 2. To discover how far parent–governors of schools were

exercising their voice in governing bodies compared to others such as industri-alists, LEA representatives, teaching staff. (There is a fear that parent–governors tend not to express their views, seeing themselves as 'only a parent'.)

Project 3. To investigate interactions between pupils and teachers in classrooms with a view to discovering any gender differences.

Project 4. To discover how teachers are responding to delivering and assessing the National Curriculum up to Key Stage 1 (7 years old).

Project 5. To discover whether 'media rich' children (those with easy access to video recorders, computers, etc. in their homes) do better or worse at school as a result compared to 'media poor' children.

Project 6. To investigate the early socialization of children in the home, particularly in terms of language development, to discover whether middle-class children have any advantages over working-class children in terms of language development and use when they come to school.

Essay questions

1 Briefly explain the role of an hypothesis in positivist educational research. (2 marks)

2 Show, with reference to studies discussed here, why some educational researchers reject positivism. (4 marks)

3 With reference to the Bennett study and any others in natural or social sciences, how far do you agree that science is a systematic method? (6 marks)

4 Interpretivists claim that human beings 'know'

things to be true in ways other than the scientific method. On what other grounds do educational researchers claim their beliefs or ideas are true? (4 marks)

5 Using examples from the studies you are familiar with, assess whether it is possible for educational research to be scientific. (9 marks)

(Adapted from AEB 'A' level Sociology June 1992, Paper 1, Question 1)

Suggestions for further reading

Useful further readings on educational research methodology are:

Wragg, E.C. (1994) *An Introduction to Classroom Observation*, London: Routledge.

Hitchcock, G. and Hughes, D. (1989) *Research and the Teacher*, London: Routledge.

The government's Central Statistical Office and the Department for Education are sources of useful secondary data. Examples of published quantitative data include:

Social Trends;

Education Statistics for the UK.

Examples of published secondary qualitative data include free OFSTED reports on schools and a list of all schools inspected so far, available from: 0181 985 7757.

Secondary data in the form of publications from the Department for Education can be obtained from:

DFE
Publications Centre
PO Box 2193
London
E15 2EU

Answer to the question on p. 49.
The students who thought that the forces in the direction of movement are exactly equal to the forces in the reverse direction were right. This is the Newtonian answer. The second answer was believed to be true before Newton's time. Similar examples are given in Prosser, M. (1993) 'Phenomenography and the principles and practices of learning', *Higher Education Research & Development*, vol. 12, no. 1.

3

Vocational education and training policy

Paul Trowler

Figure 3.1

Education and training: an exception to the rule?

 List the aspects of your education which have been work-related (that is, vocational).

Compare lists with a partner and then share your views on the experiences you have had of vocational education and training.

The background

Attempts to create a coherent system of training for work have been unsuccessful since the sixteenth century. Despite this, Britain has been economically successful: it was the first country to industrialize. During the Industrial Revolution and afterwards the administrators and those in power were schooled in Latin and Greek, while workers' education aimed to instil literacy and morality. Learning the trade 'on the job' through apprenticeships, leading to the status of skilled crafts workers was the only real training in skills for work.

One of the main obstacles to achieving a coherent system of work-related education and training has been the difference in status between them. Training is stereotyped both by philosophers of education such as Peters and Plato, and by the general population, as the narrow, rote learning of knowledge or skills. Education, on the other hand, is seen as initiation into adult life, giving people the ability to appreciate fine things and to use one's brain critically. The writer C.P. Snow described this divide as the 'two cultures'.

Even the Second World War – when nearly half a million people (mostly women) did government training courses to improve the 'war machine' – did not shift these attitudes. Immediately after it the tripartite system of grammar, secondary modern and technical schools created by the 1944 Education Act set the class-based divisions of the past – between education for self-improvement and training for work – in institutional concrete. Given these status differences it was not surprising that the few technical schools which were built following the Act were very much second-best to the grammar schools.

The school system gradually developed into the comprehensive system that it largely is today. The aim was partly to give a more rounded education and greater equality of opportunity to students. But even here the old status differences remained. The deeply entrenched nature of the two cultures meant that even where policies were put into effect to make education more vocational, a process of academic drift (inappropriate intellectualization of subjects) occurred. This happened to the polytechnics, set up to be a vocational arm of higher education (HE).

 Would you agree that doing a GNVQ (General National Vocational Qualification – see p. 98) has a lower level of prestige than doing an 'A' level? If so, why is this?

Such attitudes – and the education system they gave rise to – caused deep problems. For example, during the 1960s British governments became increasingly concerned about the ability of the poorly trained British workforce to cope with changing technology. The Labour Government under Harold Wilson promoted the idea of a bright new future for Britain, driven by the 'white heat of technological revolution'.

In 1974 the Manpower Services Commission (MSC) was set up and is in existence today, re-shaped and renamed, as the Training, Enterprise and Education Directorate (TEED). This is an arm of the government's Employment Department and, though it was originally aimed at improving vocational education and training (VET), it was quickly used to set up schemes to deal with the increasing numbers of young unemployed people leaving school during the recession of the mid 1970s. Today TEED is the power-house of the vocational thrust in government policy.

The Great Debate

In October 1976 the Labour Prime Minister James Callaghan gave a famous speech at Ruskin College Oxford, which attacked schools and colleges for being out of touch with the changing industrial world. This formally opened the 'Great Debate': a public dialogue about the education system in the UK.

Some key points of the Ruskin College Speech were that:

1 schools, universities and polytechnics were anti-industry so that students left with 'no desire or intention of joining industry';

2 science teaching in schools needed to be more related to practical applications in industry;

3 standards of teaching mathematics were in decline and inadequate numbers of mathematically qualified potential scientists were being produced;

Figure 3.2

James Callaghan

4 too much priority had been given by schools to equipping children 'for a lively, constructive place in society' and not enough to enabling them 'to do a job of work';

5 the essential job of education was to give the following tools: 'to be basically literate, to be basically numerate, to understand how to live and work together [and] to have respect for others'.

 Callaghan's speech was made around twenty years ago. With the benefit of hindsight, what critical comments would you make about it now?

One of the main concerns in the 'Great Debate' was Britain's declining industrial competitiveness compared to Germany, the USA and Japan. The 1984 Institute of Manpower Studies' publication *Competence and Competition* contrasted VET systems in all these countries and pointed to the urgent need for changes in the British system. The idea that a liberal education leading to personal development was desirable now began to be replaced by a view which saw education and training as an investment in human capital.

The **human capital** concept sees people's skills and knowledge as a form of capital. Investment in this type of capital yields greater returns for both the individual and the country than investment in machinery or conventional (non-human) capital:

It has been widely observed that increases in national output have been large compared with the increases of land, man-hours [sic], and physical reproducible capital. Investment in human capital is probably the major explanation for this difference. . . I shall contend that such investment in human capital accounts for most of the impressive rise in the real earnings per worker. . . By investing in themselves, people can enlarge the range of choice available to them.

(Schultz 1961)

Looking back on your own education, in what ways (if at all) has your personal stock of human capital been increased by your education and training?

Figure 3.3

Vocational qualifications of workforce

Figure 3.4

Destination of 16 year olds by GCSE results 1989

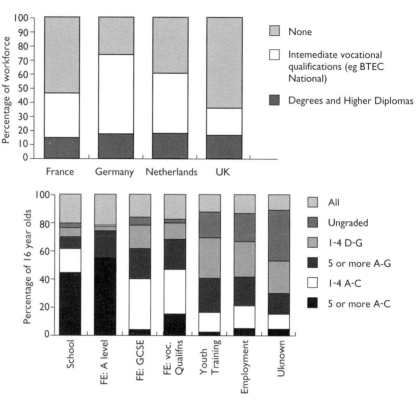

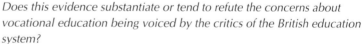

Does this evidence substantiate or tend to refute the concerns about vocational education being voiced by the critics of the British education system?

How is it done?

When teachers on the Continent are asked to account for the comparatively high attainment of most of their young people, they usually refer to features commonly found in other European schooling systems, but absent from English education:

- teaching groups of roughly similar abilities; repeating of years [for those who fail];

- different pathways, reflecting academic, technical or vocational goals, open to youngsters from the age of 12–14 onwards; invariably the vocational tracks, and often the technical tracks, begin with basic, practical studies before progressively introducing higher technology;

- access to the pathways is by choice: teachers provide parents with guidance. . . but parental choice is paramount;

- progression along pathways depends on performance and there is often a settling down from more demanding tracks to less demanding ones;

- bridging and transfer mechanisms exist which allow youngsters to move from one part of the system to any other point;

- the mark at the end of the school year, which determines whether a pupil is ready to move on to the next year, depends on all his [or her] subjects; a pupil cannot give up on a subject, say maths, simply because he or she does not like it;

- there is a range of school-leaving diplomas closely tied in with future job opportunities;

- the labour market is so organized that clear standards are demanded in all occupations, standards that are highly dependent on success in the educational system.

(Halsey *et al.* 1991)

How practicable and desirable is this model for the British system? Would you say that we have moved closer to this model over the last few years?

The new vocationalism

Another government concern was the steadily rising unemployment, particularly among the young. By 1986 the official figure was 12 per cent unemployment, representing 3 million people. Apart from the costs of supporting such numbers, a valuable resource was being wasted. What became known as the new vocationalism (although it is now not so new) was seen by the New Right as an answer to these problems. (See p. 3 for a description of the New Right perspective.) It put human capital theory into practice and attempted to strengthen the links between education and the economy. Policies to do this were introduced progressively over the 1980s.

Specifically, the aims of the new vocationalism were to:

- rationalize qualifications;

- vocationalize education in schools, further education (FE) and adult education;

- instil 'core skills' in trainees and students;

- record these and other personal attributes as well as qualifications to improve employment selection in a formal Record of Achievement (RoA);

- train the unemployed for work;

- abolish the status gap between education and training;

- improve the quality of VET.

Policies designed to achieve these aims proceeded on four fronts:

Figure 3.5

The aims of new vocationalism

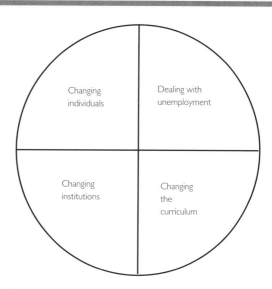

While these may have been the explicit aims of new vocationalism, a number of criticisms of the policies involved in actually implementing them have been made by academics. We summarize these below and will consider each in more detail when we look at the individual policy areas. The criticisms are:

- the state has become involved in areas of individual life and aspects of the personality that are not the concern of the education and training system or of the state;

- policy has been concentrated on the lower levels of education and training and on lower achievers rather than areas of the economy which would make British industry competitive abroad;

- training has not enhanced social mobility for individuals and groups undertaking it; rather it has tended to reproduce existing social inequalities based on, for example, race and gender;

- much 'training' has in fact been preparation for unemployment. Training schemes are simply a way of making the unemployment figures smaller and less politically damaging;

- new vocational policies have shifted power into the hands of employers and national politicians. Teachers, parents, students and the local community have lost control of education and training;

- while there has been a rash of VET initiatives, these have often been short-lived and have worked in isolation;

- political disagreements have meant confused and changing policies with too many unclear aims;

- money has been wasted on publicity for training schemes and on 'evaluations' by outside consultants while the schemes themselves have been underfunded.

Next we are going to deal with specific examples of the areas shown in Figure 3.5. These are, however, only selections from a number of VET policy areas.

Dealing with unemployment:
  Youth Training and Employment Training;

Changing the curriculum:
  the National Curriculum and vocationalism;
  recording achievement;
  adult education and vocationalism;
  vocationalism in the school and college curriculum;

Changing institutions:
  city technology colleges;

Changing individuals:

  students as enterprising consumers: EHE and training credits;
  NVQs and competence;
  core skills.

Dealing with unemployment

Figure 3.6
Alan Clark

Alan Clark, the then Minister of State at the Department of Employment (DoE), wrote in his diary in June 1983:

> Faster than I can digest them great wadges of documentation are whumped into my 'In' tray. The subject matter is turgid: a mass of 'schemes' whose purpose, plainly, is not so much to bring relief to those out of work as to devise excuses for removing them from the [unemployment] Register. . . The Enterprise Allowance Scheme, the Job Release Scheme, the Community Scheme. Convoluted and obscure even at their inception, they have been so picked over and 'modified' by civil servants as to be incomprehensible. . . my head is bursting.

(Clark 1993)

Youth Training and Employment Training

The Youth Training Scheme (YTS) began in 1983 as a one-year foundation course after a series of less ambitious schemes. It became a two-year course in 1985. By 1993 15 per cent of school leavers were attending youth training courses, though the number has been dropping recently as more stay on at school or in further education.

Schemes are administered through TEED. TEED controls them through the TEC network which funds the actual training locally, both for school leavers on Youth Training (YT) and adults on Employment Training (ET). TEED is also responsible for the allocation of training credits (see p. 93). TECs try to meet the needs of local employers when they decide where to spend money on training. Training courses are delivered by FE colleges, other training organizations (often private), and employers with a bias in recent years to moving training out of colleges and into the employers' premises.

Figure 3.7

Participation in, and qualification from, Youth Training

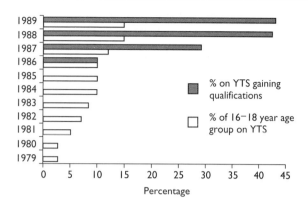

D. Lee and a team of researchers conducted a research project lasting six years into the YTS in a town they called 'Southwich' in the southeast of England. While the authors agree that 'British schooling has for too long been impoverished by rigid and elitist ideas of academic worth' (the 'two cultures' divide), their study concludes that youth training in its current form does not solve the problem. They found that trainees complained that they were being prepared for 'Noddy jobs'. Their comments illustrate this further:

> All I learned was how to make the tea. . . I used to pick up loads of potatoes and coal and load the lorry. I got all sweaty and dirty. The reason they wanted me was as a sort of dogsbody.

(Lee *et al.* 1990)

Figure 3.8

Youth training – the experience of trainees?

The researchers also found that the youth training experience was not itself marketable to employers. In some cases it even had a stigma attached to it so that the trainee's chance of getting a job was worse *after* than before the 'training'. Although a relatively high proportion of the trainees Lee *et al.* studied did get jobs after the scheme, they were often in low status or unskilled occupations. The main contribution to any success the trainees had when job hunting appeared to come from the fact that employers were using the scheme as a probationary period for potential new staff.

The perception of poor quality training in the scheme was not limited to the researchers, the trainees or the town of Southwich: the European Social Fund refused to pay over £100 million to fund the YTS because of its inadequacies – particularly the lack of training in information technology within it.

The VET literature contains a number of other criticisms of youth training. Denis Gleeson, Leslie Bash and David Coulby note that government policy on training is incoherent and mutually contradictory. One obvious paradox in the policy is, as Gleeson remarks, 'What is the point of relevant vocational education when the possibilities of obtaining employment remain limited?'

This paradox is explained by J. Wellington who suggests that the following process is in operation:

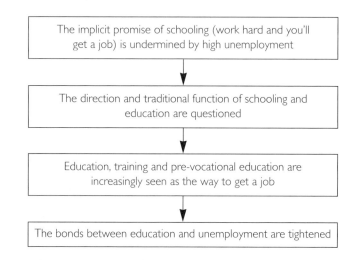

The implicit promise of schooling (work hard and you'll get a job) is undermined by high unemployment

↓

The direction and traditional function of schooling and education are questioned

↓

Education, training and pre-vocational education are increasingly seen as the way to get a job

↓

The bonds between education and unemployment are tightened

Underlying this process is the 'individual deficit' model which blames unemployment on the unemployed young people themselves for lacking the necessary skills and attitudes for the work available. If only educational institutions operated more effectively then they could correct the deficit, the argument runs.

 Adopting a Marxist perspective (see pp. 12–14), what are the possible effects on class solidarity and potential for revolution by the working class of trainees being instilled with this individual deficit model?

Gleeson also identifies less obvious paradoxes. One is between centralization and local initiative. YT is typical of many VET schemes in that it is operated locally but controlled centrally (by TEED in this case). A problem arises when innovative and useful projects develop on the ground then central funding stops and their benefits are lost. This has happened very often in vocational training schemes.

Another paradox is to do with teaching and learning styles. YT, the Technical and Vocational Education Initiative (TVEI) and other schemes have evolved progressive teaching approaches such as learning by doing, problem solving, innovative forms of assessment, and new types of relationship between teachers and students. Yet other measures, like the National Curriculum and government policy generally, favour a return to traditional subject teaching and forms of assessment.

Paradoxically too, while government rhetoric stresses the need for training in high level skills to be competitive internationally, evidence from both the UK and the USA shows that it is the low attaining students who attend 'vocational' courses, and these are usually oriented to the low status, low skilled, occupations. These courses often restrict access to the higher status and better paid jobs because of the stigma that discredits their appeal.

In terms of equal opportunities, too, the rhetoric and the reality do not match. YT and TVEI schemes stress equality of opportunity in terms of ethnicity and gender and special needs. Yet, as Gleeson points out:

> in the specific case of female participation in nursing, child care and other gender-specific courses. . . vocational training represents little more than a reinforcement in gender roles and apprenticeship in home crafts. . . [while] evidence regarding black youth on [YT] courses indicates that they are consistently more likely to be allocated to schemes offering inferior opportunities of subsequent employment.
>
> (Gleeson 1989)

The freelance writer and researcher Paul Willis (1987) makes the same point, saying 'the more the school curriculum is vocationalized, the deeper and earlier will class reproduction take root'. Even where, for example, women trainees are offered opportunities for training in non-traditional areas, they have to face a multitude of pressures. J. Tizard reports a female trainee's comments:

> Who do you sit by at tea break? You aren't one of the boys, you can't join in the discussion of sexual exploits and you probably don't want to talk about fishing and football. . . what do you do when the lads are leaning out of the window whistling at another woman, or discussing a pin-up?
>
> (Tizard 1984)

Roger Dale (1985) agrees with these criticisms: YT and similar schemes are aimed at the lower ability 14–18 year olds, not those who take the traditional academic curriculum; they are aimed not only at training people for jobs but also at preparing them for a status somewhere between work and non-work; they legitimate gender and ethnic inequalities; and the new vocationalism of which YT is a part is often not supported by those involved in implementing it – teachers, educators, administrators and the young people themselves.

This last argument is explored in Andrew Pollard's book which describes and analyses the experiences of the young people and teachers who have been affected by the new vocationalism. Carol Buswell's chapter on 'Flexible workers for flexible firms?' gives the results of research conducted between 1985 and 1986 in which she interviewed fifty-five young people on a YTS. She argues that these young people were being trained for 'responsible autonomy' whereas the sort of work they would get (clerical and retailing in this case) really only required the simple following of instructions. This led to an uncomfortable experience for the trainees. The quotes below illustrate this contradiction:

Clerical lecturer: 'In further education we try to treat you like young adults – so you see me like a supervisor at work.'

Retail lecturer: 'This isn't meant to be like school – we won't dictate notes, you'll have to find out for yourself.'

Clerical girl, small building firm: 'There's nothing to do most of the time, so I took me book in one day and got wrong [told off] for reading – we've got to sit and do nothing. They stand right over you when you're typing and make comments. The only decent time is when they go off and play golf on a Wednesday and we've got the office to ourselves.'

Retail girl, department store: 'The manager had me in his office one day and was trying to tell me my skirt was too short – so I said "Are you saying I'm not good enough for this shop?" So then he started saying me shirt collar hadn't been ironed, and he told me to save up for a new skirt.'

 Have you had any experience of this sort of contradiction?

One telling example which illustrates the mixed motives and contradictory aims of the government's VET policy is noted by the Greater London Training Branch of the Greater London Council (now abolished) in 1984:

Trade unions, local education authorities, training boards, skill centres, standard setting bodies are all being systematically undermined [by government]. . . Government VET policy seems to be to dismantle the basic infrastructure of training! The effect of this is to remove all control from training policy except for that of government and the employers. Meanwhile, the study of politics and an understanding of the context of work are strictly off the agenda in these schemes. The Manpower Services Commission made this clear when it wrote to training providers telling them not to become 'involved in any activity of a political nature', a sentiment reiterated by government minister Peter Morrison who said that youth training is 'all about the world of work, and I don't want it to get a bad name if politics get involved'.

 Refer back to the list of criticisms of the new vocationalism on p. 73.
Put a tick next to those which apply to this aspect of government policy in your view.
Now put them in order. Which is the most important criticism, which next and which the least important?
In pairs, explain to each other why you prioritized the criticisms in the way you did.

Changing the curriculum

Curriculum comes from 'curricule': a two-wheeled carriage or racing chariot. Curriculum thus related to a racecourse, but now usually refers to a course of study: the subjects offered by an educational institution. Some definitions are rather broader though, for example the educationalists Neagley and Evans define it as 'all of the planned experiences provided by the school to assist the pupils in attaining the designated learning outcomes to the best of their abilities'. Some authors are more cynical. For example, Musgrove believes it is 'an elaborate device for filling the time available'.

The National Curriculum and vocationalism

The 1988 Education Act introduced the National Curriculum: ten subjects which are compulsory for all students from 5 to 16 years. Spours and Young note:

> the National Curriculum itself can be seen as a form of vocationalism. Though not related to particular jobs, it does very much reflect the kind of response given by employers when asked their views about education. With an emphasis on standards and discipline, it is clearly concerned with the kind of model citizen envisaged by many employers.

> (Spours and Young 1990)

In terms of content, though, the National Curriculum is a very traditional curriculum, reproducing almost exactly the curriculum prescribed by the 1904 Board of Education Regulations:

Table 3.1	A comparison of the curriculum in 1904 and 1988 – how much has it changed over eighty years?
1904	*1988*
English (> 4.5 hours per week)	English
Maths (> 3.5 hours per week)	Maths
Science (> 3.5 hours per week)	Science
History (> 4.5 hours per week)	History
Geography (> 4.5 hours per week)	Geography
Physical Exercise	Physical Education
Drawing	Art
Foreign Language (3 hours per week each)	Modern Foreign Language
Manual Work	
Domestic Subjects (in girls' schools)	Technology
(Music added soon afterwards)	Music

 Ivor Goodson, a pioneer of curriculum history, argues that:

> *The similarity between 1904 and 1988 questions the rhetoric of 'a major new initiative' employed by the government, and points to some historical continuities in social and political purpose and priorities.*

> *(Goodson 1990)*

> *What might these 'continuities in purpose and priorities' consist of? What would your ideal curriculum consist of? (Think particularly about the balance between vocational and non-vocational education and training.)*

One subject in the National Curriculum – technology – is directly oriented to vocationalism while a second – the modern language – is indirectly aimed at working in a European context. The subject of technology held out hopes for National Curriculum enthusiasts. Duncan Graham, the first chair and chief executive of the National Curriculum Council (1988–91) wrote:

> Because it is compulsory for all, from the very brightest child to the less able, technology can become the vehicle for breaking down the academic and vocational divide which has bedevilled British education for so long.
>
> (Graham 1993)

Because it was compulsory, technology would also help to ensure that more girls entered science and technology fields. However, two problems have beset the teaching of technology in schools since it was introduced:

1 The cost to schools of students actually making things. The basic aim of the technology syllabus is for students to identify a need and fulfil it through designing and making a solution. In practice, though, the emphasis is on the cheaper stages of assessing need and planning a solution rather than actually doing and making. Some writers, for example the authors of *Every Child in Britain*, have seen this as partly the result of academic drift: the need to verbalize 'design briefs' is given priority over actually making things and this disadvantages those of less academic ability. For other writers it is simply the result of inadequate resourcing of the National Curriculum.

2 The lack of teachers trained to deliver the technology syllabus. Those who teach have experience in craft, design and technology (CDT) or home economics – very different subjects from the National Curriculum's technology.

 Discuss your experience of learning technology-type subjects. In what ways would you have changed it?

However, it may be that employers are enthusiastic about the National Curriculum because of its very traditional nature, not its content. A tightly structured, rigidly delivered and rigorously assessed school experience creates a hidden curriculum which draws the school and work experiences closer together (see p. 155).

> **Correspondence theory** argues that there is a correspondence between school and work in that school trains people for work not so much through the formal curriculum but through the hidden curriculum. School requirements of discipline and order, punctuality and deference to the teacher, anticipate the requirements of work, except that the boss replaces the teacher. More subtly, Paul Willis (1978) argues that school prepares people for the boredom of work: at school they learn how to cope with boredom and develop strategies to prevent it.

Correspondence theory alerts us to the fact that the formal curriculum and the hidden curriculum are important in VET.

 1 What other areas of correspondence are there between school (or ET) and work? Complete the boxes in figure 3.11.

2 List the coping strategies you have developed over the years to deal with boredom. Could they be applied in a work context too?

Refer back to the list of criticisms of the 'new vocationalism' on p. 73.

Figure 3.9

Correspondence theory

School
Teacher in charge School uniform Punctuality Subjects not projects

Work
Manager in charge Acceptable dress 9 to 5 work Division of work into small parts

Put a tick next to those which apply to this aspect of government policy in your view.

Now put them in order. Which is the most important criticism, which next and which the least important?

Explain to a partner why you prioritized the criticisms in the way you did.

Recording achievement

Two parallel schemes of recording achievement began in the mid-1980s. One was backed by the DoE and was used to record competences achieved through National Vocational Qualifications (NVQs). This was the National Record of Vocational Achievement, or NROVA. A square grey box was issued to keep the certificates of competence in. It looked just like a pizza box, and this is what it became known as.

The other was sponsored by the Education Department and was called the National Record of Achievement, or NRA. A burgundy coloured folder with gold trim was issued to keep the various statements of achievement in. It had plastic inserts to protect the contents and elaborate lettering on the front. It looked just like a wine list, and this is what it became known as.

These two schemes represented conflicting ideologies over the aims of the RoA policy. From the New Right perspective (and that of the DoE), the aim was to keep a record of training and work success in the NROVA. It represented proof for employers of what its owner could do:

> You can use your **NROVA** to show employers what you can do already and you can go on adding to these achievements throughout your life.
>
> (NCVQ The National Record of Vocational Achievement)

This approach stresses the importance of the product, which essentially is a profile of the person. This profile (the RoA itself) is the primary interest because it is useful in moving the young person from training to employment, showing what he or she can do. For this reason it is a central element of vocational programmes like TVEI and NVQs. The importance of having a personal profile is summed up in the following quote from the Further Education Unit:

> A central principle of recording achievement is that qualifications, the possession of certain skills and knowledge, do not represent all that is important about a person. Personal qualities and general skills are central to our ideas of what a person is, and [. . . are] at least as important to potential employers as the more specific material often identified in examination syllabuses and occupational standards. . . It is for these reasons, among others, that notions of 'core skills', 'personal transferable skills'

and 'personal effectiveness' have entered the debates on post-school education.

Which of your personal qualities and general skills would you like to have publicly recorded and which not? Why?

The NRA, on the other hand, was based on the view that student-centredness in schools and colleges should be increased. This aim was promoted by the DES and by some teachers and academics. The student and his or her teachers sit down together and discuss progress and achievements and make plans for future. The idea behind it is that the student's educational experience becomes richer, more collaborative, and personalized. This happens because students can then identify their own strengths and weaknesses, use action plans to improve on weak areas, and take responsibility for their own learning. The supporters of the NRA, then, are advocates of the process of recording achievement and tend to hold the humanist perspective we described in Chapter 1.

In 1993 the DoE took over responsibility for the NRA from the DES. The NROVA had been dropped but the 'process' advocates began to worry that the 'product' was assuming too much importance under the NRA's new ownership. Patricia Broadfoot, an expert in the field, began to view with concern the increasing desire in some quarters to use RoAs as an instrument for recording progress and achievement within the national assessment system, and for evaluating pupils against pupils, schools against schools. She feared it would simply become an instrument for supporting the government's attempt to bring market forces to education and training through its use as an information source for consumers to make choices. This prospect was, she argued, 'deeply incompatible with the [original] philosophy and purposes of RoAs'.

As well as the New Right and humanist perspectives, a third group have written about RoAs: the critical theorists. They are very sceptical about any form of recording achievement. They see it as a means of the 'Big Brother' state keeping tabs on citizens.

The French social philosopher Michel Foucault is best known in this context: he raises the spectre of education as part of a modern panopticon. The panopticon was originally a Victorian device which allowed 360° surveillance from a central position, but the term was used by Foucault to refer to the increasingly intrusive surveillance of individuals by the state. Once, education was only interested in a person's intelligence and memory; now it concerns itself with all aspects of the character. The student's attitudes to authority, sociability and commitment are documented and carried with them for their whole life. Foucault notes that the traditional end-of-year examination system 'places individuals in a field of surveillance. . . situates them in a network of writing [and]. . . engages them in a whole mass of documents that capture and fix them'. This is even more true of the process of recording achievement.

Anthony Giddens and Denis Gleeson also number among those concerned about state surveillance and who would see RoAs as an example of this.

Records of Achievement: information for employment selection, improved teaching and learning, or surveillance?
Which approach is a more accurate description of the process of recording achievement in your experience? Discuss your opinion with another member of the group.

A further problem with recording achievement is that, like many educational initiatives, it has attracted a group of advocates who are relatively uncritical of it. As in other areas of education, an 'industry' has developed around RoAs. The uncritical advocates in this industry often make us lose sight of the real effects of their favourite project: its problems as well as its benefits. In the case of recording achievement this group contains members from both the humanist perspective and from the New Right. The former take most interest in the process of recording achievement; the latter in its product: the record.

Item A

> where pupils had received a record of achievement at sixteen, these were much valued by the pupils themselves; many employers responded very positively to the initiative, getting involved with development work in schools and schemes as well as finding the summary documentation useful; pupils' enthusiasm for learning increased where teachers gave them more of a partnership role and provided opportunities for individual discussion: teachers were becoming increasingly aware of the powerful formative role assessment could play in supporting the curriculum.

(Broadfoot 1988)

Item B

	% M Agree	% F Agree	% All Agree	% M Disagree	% F Disagree	% All Disagree
Profiling helped me to improve my schoolwork	2.6	2.9	27.4	50.6	45.8	48.2
Profiling helped me to understand myself better	33.3	38.7	35.8	42.3	36.5	39.5
Profiling helped me get on better with the teachers	41.6	44.1	42.6	32.1	36.7	34.6
I think my profile would help me get a job if I showed it to an employer	32.5	36.7	34.6	41.1	34.7	38.1
Profiling helped me to decide what job I wanted to do	7.2	8.4	7.9	74.3	76	75.1
Teachers seemed really keen on profiling	47.2	48.4	48.1	23.5	21.4	22.2
Profiling was too much effort for what I got out of it	32.4	25.2	29.1	41.8	48.7	45.3
I couldn't see the point of profiling	36.5	31.4	34	44.8	51.1	47.9
I never really knew what to put in my profile	6.8	35.4	35.9	43.7	48.5	45.9
Profiling made me feel uncomfortable	22.7	15.7	19.5	50.6	57.9	54.1
Profiling seemed to make the teachers feel uncomfortable	7.5	2.2	4.8	54.6	64.4	59.5
The teachers didn't give me a chance to say what I wanted	15.6	10.8	13.3	68.4	76.1	72.4
We were meant to do profiling but we didn't do it much	34.1	30.3	32	49.2	55.4	52.6
There wasn't enough time to do it properly	37.7	37.5	37.9	47.3	44.8	46.3
Response of 3,000 16–17 year old students across the TVEI authorities to a questionnaire about their experiences 1 or 2 years previously of profiling for a record of achievement. Favourable statements about profiting in bold type.						

Source: Adapted from Helsby, G. (1991) *TVEI Pilots in Profile* in Hopkins, D. (1991) *TVEI at the Change of Life*, London: Multilingual Matters

Item C

> the success of the NRA has been phenomenal; to date over 2 million copies [of the free folder] have been ordered and at the end of the 1991/1992 academic year, it is expected that the majority of school leavers will leave with a copy of their completed NRA.

(North West Record of Achievement Working Group 1992)

1 Which of the three items reflects most closely your experience of recording achievement?

2 How far could item B be considered reliable evidence of the effectiveness of recording achievement generally?

3 Critically examine the accounts of the evidence contained in items A and C.

In a small group, discuss your conclusions.

Refer back to the list of criticisms of the new vocationalism on p. 73.

Put a tick next to those which apply to this aspect of government policy in your view.

Now put them in order. Which is the most important criticism, which next and which the least important.

Divide into pairs. Explain to each other why you prioritized the criticisms in the way you did.

Adult education and vocationalism

Over 5 million adults engage in formal education each year. Some 45 per cent attend adult education centres, 28 per cent go to FE colleges and 16 per cent to universities, with the Workers' Education Association (WEA), the Open University, the Basic Education Service and residential establishments accounting for the rest at around 2 or 3 per cent each.

The development of adult education has undergone a number of discrete phases in terms of its purposes and therefore its curriculum content. We could summarize these as:

Education for salvation (seventeenth century onwards). Religious groups such as the Quakers and Methodists supported adult education and oriented it to the propagation of religious knowledge and associated literacy.

Education for vocation (nineteenth century). The first 'mechanics institute' was set up in Edinburgh in 1821, and by 1850 there were about 700 throughout the UK. They were often funded by private donations. These institutes aimed to improve the skills and understanding of working people and to make their businesses more profitable. Many mechanics institutes later became technical colleges, libraries or museums, or polytechnics.

Education for civilization (also nineteenth century). Other institutes were sometimes set up as a reaction to the vocational emphasis of the mechanics institutes. They taught subjects such as Greek, Latin, history, logic, literature and modern languages. Examples are the London Working Men's College and Leicester College, now the extra-mural teaching centre for Leicester University (Vaughan College). From the 1870s, university extra-mural work became increasingly important in non-vocational adult education. (Extra-mural – literally 'beyond the walls' – means education for the community outside the university.)

Education for participation (end of the nineteenth, early twentieth century). This was stimulated by the need to educate members of the working class as they gained the vote. By 1900 male householders had the franchise and this was gradually extended to broader groups, including women. The WEA was created in 1903, supported by the cooperative movement, trade unions and universities. The work of the WEA was rooted in the liberal humane philosophy of the universities. In 1924 the WEA gained funding from central government and began to split from the universities.

Education for recreation (post Second World War). The 1944 Education Act set up adult education centres offering a wide range of provision. The number of adult students in evening institutes rose from 300,000 in 1947 to more than a million in 1967. By 1970 vocational education was under the control of LEAs and colleges of commerce, art and technology. Non-vocational education was taken care of by LEAs, university extra-mural departments and the WEA, all with financial assistance from central government. Around half of adult education became oriented to 'leisure', for example courses on cooking, flower arranging, yoga, painting, arts and crafts and assorted hobbies. The high point of this phase was probably 1973 with the Russell Committee's report proposing a large-scale expansion of non-vocational adult education to give a comprehensive service which would enable education to be continued throughout a person's lifetime. However the next phase began before this happened.

Education for vocation (1970s to today). The government began to question expenditure on education for leisure and began to withdraw support; in response the LEAs, the WEA and university extra-mural departments gradually began to offer less of it. John Daines conducted a survey into changes in adult education in Derbyshire between 1976 and 1981. He found:

> *an increase in fee levels at three times the rate of inflation, towards*
> *the economic cost of courses;*
> *a 28 per cent drop in participation overall;*
> *an increase in the participation of the middle class from 61 to 75 per cent;*
> *an increasingly work-related motivation for joining adult education*
> *(from 10 to 22 per cent).*

The New Right argument underlying government policy for the vocationalization of adult education is that adult education is best left to voluntary agencies, the family and market forces. For Milton Friedman, for example, state intervention measures:

> *weaken the family; reduce the incentive to work, save and innovate;*
> *reduce the accumulation of capital, and limit our freedom. These are*
> *the fundamental standards by which they should be judged.*

The New Right would argue that where subsidized non-vocational leisure activities such as basket weaving or flower arranging are provided, these deflect people from the social goal of improvement of the economy which leads to long-term benefits. Furthermore vocational education helps people achieve a better social position and is also good for society (the human capital approach). Non-vocational education leads to personal enjoyment and perhaps enlightenment but does not lead to any social good and therefore should not be subsidized. In a country with economic problems, we need to concentrate on vocationalism: we can't afford education for leisure any more. Increasingly people will choose VET if they are asked to pay the real costs, as they should do.

The Conservative Government's White Paper *Education and Training for the 21st Century* (1991) and the Further and Higher Education Act 1992 which followed it applied the New Right type of ideas to adult education. Funds for FE would only be available to help adults 'improve their qualifications, update their skills and seek advancement in their present career or in a new career'. The FE funding councils would now only support full-time and part-time education for adults which lead to:

- NVQs (and before NVQs were fully established, to other vocational qualifications which were not yet approved as NVQs);

- GCSEs, 'AS' and 'A' levels;

- access to HE;

- access to higher levels of FE;

- acquisition of basic skills (literacy and numeracy);

- proficiency in English for speakers of other languages;

- courses for adults with special educational needs.

These areas of the curriculum came to be known as 'schedule two' courses: those which had funding with them or for which institutions outside FE could bid to provide. Courses outside schedule 2 – the non-vocational ones – suffered even more after the 1992 Act. There was a 5 per cent cut in funding in 1992 overall and some authorities drastically cut leisure course provision. One response was to 'vocationalize' previously non-vocational courses by, for example, making students work towards an NVQ certificate. Adult students often don't want the pressure and rigidity this brings, but it is necessary to attract funding.

1 One of the criticisms of these changes to adult education is that they make too simple a distinction between 'vocational' and 'non-vocational' education. How could you argue that there is no clear dividing line between the two?

2 Complete the right-hand boxes in Table 3.2.

Table 3.2	Arguments for and against the vocationalization of adult education.
Arguments in favour of the vocationalization of adult education	*Arguments against the vocationalization of adult education*
❑Subsidized non-vocational adult education is unnecessary: most adult learning is informal or conducted through clubs and voluntary organizations.	
Keith Percy's study indicates that 'Perhaps a third of all learning is undertaken through voluntary organisations' and suggested that 'working class men and women, senior citizens and members of ethnic groups are more likely to engage in learning in voluntary organisations than in formal adult education'. Similarly Allen Tough suggests that 'self-planned learning' is far more prevalent than 'professionally planned learning' – 81% compared to 19%.	

❏The main recipients of non-vocational education are the middle class and that the state should subsidize the poor, not the middle class.

The Further Education Unit's 1987 survey found that participation was skewed towards the young, higher social grades, owner occupiers and those with access to a car. J LeGrand's 1982 study showed that post-compulsory education in general benefits the well off and redistributes resources towards them; the opposite of the intentions behind the welfare state. The 1992 Further and Higher Education Act is therefore justified in targeting the needy; for example those needing basic literacy and numeracy, English for speakers of other languages and courses for adults with special educational needs. So, while it is well-known that those with some education will be more likely to seek more (the 'Trenaman effect', named after the researcher who identified it), it is not the state's responsibility to fund this.

❏Adult education reinforces and sustains an unfair society:
Janet Finch (1984) argues that adult education removes the upper working class (who use it most) from their community and culture and this harms the interests of the working class as a whole. Political leadership is removed from them. John Daines found that 16% of participants in Derbyshire's adult education came from the upper working class (class C2) compared to 8% from classes D and E combined. Nell Keddie in Thompson argues that adult education incorporates an individualistic self-help ideology. For example adult basic education implicitly blames the victim: it is the individual's fault that they cannot read or write adequately and it is they who are in need of correction (the 'individual pathology' model). This reflects back social problems to the 'imputed inadequacies of individuals' – there is no critique of the system which fails to address these problems.

❏Non-vocational adult education reproduces and reinforces women's domestic roles.

Hughes and Kennedy found that around 74% of those attending LEA funded adult education were women, and many of these classes are domestically oriented.

' . . . prejudiced attitudes and power have been used as a means of social control – the dominant over the subordinate, men over women – in ways that hinder change.'

They quote a number of examples to illustrate the point:
* The proliferation of courses in 'ladies keep fit' and 'women's weight training' in 'hostess cooker' and 'dressmaking'.
* A 'Mainly for Men Cookery' at a local evening institute (the only one in which ingredients were supplied).
* A course in an outer London borough entitled 'Car Maintenance for Ladies of Little Ability'.
* Prospectuses refer to women tutors as 'Mrs/Miss M Block' but men as 'I Block', or 'E Block Esq'.

3 Investigate the provision of adult education in your area. Interview staff involved about recent changes and how they feel about them.
Now, refer back to the list of criticisms of the new vocationalism on
p. 73.
Put a tick next to those which apply to this aspect of government policy in your view.
Now put them in order. Which is the most important criticism, which next and which the least important?
Explain to another member of the group why you prioritized the criticisms in the way you did.

Vocationalism in the school and college curriculum

During the 1980s the DoE became increasingly involved in the school curriculum. It spent so much money on a variety of schemes that there were worries that the influence of the DES would be almost completely displaced, at least in the 14–19 year groups. DoE schemes such as the TVEI and school-industry link schemes like the Compacts were often well funded and attractive to hard-pressed schools. Involvement with TVEI, for example, meant half a million pounds' extra income over five years, or £600 per pupil for each school or college participating (though this was much reduced as the scheme expanded).

The involvement of the DoE became so extensive that it has even been suggested that one of the motivations for the introduction of the National Curriculum in schools was to enable the DES to reassert its authority. DoE schemes are less important now than prior to the introduction of the National Curriculum, but it is worth examining one of them, the TVEI, more closely.

TVEI was introduced in 1983, funded by the Manpower Services Commission, an arm of the DoE. It aimed to help make young people better equipped for working life in a rapidly changing society. There were fourteen pilot projects, affecting 10,000 pupils between 14 and 18 years old. TVEI worked in both schools and colleges and the aim was to achieve better integration between them: as pupils moved from one to the other, TVEI moved with them. Anne Jones, then head of the Education Programme Directorate at the Training Agency, stated that TVEI was designed to achieve its aims by:

- using every opportunity to relate education to the world of work, using concrete examples where possible. TVEI-funded teacher placements in the business world helped achieve this;

- making sure that young people received the knowledge and competencies they needed in a world economy by, for example, providing them with computer equipment;

- making sure that young people received direct opportunities to learn about the nature of the economy and work through work experience, work shadowing, projects in the community and so on;

- making sure that young people learned how to be effective people, solve problems, work in teams and be enterprising through the way they were taught (i.e. in a student-centred way with less front-of-class teaching);

- making sure that young people had access to initial guidance and counselling and then education and training and opportunities for progression throughout their lives. The Record of Achievement (see p. 81) was one means of achieving this.

Initially there was also a lot of suspicion from teachers and lecturers in schools and colleges. They saw TVEI as reintroducing the old distinctions between academic and technical streams that existed in the tripartite system of grammar, technical and secondary modern schools. Norman Tebbit, the Employment Secretary at the time, actually referred to 'the rebirth of technical education' and this confirmed people's fears. However the money helped calm these worries.

Each school and college involved appointed a TVEI coordinator who liaised with the MSC about how they would spend the TVEI money. In practice the coordinator and the school or college had a lot of power in deciding how the money was spent. Each scheme was different, but what tended to happen was that instead of a particular group of students getting the money for special work-related courses, the money was spread around all pupils and all types of courses. In some schemes it became difficult to identify anything that was specifically 'TVEI' in a school, but easy to say 'that was bought (or done) with TVEI money'. Lots of computer technology was bought and the extra money also helped schools and colleges to work more closely with students in a student-centred way. One English teacher said:

> The great thing about TVEI was that it impressed upon management that we could have kids sitting around tables instead of in rows. They could do work in rough and produce a final version on wordprocessors, or work with felt

pens on large sheets of paper to sketch out their ideas. . . As a result the school has been transformed. It was at the bottom of the [local education] authority's league table on every point. In fact, to say it was a hell-hole would be an understatement. It was worse than that! But now relationships have changed from very much 'them and us' because when TVEI introduced residential weeks away and allowed us the time for personal counselling on a one-to-one basis, staff actually had to start talking to students.

(Quoted in Ainley 1990)

What happened to TVEI was that teachers took control of it and moulded it to suit their pupils' needs. After they saw that they could do this, teachers' attitudes towards the scheme changed considerably: they became very enthusiastic about it. The government, in contrast, began to lose interest. In 1986 the White Paper on education and training had predicted that all 14–18 year old students would have a TVEI-type experience and long passages in the paper praised the scheme. But in a consultation document on the National Curriculum in 1987 there were only two passing mentions of TVEI and since then its role has been reduced.

TVEI gives us some interesting lessons about how policy can change as it is being put into practice. It is easy for governments to think that to get things done it is only necessary to make policy, to provide the resources and to tell those on the ground (teachers and others) what to do. The case of TVEI shows that those who put policy into practice can actually change the policy to suit their own ends.

Reynolds and Saunders have researched this and developed the idea of an implementation staircase. Policy travels up and down this staircase, changing all the time; bits of it are overlooked and drop out of sight, other parts are reinterpreted, further parts are implemented in ways which were not foreseen by government. The finished product (in this case TVEI as it actually came to be) turns out to be quite different from the vision its inventors in government had.

The implementation staircase

Central government makes TVEI policy and allocates funds for it to be carried out — National

Head teachers and LEAs meet to decide on implications and how best to use the scheme — Regional

School heads and TVEI coordinators decide how to meet needs, avoid jealousies among teachers and sort the practical from the impossible. They produce written rationales for what they decide — Local

Year teachers set classwork that is appropriate to their pupils. Some trade off with them is necessary to make things work smoothly. Teachers adapt TVEI according to their preferences, the context, their pupils etc. — Classroom

Pupils get away with what they can, balancing time and effort with risks and rewards.

(Adapted from Reynolds and Saunders 1987)

Refer back to the list of criticisms of the new vocationalism on p. 73.

Put a tick next to those which apply to this aspect of government policy in your view.

Now put them in order. Which is the most important criticism, which next and which the least important?

Explain to each other why you prioritized the criticisms in the way you did.

Changing institutions

City technology colleges

City Technology Colleges (CTCs) were first proposed in 1985 and the first three were opened in 1988–89. The idea was that they should prepare young people for the high technology industries of today and tomorrow and that industry would largely pay for them. They were, in effect, a modern, high status equivalent of the tripartite system's technical schools. They are exempt from the National Curriculum, though many follow it quite closely. Their supporters argue that though small in number, they will act as 'beacons of excellence' for others to follow. The very first was Kingshurst in Solihull, and others have since been opened.

CTCs do seem to be successful at what they do. The 1991 HMI (Her Majesty's Inspectorate) report on the Kingshurst CTC said, for example:

> By its third year of operation the college had established itself as a popular, innovative and largely successful institution. . . [it] provides a broad and balanced education with some unusual and valuable additional features. . . [students are] highly motivated and their expectations have risen.

There are, however, critics of CTCs. The aim of establishing twenty by 1990 was not achieved, largely because of the lack of funding from the private sector which was to 'wholly or substantially' support them. The director of the Industrial Society said that the government must be living 'in fantasy land' if it thought that many companies had £6 million to invest in a local CTC. Companies were also worried about being seen to subscribe to a partisan education policy: they were happy to support education, but not a policy so clearly rooted in New Right philosophy. This meant that by 1991–92 the government was planning to spend over £122 million on CTCs, compared to only £43 million from the private sector.

Academic drift seems to be occurring even in Kingshurst. Walford and Miller note that the school has recently introduced the International Baccalaureate (IB) alongside the vocational BTEC programmes for its post-16 students. Probably half of its students would take up the IB which would, researchers Walford and Miller predict, gain a higher status than BTEC.

The critics of CTCs argue that:

- they threaten the existence of nearby schools (Simon Digby school near Kingshurst has since closed);

- they have little effect on the relevance of education to work: only a small number of students attend them;

- they represent unfair competition; over £9 million was spent on building one CTC in Nottingham. The LEA there has a total annual budget of £2.5 million for capital expenditure on schools. One estimate is that it would cost £2.8 billion to equip every secondary school in the UK to the same standard as Kingshurst;

- where good results are achieved this is because of the high capital expenditure, low staff-student ratios, higher pay for staff which attracts the well qualified, and surreptitious selection of students.

The HMI report on Kingshurst also noted some problems. Surprisingly, these mostly concern the exact subjects CTCs are supposed to specialize in: science and technology, and modern languages, the very areas crucial to international competitiveness:

> Work is less satisfactory. . . in those aspects of technology concerned with designing and making. . . [Technology and science in particular] lack clearly stated general aims and a co-ordinated approach to classroom practice. . . The good work in information technology is not matched in technology as a whole. . . In modern languages. . . some very poor lessons occur where staff are insecure in the foreign language or are linguists without teaching qualifications.

Find out where the nearest CTC is to you.
What are its admissions policies?
What are its special features compared to other schools locally?
Compare its facilities to other local schools.
If you can, interview teachers in the CTC and local schools about the CTC debate.
Find the names of other CTCs in the country and telephone OFSTED (the number is given at the end of this chapter) for a free report on the school. If you are working with a group, prepare a summary of your local CTC for them.

Refer back to the list of criticisms of the new vocationalism on p. 73.
Put a tick next to those which apply to this aspect of government policy in your view.
Now put them in order. Which is the most important criticism, which next and which the least important?
Explain to each other why you prioritized the criticisms in the way you did.

Changing individuals

Students as enterprising consumers: EHE and training credits

Much of the government's VET policy is essentially about changing individuals, especially to make them more enterprising. Its Enterprise in Higher Education (EHE) initiative, funded by TEED, says that every HE student should become:

> a person who has belief in his [sic] own destiny, welcomes change and is not frightened of the unknown, sets out to influence events, has powers of persuasion, is of good health, robust, with energy and willing to work

beyond what is specified, is competitive, is moderated by concern for others and is rigorous in self evaluation.

(MSC press release November 1987)

Millions of pounds have been spent by the DoE, through TEED, on setting up EHE initiatives in British universities. Each scheme is unique, but common aims are:

- to involve employers in HE more;

- to give students core transferable skills (see p. 99);

- to make HE more relevant to the world of work;

- to promote new initiatives in teaching and learning which put the student at the forefront.

Russell Keat notes that the sceptics see the 'enterprise culture' EHE seeks to create as one characterized by 'fear, greed [and] opportunism. . . human qualities whose actual character is dignified and sanitized by the rhetoric of enterprise'. Critics of the aims of EHE say that it is trying to change HE into merely training for work, an aim which loses sight of what makes it distinctive.

 Contact your local university and find out whether it has an EHE unit. If you can, find out what its specific aims are, how it has gone about achieving them, and how successful it feels it has been.

As well as enterprise, government policy has focused on individuals as consumers. Training credits are one example of this. A training credit is a voucher, credit card, cheque or passport given to young people who have left full-time education for them to 'buy' training from an employer or other training provider. It is designed to look as much like real money as possible, displaying a monetary value of anything between £500 and £5,000.

The basic idea of vouchers to buy education has been around in New Right circles for some time, though the specific idea of training credits was developed by the Confederation of British Industry in its report *Towards a Skills Revolution*. Much emphasis is placed on in-depth advice to young people on their career plans and training needs, so that they spend their credits wisely.

The explicit aims of the training credits scheme are to:

- motivate more young people to train for work;

- increase the quantity and quality of training provided, especially by employers;

- bring the rigours of the marketplace to training provision by turning students into 'customers'.

The idea is also to instil in young people an appreciation that training is a valuable resource that has to be paid for, and that it should be taken as seriously as any other costly item.

Training credits were piloted in eleven areas in the UK beginning in April 1991.

Another nine areas joined in 1993. All 16–17 year olds who had left full-time education were eligible, whether or not they were in employment. In almost all cases the local TEC administered the scheme. The Department of Employment *Progress Report* tells us that after a year 60 per cent of the eligible young people (around 21,000) in the eleven areas had 'started to use' their training credits and that the first year of the scheme cost around £125 million to set up and run. A lot of this was spent on eight different evaluations of the schemes. The consultancy firm Coopers & Lybrand Deloitte conducted three of them, as well as coordinating a final 'report of reports' for the government.

 Examine the language being used in these quotes from the evaluation. What comments do you have about it?

Over 21,000 young people had started to use their training credits.

Young people have a poor understanding of the fact that credits gave them purchasing power.

The immediate impact on the FE curriculum has been modest. A number of positive benefits were expected in the medium term. These included the modularization of full-time courses to permit part-time participation and the adoption of a more market-led approach to training.

(Department of Employment 1992)

How did the young people feel about the credits? While the evaluation made much of the fact that 'between 60 and 90 per cent of the young people in the eleven areas had heard of training credits', their attitude towards them was mixed, as the Credit Holders Survey shows:

Hasn't affected me at all   44%

Made me think seriously about training   28%

Made me feel I had more control over my training   24%

Made me keener to leave full-time education   11%

Helped me change my mind about my choice of career   6%

Made me keener to get a job without training   4%

Even the DoE evaluation admitted that although young people might be aware of the existence of training credits, most did not really understand them. The holding of a credit made little impact on the choice of employer. They didn't appreciate either, that the real cost of training was higher than the value of the credit.

As far as employers were concerned, only between a third and a half had even heard of the credits while 'the majority' felt that credits had not had any impact on their recruitment and training strategies.

Despite all this, the 1992 Conservative Party Manifesto said: 'We intend to make training credits available to all 16 and 17 year olds within the lifetime of the new parliament' and aimed to make the scheme national in 1996. The White Paper *Competitiveness*, published in May 1994, announced that the government intended to give all 16 year olds a £2,000 voucher to spend on education or training. The Secretary of State for Education at the time said that this and other measures meant that 'the 16 year old school leaver would be as dead as a dodo by the year 2000'.

What is your view on being given training credits to 'spend'? Would you be a careful consumer?

Refer back to the list of criticisms of the new vocationalism on p. 73.

Put a tick next to those which apply to this aspect of government policy in your view.

Now put them in order. Which is the most important criticism, which next and which the least important?

Explain to each other why you prioritized the criticisms in the way you did.

NVQs and competence

Since 1986 the government has been working towards setting up a scheme of National Vocational Qualifications (NVQs) through the National Council for Vocational Qualifications, based in London. Around 80 per cent of the workforce are now in occupations which have NVQ qualifications. The aim of the scheme was to rationalize what had been a confusing multitude of vocational courses and awards into a single coherent system of qualifications at five distinct levels. Each qualification states very explicitly what its holder can do by giving clear statements of competence which they must achieve to be awarded it. These competence statements have been formulated by industry and commerce to ensure that they match what people need in the workplace.

The qualifications are modular in design. This means that the programme of study is broken into separately assessed smaller pieces so that people can achieve small sets of competencies at different times, until all those required for the qualification are attained. For people with families or with shifting work patterns or other responsibilities, modular programmes are ideal, giving access to qualifications and easy part-time study. Also, people who can demonstrate that they have already acquired some competencies can get certificates to prove this without needing to follow a course. This process is called the accreditation of prior learning (APL).

NVQs: the levels

> Level 5: competence which involves the application of a significant range of fundamental principles and complex techniques across a wide and often unpredictable variety of contexts. Very substantial personal autonomy and often significant responsibility for the work of others and for the allocation of substantail resources feature strongly, as do personal accountabilities for analysis and diagnosis, design, planning, execution and evaluation.

> Level 4: competence in a broad range of complex technical or professional work activities performed in a wide variety of contexts and with a substantial degree of personal responsibility and autonomy.

Responsibility for the work of others and the allocation of resources is often present.

Level 3: competence in a broad range of varied work activities performed in a wide variety of contexts most of which are complex and non-routine. There is considerable responsibility and autonomy, and control or guidance of others is often required.

Level 2: competence in a significant range of varied work activities, performed in a variety of contexts. Some of the activities are complex or non-routine and there is some responsibility or autonomy. Collaboration with others, perhaps through membership of a work group or team, may often be a requirement.

Level 1: competence in the performance of a range of varied work activities, most of which may be routine and predictable.

DES (1991) *Education and Training for the 21st Century*, HMSO

NVQs: an example of competencies

Production Machine Sewing. Level 2.

1. Create and maintain relationships with supervisory staff.

2. Create and maintain relationships with colleagues.

These are called 'elements of competence'. More specific details about what candidates must demonstrate are given by 'performance criteria'. In this case these are:

* Assistance is requested in a clear, polite manner.

* Instruction or advice is responded to by an indication of understanding or request for clarification.

* Verbal responses offered and/or actions taken in such a way as to satisfy. . .

* Disagreements conveyed in a tactful manner.

* Responds to reasonable requests in a positive, supportive manner.

Employment Department and NCVQ (1991) *Guide to National Vocational Qualifications*, HMSO

The candidate must demonstrate that she/he can do this in a variety of contexts. These are specified by 'range statements'. In this case, an example is that the candidate must be able to do the above with 'supervisory staff who may be both familiar and unfamiliar to the candidate'.

The above elements of competence, performance criteria and range statements are part of one unit of several. The demonstration of competence in all the units leads to the NVQ level 2 qualification in production machine sewing. NCVQ considers it best if competence is proven in the workplace rather than tests at college, or at least in a 'realistic working environment' – a simulation.

Table 3.3   The claimed benefits and criticisms of the competence approach

Benefits	*Criticism*
Assessment of obsrvable performance is far more reliable than non-observable things like knowledge and understanding. It is better, therefore, to assess behaviour than knowledge. If students can show themselves capable of carrying out specified tasks, the necessary knowledge must have been acquired and does not need to be separately assessed anyway.	While it is relatively easy to describe physical skills in terms of a series of statements of competence, it is less easy to describe knowledge, understanding, values and motivation. For this reason competence based schemes lose sight of these areas. It is possible to train a car mechanic to change a car part, but does s/he understand the reasons why it went wrong? Is s/he motivated to do the job well every time? Does s/he understand the principles underlying the car's various systems?
Assessment in NVQs is one-to-one and only takes place when the individual is ready. This is true personalized training.	The competence based approach is individualistic, accrediting the competence of one individual to perform a task. However modern industry and commerce is based upon team-work and co-operation.
Rigorous assessment and accreditation of small elements of competence means that employers will know exactly what job applicants are capable of doing.	This approach assumes that it is possible to transfer competence from one context to another once it has been achieved. However a number of context-specific factors influence the ability to perform well. Psychologists have shown that memory is context-dependent to a certain extent, for example.
Explicitly setting out units and elements of competence with associated performance criteria and range statements means that assessment is fair and objective. What is being tested is clear to all, including (and especially) the student.	There are doubts over how rigorous the assessment of competence can be. The assessment process can be subjective, despite the apparent specificity of the descriptions. Where assessment occurs in the workplace, candidates may be disadvantaged by the lack of equipment or facilities there to achieve and then demonstrate certain competences.
Competence statements are based on a careful functional analysis of jobs. Employers are involved in this through the Lead Bodies. The learning is thorough and job-related. There is neither too little nor too much learning and it is all relevant.	Dividing learning down into minute statements is reductionist. The whole is greater than the sum of the parts, so that though an individual may successfully demonstrate all the necessary competences in, for example, teaching, they may still not be a good teacher.
Training institutions like colleges are paid by results; the number of students successfully gaining competences. This is known as output-related funding. This means they are motivated to achieve high quality training so the pass rate is high and they get more money.	Output related funding has tempted colleges to pass students who would otherwise fail. BTEC became aware of this happening in 1994 and had to increase their monitoring of standards. Lecturers knew it was happening but could not say anything for fear of their jobs.

Most vocational qualifications at the lower levels have now been 'NVQ'd'. The NVQ approach will be applied in higher education at levels 4 and 5. This will have all the advantages of currently available NVQs, particularly their vocational relevance, clearly stated learning outcomes and objective assessment.	While a competence-based approach may be appropriate for the lower levels of training, where observable skills are more important, transfer to higher levels is very difficult and may actually lower standards there. NVQs were first applied to the lower levels and so this was not immediately apparent, but as attempts are made to make levels 4 and 5 competence based it is becoming increasingly obvious.

For Peter Ashworth, Judy Saxton and Professor Alan Smithers, the adoption of the competence-based approach to VET is a backward step. They and other authors criticize the competence approach on a number of grounds, summarized in the right-hand column of the above table.

GNVQs (General National Vocational Qualifications) have been introduced to reduce the gap between vocational qualifications and academic qualifications. They are designed to give vocational qualifications equivalence to 'A' levels and GCSEs. Students can take GNVQs alongside academic qualifications so that individuals are not solely on an academic or a vocational track. GNVQs link in to other aspects of VET policy that we have been examining in that they are aimed at the needs of employers: they focus on general skills in communication, numeracy and use of computers as well as more specific vocational skills, and they are also designed along modular lines.

The aim is that one in four people aged 16 will take GNVQ courses in the short term, with half of all 16 and 17 year olds taking one at some level (these are Foundation, Intermediate or Advanced – corresponding to GCSE grades D-G, A-C and 'A' level respectively) 'in the longer term'. Just five subjects were available in 1993: Art and Design; Business; Health and Social Care; Leisure and Tourism; and Manufacturing. These were only available at Advanced and Intermediate levels but the plan is to expand this in the future. The 1994 White Paper *Competitiveness* included a proposal to spend £300 million on this expansion between 1997–98. One of the measures is to provide 'accelerated modern apprenticeships' for 18 and 19 year olds with 'A' levels or GNVQs. These will lead to qualifications at NVQ level 3.

 Read the literature on GNVQs published by the DoE and the Department for Education (the addresses are at the end of this chapter). Design a questionnaire aimed at students taking GNVQs. It should establish how far their views about the qualifications correspond to the aims that the government has for them. Apply the questionnaire to a suitable sample of students, analyse the data and write up the results.

National Training Targets have been set by the government. Local TECs, in collaboration with colleges and others, will determine local needs and priorities in order to ensure that they are met. The targets are as follows:

Foundation learning:

1   by 1997 80 per cent of young people should reach NVQ 2 or equivalent;

2   training and education to NVQ 3 or equivalent should be available for all young people who can benefit;

3   by 2000, 50 per cent of young people should reach NVQ 3 or equivalent;

4   education and training should be provided to develop self-reliance, flexibility and breadth.

Lifetime learning:

1   by 1996, all employees should take part in training or development activities;

2   by 1996, 50 per cent of the workforce should be aiming for NVQs or units towards them;

3   by 2000, 50 per cent of the workforce should be qualified to at least NVQ 3 or equivalent;

4   by 1996, 50 per cent of medium to larger organizations should be 'investors in people'.

Consider these targets critically. What barriers are there to them being met?

Refer back to the list of criticisms of the new vocationalism on p. 73.

Put a tick next to those which apply to this aspect of government policy in your view.

Now put them in order. Which is the most important criticism, which next and which the least important?

Explain to each other why you prioritized the criticisms in the way you did.

Core skills

The recent emphasis on core or transferable skills is designed to ensure that whatever students study, at whatever level, they are also equipped with general skills and understanding that would be required whatever the occupation the students eventually enter. The idea of transmitting core skills has been incorporated into most vocational qualifications including BTEC, TVEI, NVQs and GNVQs, and is now moving into the academic arena. The National Curriculum Council advocates the addition of six core skills to 'A' levels and EHE is working in universities to ensure that core skills become a central part of the HE curriculum. The list on p. 101 indicates some of the core or transferable skills which various bodies advocate teaching to young people as part of more specific syllabuses.

Some of the arguments against these ideas are:

• These skills are often referred to as transferable skills: the idea is that, having learned them, they can be transferred from one context to another. However, skills do not exist in their own right, they reside in people. An individual may 'have' a skill, for example basic numeracy, but may be more or less inclined or able to apply it in different situations, or to adapt and build on it as circumstances change.

Similarly many of these skills are particularistic, that is, they depend upon the particular circumstances in any given context. Interpersonal skills, for example, depend upon groups of individuals who have built up working relationships together over a period of time. These can never be exactly reproduced elsewhere.

• While the attraction of core skills is that they appear to address the practical problems that may affect young people at work, the reality has become an agenda which aims to fit young people into society rather than teach them about it. The young person's attitudes, deference to authority, demeanour, appearance and other personal characteristics have now become part of the curriculum and subject to discussion and evaluation. As researcher Cynthia Cockburn points out, the core skills talked about in, for example, YT:

> *are so basic as to lend themselves to parody: learning to push, learning to pull. Learning to stand up without falling over. Life and social skills, intended. . . to be a core element of all youth training schemes are widely regarded as a patronizing slur on young people's personal qualities. Under this scheme they are invited to improve their appearance, their interview technique and their approach to authority.*

• Denis Gleeson (1990) argues that the emphasis on generic skills has more to do with regulation of the individual than with preparation for work. We should consider this emphasis in relation to the government's overall political and economic strategy which is, he says, 'designed to alter social relations in the workplace and to restructure curricular priorities around a greater appreciation of economic values and the market'.

• The policy has gone beyond the Ruskin Speech which simply aimed to alter the content of the curriculum towards the needs of the workplace, to change notions of the individual and his or her role in society.

How are transferable skills taught in courses you are involved in?
What are the arguments in favour of expecting people to leave education in possession of 'core skills' (See Table 3.4, p. 101)?
Refer back to the list of criticisms of the new vocationalism on p. 73.
Put a tick next to those which apply to this aspect of government policy in your view.
Now put them in order. Which is the most important criticism, which next and which the least important?
Explain to each other why you prioritized the criticisms in the way you did.

VET policy: conclusion

In this chapter we have reviewed just some of the initiatives designed to create a closer link between education, training and employment and to improve standards of training generally. While there have been some successes, there have also been a number of failures.

Table 3.4

Core skills.

	Clear meaning?	Skill easily assessed?	Appropriate to assess this skills?	Useful for employment prospects to have certificated?	Easily transferable to different situations?
Communication (HMI, BTEC, GNVQ, CBI, NCC)					
Applying numeracy (HMI, BTEC, GNVQ, CBI, NCC)					
Problem solving/management tasks (HMI, BTEC, GNVQ, CBI, UDACE, NCC)					
Working co-operatively (HMI, BTEC, GNVQ, CBI,MCI)					
Improving learning performance (GNVQ, MCI)					
Using knowledge about I.T. (HMI, BTEC, GNVQ, CBI, NCC)					
Knowledge about society and the environment (HMI)					
Practical skills (HMI) ☐ Applying design and creativity (BTEC)					
Adaptability (HMI)					
Values and integrity (CBI)					
Understanding of work and the world (CBI)					
Positive attitude to change (CBI, UDACE)					
Concern for standards (UDACE, MCI)					
Pro-activity (UDACE)					
Systematic thinking (UDACE)					
Conceptual thinking (UDACE)					
Information seeking (UDACE)					
Self-confidence (UDACE, MCI)					
Accurate self-assessment (UDACE)					
Leadership (UDACE, MCI) ☐					
Persuasion (UDACE)					
Perception (UDACE)					
Managing stress and personal emotions (MCI)					
Personal skills (NCC)					
Modern languages (NCC)					

BTEC = Business and Technician Education Council

CBI = Confederation of British Industry

GNVQ = General National Vocational Qualification

HMI = Her Majesty's Inspectors

MCI = Management Charter Initiative

UDACE = Unit for the Development of Adult and Continuing Education, now part of the Further Education Unit (FEU)

NCC (National Curriculum Council in their publication Core Skills 16-19)

One of the most striking features of the period since 1979 is the large number of schemes there have been and how quickly they have changed, come and gone. This volatility has meant unemployment for trainers, closure for training companies and uncertainty for trainees. It has also meant, though, that VET policy has been able to change and in some cases improve. For example, there is evidence that the National Council for Vocational Qualifications has listened to some of the criticisms listed on pp. 97-8 and that it is now moving away from the harder form of behaviourism it began with in 1986.

A major problem for VET policy, however, is that the attractiveness of training is affected by factors outside the control of the education and training system. For example, students who achieve high 'A' level grades tend to opt for law, humanities and the social sciences, not engineering or chemistry, even when they studied science and maths at 'A' level. Government blames this partly on the anti-industrial bias of teachers. However it is a rational decision by students as long as engineers, scientists and technologists are underpaid and given poor job security and low status in Britain. Trying to change the education and training system tackles only one half of the problem: changes need to occur in economic policy and the job market to attract students to VET.

Another major problem is, as Spours and Young note, that there is a too narrow a focus in VET and this means that there is a lack of continuity in the 14–19 curriculum. Vocational courses are in an enclave, separated from academic subjects, and this causes problems of progression. Changing both the academic and vocational is the only way to solve these problems of progression. Coulby and Bash (1991) agree, arguing that:

> the structures and content of education which currently enforce a divide between academic and technical knowledge, between education institutions and the workplace, are the ones in particular need of reform.
>
> (Bash and Coulby 1991)

The two cultures we discussed at the start of this chapter are remarkably persistent, despite the efforts to unite them that we have reviewed in this chapter.

 What policies would you wish to see implemented in the vocational education and training system in England and Wales?

Essay Question

Education prepares people for work, not only in the obvious way of providing vocational skills, but also in developing certain attitudes and values. Explain and discuss. (AEB 1990)

Suggestions for further reading

Specific sources for this chapter

Recent books on vocational education and training have attempted to expose and explore the perceptions and experiences of young people and teachers affected by policies in these areas. In conducting investigations you may wish to compare your experiences or those of people you study, to those described in books such as:

Lee, D. *et al.* (1990) *Scheming for Youth*, Milton Keynes: Open University Press.

Pollard, A. *et al.* (1988) *Education, Training and the New Vocationalism: Experience and Policy*, Milton Keynes: Open University Press.

Tomlinson, H. (ed.) (1993) *Education and Training 14–19: Continuity and Diversity in the Curriculum*, London: Longman.

Literature on government policy in the VET area is available from:

> The Department for Education
> Publications Despatch Centre
> Honeypot Lane
> Stanmore
> Middlesex
> HA7 1AZ

The address for TEED publications is:

> TEED
> Department of Employment
> Moorfoot
> Sheffield
> S1 4PQ

OFSTED reports on schools can be obtained from:

> OFSTED Publications Centre
> PO Box 151
> London
> E15 2HN
> Tel: 0181 985 7757

Reports on vocational education and training in FE can be obtained from:

> The Further Education Unit (FEU)
> Information Centre
> Citadel Place
> Tinworth Street
> London
> SE11 5EH

The *Training and Enterprise Yearbook* is published annually by the Planning Exchange. This should be available in your library and gives details of local TECs, etc.

A number of other useful addresses can be found at the back of the *Charter for Further Education*. To obtain this write to:

> Charters
> FREEPOST EDO 3138
> London
> E15 2BR

4 Racism, ethnicity and education

Stuart Billingham

Figure 4.1

A class on racism and ethnicity in education.

In this chapter we will look at educational perspectives and research evidence on racial and ethnic inequality in education, focusing on:

- the racialization of education;

- the main ideologies concerned with ethnic diversity in education;

- evidence on minority ethnic achievement and 'underachievement' in schools, and possible explanations for these phenomena;

- other aspects of education which have recently concerned researchers, such as racial violence in schools;

- feminist thinking related to ethnic diversity in education;

- evidence on ethnic inequality and participation in post-compulsory education.

The racialization of education

Many people believe that **'race'** is a valid scientific concept which describes and explains the division of humankind according to physical characteristics (such as skin colour). However, the validity of this view is now rejected by science itself. Many people still behave, though, as if 'races' do exist in this sense. Many writers and researchers therefore place this concept in inverted commas to show that they do not accept its validity but do recognize its social significance. They are acknowledging, in this way, that 'race' is a socially constructed not scientifically objective concept.

Ethnicity refers to the sense of shared cultural identity which binds a community together. It is used to distinguish one community from another and can be the basis for collective action by, and conflict between, communities.

Ethnicity is often expressed through religious values and practices, language, dress, cuisine, and other cultural traditions and beliefs. This way of understanding relations between groups is known as the ethnic relations perspective.

Racialization refers to the development of policies and practices which focus on ethnic identities and categories. For example, if the educational policies and practices of government, schools or colleges are based upon supposed racial or actual ethnic differences between individuals or groups, then those policies can be said to be racialized.

A major feature of the racialization of education in the UK has been the development of educational ideologies and policies concerned with the multiracial and multiethnic character of education. These perspectives have suggested ways in which ethnic diversity in schools and colleges should be tackled by policy makers, teachers and others. These policies and ideologies have been given different labels by different people, but we will refer to them as:

- assimilationism;

- multiculturalism;

- antiracism.

They have been very influential not only in educational research but have also influenced the educational experiences of school pupils, college students and teachers since the 1960s.

Some practices associated with these perspectives in education may be seen as positive: for example, the activities of those teachers, students and others who campaign against racism such as NAME (National Antiracist Movement in Education) or EYTARN (the Early Years Trainers' Antiracist Network). Others may be seen as negative: for example, the activities of extreme right-wing or fascist groups both inside and outside schools and colleges.

Some government education policies in the 1960s (such as Circular 7/65), or 1990s (such as the 'new' Section 11), which reinforce stereotypes of minority ethnic pupils and communities, may also be seen as negative as we shall see on p. 107. Whether positive or negative, these policies or practices share a focus on racial and ethnic dimensions of education: they are 'racialized'. We deal with them in turn.

Ideologies and ethnic diversity in education

Assimilationism and education

Immigration from the New Commonwealth (mainly India, Pakistan and the Caribbean) began to increase in the late 1950s. During that time few people considered that this would affect education: the view was that the migrants would not stay in this country. However, by the early 1960s it was clear that migrant workers were settling and being joined by their families or starting families here. Throughout that period, sociological research and popular debate saw the issue as one of immigration and race relations.

This research suggested that racial harmony would only come about gradually, as immigrant and non-immigrant communities came to understand one another more fully. It was argued that one factor that would help or hinder this process was the extent to which immigrant communities adopted 'the British way of life'. This was the ideology of assimilation.

> **Assimilationism** can be summarized with the phrase: 'When in Rome do as the Romans do.' Assimilationists argue that the migrant settlers should adopt the values and lifestyles of the society in which they have settled. It assumes that members of our society all shared the same values and traditions before the migrant settlers arrived. The minority ethnic communities should endeavour to learn these values and traditions which, by clear implication, means they should abandon the values and traditions of their original cultures.

The following extract from a report of the Commonwealth Immigrant Advisory Council in 1964 shows how this perspective was applied to education:

> A national system of education must aim at producing citizens who can take their place in society properly equipped to exercise rights and perform duties the same as those of other citizens. If their parents were brought up in another culture and another tradition, children should be encouraged to respect it, *but a national system cannot be expected to perpetuate the different values of immigrant groups.*

One example of the way this view influenced what happened in schools is found in the so-called monocultural or Eurocentric curriculum. This is an approach to teaching subjects which ignores or, at worst, devalues cultures and histories other than those of white people in Britain and/or Western Europe.

Ethnographic evidence from the 1960s shows what this approach to the curriculum could be like for 'immigrant pupils' and the impact which assimilationist ideology could have upon them:

> A West Indian/British male
>
> I remember the first day I went to school in Leeds. . . There I had to be much more aware of black kids because we all seemed to be lumped together in the same class and I suppose because we were all black we just got on. . . The really ridiculous thing was that we had to read as a class book *Little Black Sambo* and the teacher used to read it and we used to follow it. So I read it on my own and put it back but I had to read it again and again and again.

A Pakistani/British female

On starting school we were put into the 'immigrant' class at school, along with other Asian children for the first year. We had special reading sessions with the headmaster a few times a week, for which the group was termed 'backward readers'. . . The time at primary school (up to 11 years) I can remember as one of happiness overall. . . I can remember feeling very proud when the teachers praised my father for taking so much care over our education. He would come in and talk to our teachers, more so than English parents, about our progress at school.

A Gujerati/British male

As far as I was concerned, at that time, there were no differences in colour, the visual difference to me was that they were just richer and better off materially than we were. If we were to achieve that standard, we would have to adopt their way of life, values, attitudes, etc. . . Being about 5 years old when I came to England, I had few memories of India – I had not formed my Indian identity yet. Having emigrated to England, I was to form two identities alongside each other: that which my family and community socialized me into, and that which the white society wanted.

(Husband 1982)

The recollections of the Pakistani/British woman recall the *English for Immigrants* project established by the Ministry of Education in 1963 and implemented by hundreds of multiracial primary and secondary schools mainly with Asian children. Here, there was no place for bilingual or 'mother-tongue' teaching, only an attempt to get Asian children speaking and writing English as their main language as soon as possible. As the woman's experience shows, the special classes for English were labelled as being for 'backward' students.

Studies in Inner London in the mid-1960s showed that as many as 70 per cent of pupils in ESN schools (i.e. schools for the 'educationally subnormal' as they were then named) were of West Indian origin. Some of the reasons for this very high rate were captured by Coard's study which showed how teachers often interpreted the Creole language of the child as an indication of educational subnormality. That is, they often saw it as an inferior form of English and so a sign of, for example, low intelligence rather than as a separate language in its own right.

The idea of special provision to enable assimilation was also the basis of Section 11 of the Local Government Act (1966). This section of the Act allowed LEAs to bid for additional money from central government to support projects aimed at overcoming cultural barriers to assimilation. The DES Circular 7/65 was based on the same idea. This advised LEAs to 'bus' children around their area if the proportion of 'immigrant children' was more than 30 per cent in any one school. The basis upon which the DES put forward this policy was that if a school had more than 30 per cent immigrant children, then their 'fitting-in' was likely to be much more difficult. Also, and significantly, the DES argued that the educational progress of the white (or indigenous) children could be threatened since teachers would be spending more time with the 'immigrant children'.

Sometimes the impression is created that assimilationism is an ideology that belongs to the distant past. However, the following quotation is taken from the *Daily Mail* in March 1989:

> We must do nothing through legislation or the use of public money to pre-serve alien cultures and religions. Likewise, they must seek to be assimilated. . . They have chosen to dwell amongst us. In Rome do as the Romans do.

> (*Daily Mail* March 1989)

With a partner, choose a textbook from any of the subjects you are now studying.

Together, examine its content and any pictures it may contain.

Note any examples which reflect a monocultural, Europe-centred or assimilationist view.

Multicultural education

Multicultural education sees ethnic diversity in education as good for all students: positively acknowledging children's cultures will increase their self-esteem and this will improve their performance at school. At the same time, by learning about other cultures prejudice among 'white' children can be reduced. Supporters of multicultural education believe that schools and other educational institutions should introduce a multicultural dimension into all aspects of the institution's life (e.g. the school meals' menu, multilingual signs around buildings and multicultural elements in the syllabus). They feel education must reflect the multicultural world in which we live.

Multiculturalism is based on the idea of integration. One of the most famous definitions of integration was given by Roy Jenkins, the Labour Home Secretary and a prominent politician in the mid-1960s, who said that multiculturalism was 'not a flattening process of assimilation but equal opportunity, accompanied by cultural diversity, in an atmosphere of mutual tolerance'.

The multicultural critique of assimilationism starts with the observation that the UK is not, and never has been, a culturally homogeneous society. It is therefore impossible for minority ethnic groups to 'join' something that doesn't exist. It is also unreasonable to expect them to want to 'join' something which regularly devalues them, their cultures, and discriminates against them.

You are asked by a college admissions tutor to describe in your own words your ethnic origin, and to write it in the limited space provided on the admissions form. She explains that this is part of the college's multicultural policy and will enable it to establish whether it is recruiting from all sections of the community. Try doing it.

This task can be quite difficult especially since not all of us are used to thinking of ourselves as belonging to an ethnic group.

This exercise highlights the point that the concept 'ethnic' is not applied universally to all groups and communities, either in everyday conversation or in academic research. It has taken on a specific meaning and is used in specific ways and about particular communities in society.

These ideas on multicultural education quickly gathered support through the 1970s and into the 1980s, especially among teachers working in multiethnic schools. They received official recognition in the 1985 Swann Report. Its title, *Education For All*,

Figure 4.2

Working in a multiethnic school

summed up the philosophy of multicultural education. However, just as *Education For All* had its critics, so too did multiculturalism.

Antiracist education

Racism is an ideology and refers to:

* ideas;
* purposeful actions (it describes the intentional behaviour of individuals and institutions);
* the unintended outcomes of action which are negative about, or disadvantage people because of, their ethnic origin or supposed 'race'.

Two forms of racism have been the main focus of attention in educational research:

* individual racism;
* institutional racism.

Individual racism refers to the prejudiced ideas and discriminatory actions of individuals against people on the grounds of their ethnic origin or supposed 'race'.

Institutional racism refers to rules, regulations or practices which disadvantage members of minority ethnic communities whether intentionally or unintentionally, directly or indirectly.

Antiracism is an ideology and political movement which stresses the connection between racism and other forms of inequality and injustice such as class and gender. Antiracists argue that the focus for change should therefore be upon the structures of power in society.

Antiracist educators argue that it is racism – in its various forms but especially institutional racism – which is the problem facing minority ethnic students in education and not their cultures nor the cultural ignorance of the white majority. Multiculturalism tends to ignore racism – instead its explanations and solutions place too much emphasis on culture and ethnicity.

For example, multicultural education sometimes takes the so-called 'steel bands, saris and samosas' approach: special class sessions, or whole school special days, looking at obvious and relatively easy aspects of different cultures. Antiracists say that this is patronizing to black and Asian people. Also there is no evidence that it has any significant impact on the issue of most concern to black and Asian parents: their children's performance in school.

An example of institutional racism in education is the entry requirements to college or university, such as having to have a GCSE pass in a modern foreign language. This disadvantages applicants from minority ethnic communities compared to others, given the relative numbers who sit such examinations. If a requirement like this is not essential for the successful completion of the college course, it could be a form of indirect discrimination and institutional racism.

Divide into groups of two. Find out about the entry requirements for courses at your college.

Are all of them absolutely necessary as preparations for the course? Ask teachers.

Does the college encourage and accept qualifications other than the traditional GCSE, BTEC, etc.?

Do you think that any of the college's entry requirements might be indirectly discriminatory (i.e. they may not be designed to discriminate unfairly against certain groups but they have the effect of doing so)?

What evidence would you need to demonstrate this?

Design and carry out a small-scale project to investigate this issue in college.

Antiracist education argues for 'the politicization of schooling', especially the inclusion in the curriculum of 'the politics of knowledge'. Knowledge is not neutral and school pupils and students should be exposed to the ways in which the subjects they study are related to, and influenced by, wider social, political and economic processes. If this is done students will be able to explore issues of injustice and inequality through every aspect of the curriculum, and not just if they study sociology or politics. In this way institutionalized racism in education can be exposed and challenged.

Robert Young, a professor of psychoanalytic studies, explores how this might be done in science teaching; he argues that an antiracist science curriculum would encourage the critical understanding of scientific knowledge and method. It would do this by linking science to culture and history, to economics and power. Students should explore, for example, the relationship between the scientific revolution, the Protestant revolution and capitalism. This approach fosters the discussion of the connections between science and inequality and science and liberation. In biology the teaching of genetics could include not only an overview of basic genetic theory but also a discussion of the role of science and scientists in reproducing racist genetic theories (e.g. in Nazi Germany), and of other scientists subsequently challenging such theories.

Students should pair up to complete this activity.

Which topics in subject areas such as science, technology, arts and humanities, might allow the discussion of ethnic and racial inequalities and injustices?

Each of you should choose one of these subject groupings.

Use your library to examine a sample of syllabuses for one or two subjects in your chosen area, and list those topics which you think might provide an opportunity to discuss these issues.

Discuss your ideas with each other and a teacher or teachers of these subjects in your college.

What constraints operate to prevent this way of teaching? Are some subjects already taught in this way? If so, which ones? If not, why not?

Antiracism has, like multiculturalism, received support from researchers, teachers and others and probably reached its height of influence in the early 1980s. However, it has also had its critics.

- Many teachers have complained that whilst antiracist education is strong on theory it is very weak on practice. For example, how should teachers translate the principles into classroom practice? How can you make mathematics or car maintenance antiracist? How should teachers tackle racism among students or among their colleagues? What can teachers do if the syllabuses, set by examination bodies, ignore these issues or require reading which reinforces racial stereotypes?

- Rattansi has argued that despite claiming to see racism as connected with other forms of inequality, antiracism most often reduces all forms of inequality to the problem of racism. So, it can be criticized in the same way that antiracists have criticized multiculturalists: that is, it searches for a single cause for what are complex issues. This is sometimes referred to as reductionism or essentialism.

- Others have argued that antiracism can only explain working-class racism as some form of false consciousness and this portrays working-class people as 'cultural dopes'.

- However, perhaps the most publicly influential attacks on antiracism have come from the New Right (see p. 3). It has claimed that antiracism is an interference with freedom of the individual, is subversive and is itself a form of racism – against white people.

The New Right ideology brings us full circle. It rests upon many of the assumptions of assimilationism. For example, it uses English nationalism as a basis for curriculum policy. Whitty and Menter see this in:

> The very emphasis of 'National' in the National Curriculum, the centrality of a notion of national testing with all the cultural and linguistic bias which that implies, the failure to recognize languages other than Welsh and English as a pupil's first language, and the omission in any of the Consultative papers, let alone in the Act, of any reference to the 1985

report of Lord Swann's Committee of Enquiry into the Education of Children from Ethnic Minority groups *Education for All*.

(Whitty and Menter 1989)

Some commentators see this as reflecting a de-racialization education. That is, all explicit reference to 'race' or ethnicity has been removed from the language of educational policy. Underneath, however, the objectives remain the same as those of the assimilationist period in educational policy.

Essay Question

Compare and contrast the assimilationist, multicultural and antiracist perspectives on the curriculum.

Minority ethnic achievement and 'underachievement'

Assimilationism, multiculturalism and antiracism have all influenced research into ethnic diversity in education. This has sometimes been directly and obviously, but also less obviously by creating a climate which 'sets the agenda' for researchers: suggesting particular questions and approaches to study.

Table 4.1	Major research approaches		
Discipline base	*Key concept(s)*	*Representative studies*	*Ideological context*
Psychology	Intelligence (IQ)	Jensen/Eysenck	Assimilationist
Social Psychology	Self-Esteem Racial Prejudice	Milner	Multicultural
Functionalist Sociology	Cultural Deprivation	Rutter	Assimilationist
Interpretive/ Ethnographic	Teacher/Pupil Relations	Wright/Mac an Ghaill/ Fuller	Multicultural Antiracist
Structural/Conflict Sociology	Discrimination	Rex & Tomlinson	Multicultural
Marxist Sociology	Racism-Class	Sarup/Miles	Antiracist
Black Feminism	Racism-Sexism	Bryan/Carby/ Yuval-Davis	Antiracist/Feminist

Whatever differences exist between these studies one theme recurs: the issue of underachievement.

Underachievement can be defined in a number of ways, for example, not achieving according to some measure of potential or not achieving certain stated objectives. Some studies have defined and measured it by looking at student performance on verbal reasoning tests or even IQ tests. However, it has mostly been defined in terms of patterns of success and failure in national examinations. Typically, this has involved comparing the examination results of minority ethnic students to those of white students.

Study the following summaries of research into patterns of educational achievement and underachievement.

- *A study by Scarr, a developmental psychologist, carried out in the West Midlands in 1980, showed Indian and Pakistani children made significant gains in IQ test scores between the ages of 8 and 11 compared to both white and West Indian children who improved very little. The differences measured at age 12 between these students were maintained through to GCE and CSE examination.*
- *Drew and Gray, prominent empirical researchers, studied fifth year examination results in 1985 across a random sample of 2,362 maintained schools in England and Wales. The study involved nearly 14,500 pupils, and found that 20 per cent of all pupils, 19 per cent of Asian pupils and 7 per cent of African-Caribbean pupils achieved five or more 'higher grade' GCE/CSE passes. Some 51 per cent of all pupils compared to 38 per cent of African-Caribbean pupils obtained one or more 'higher grade' passes. This study examined the influence of gender and social class as well as ethnic origin.*

Table 4.2   Highest qualification by ethnic group, all persons of working age, 1988-90

	All origins	White	Total ethnic minority	Afro-Caribbean	African Asian	Indian	Pakistani	Bangla-deshi	Chinese	Other African	Other/Mixed
All persons (16-59/64)											
GCE A level/equivalent or higher	38	38	31	35	34	31	14	10	33	50	41
Of which: degree/equivalent	8	8	9	3	13	12	4	6	13	14	16
Higher Education below degree level	6	6	6	8	4	4	1	1	10	13	7
GCE A level/equivalent	24	24	16	24	17	14	9	4	11	24	18
Of which: BTEC (general)/ONC/OND	2	2	2	3	3	2	1	0	1	6	3
City & Guilds	9	9	5	10	4	3	2	0	1	6	3
GCE A level or equivalent	6	6	6	5	7	6	4	2	6	8	8
Trade apprenticeship	7	7	3	6	3	2	1	1	2	3	3
GCE O level/equivalent	17	17	13	16	17	11	8	8	9	19	15
CSE (not grade 1)	5	5	5	9	5	4	3	4	1	2	4
Other	7	7	11	5	14	12	11	10	10	11	16
None	32	32	38	33	29	39	60	68	44	17	23
(Never received any education)	0	0	6	1	1	6	18	15	7	2	1
Not stated/not known	1	1	2	2	2	3	3	1	2	2	1

*Within your group, discuss and critically evaluate the information.
Identify any problems with the studies and with their findings.*

Here are some issues that have been raised about this type of research evidence.

The issue of social class

Most research into the educational achievement of minority ethnic pupils has not
studied social class variations between ethnic groups. This is an important omission
since we not only know that social class has a significant influence on educational
opportunity and success, but we also know that the social class make-up of ethnic
groups varies.

Table 4.3, for example, shows the results of one study on 15–18 year olds by
Egglestone, a professor of education and leader of the team which produced the
pioneering study *Education for Some*.

Table 4.3	Social class of father, 15–18 year olds		
Social class of father	*White*	*Afro-Caribbean*	*Asian*
Professional	24%	11%	20%
Skilled manual	50%	56%	32%
Semi skilled or unskilled manual	19%	31%	41%

However, some studies have tried to compare the influence of social class and ethnic
origin. For instance the leading researchers Craft and Craft found that African-
Caribbean pupils' examination performance 'lagged behind that of all the other
groups, even when controlled for social class'. In their 1990 study Drew and Gray's
analysis concludes:

> All three factors (gender, ethnicity and class) were statistically significant
> but, of the three, socio-economic group accounted for by far the largest
> part of the total variance that could be explained. However, and this is an
> important caveat, the three factors together only accounted for about 10
> per cent of the total variance. Simple and crude descriptions of pupils'
> social class do not appear to provide very much purchase on the question
> of why ethnic differences in attainment occur.
>
> (Drew and Gray 1990)

It seems that for minority ethnic pupils social class is not the key to educational
success. We should remember, in any case, that the significance of social class on the
achievements of minority ethnic groups in school will vary not only between but also
within ethnic groups.

Figure 4.3

Race? Which race?

The issue of within-group difference

With very few exceptions, studies of achievement and underachievement of minority ethnic pupils have divided their samples into 'white', African-Caribbean (or West Indian) and Asian. Egglestone does this, as we saw on p. 114. There are several problems with these categories. Perhaps the most important is that they can lead to over-generalized or even misleading conclusions.

For example, the category 'white' in the data reported in the Swann Report is actually 'All other school leavers'. However, this could include minority ethnic pupils (other than Asian and West Indian who have their own categories) such as Turkish and Greek Cypriot and Italian. The educational performance of these groups, where they are present, will influence the data in this category. At the same time in the Swann Report, 'Asians' includes 'Other Asians'. It is not clear what this means.

 Your college or school is required by the Department for Education and Employment to provide data on the number of students in different ethnic categories. Many colleges obtain this information by asking students to complete an ethnic origin question on the enrolment form.

Ask your college for a copy of its form and try to construct a different list of ethnic categories taking into account the points raised in this section on 'intra-group differences'.

Consider also, the possibility of using an 'open question' on the form to obtain this information. What are the advantages and disadvantages of this approach?

In pairs, try to construct such a question.

Apart from these confusions, we should also remember that there are significant differences in educational performance within these categories. Using such broad categories may easily distort the picture. This is shown in the case of Asian school performance. Research which uses these broad categories shows that pupils of Asian origins are doing at least as well as 'white' pupils (and some studies suggest they are doing rather better), and doing much better than pupils of African-Caribbean origin.

However, when we break down the category 'Asian' and examine the performance in examinations of Indian, Pakistani and Bangladeshi students, we find significant differences.

For example, the Inner London Education Authority (ILEA) study of the examination results of fifth year Asian pupils in 1986 showed that:

- whereas nearly 21 per cent of Indian and just over 16 per cent of Pakistani students achieved five or more GCE 'O' level passes, the percentage for those of Bangladeshi origin was only 3.6 per cent;

- whereas just over 60 per cent of Bangladeshi pupils attained at least one CSE, nearly 90 per cent of Indian and Pakistani pupils did so.

This failure of many studies to distinguish groups within the broad categories is one reason why some researchers claim that research has helped to create and sustain 'the myth of underachievement' and, in the case of Asian students, 'the myth of over-achievement'.

In addition, there are other minority ethnic communities who seem to be ignored in studies of achievement. For example, there are significantly large Chinese, Italian, and Jewish communities in the UK. There are also large numbers of people of Irish origin living in mainland UK. Members of these communities argue that they too experience discrimination, disadvantages and racism in the education system, yet they have been almost completely ignored in research into achievement and underachievement.

Why do you think these groups have been largely ignored in educational research into racism, ethnicity and education?
   Using your library, try to find studies which include reference to any of these groups.
   Are there any?

The issue of research design

A common feature of statistical studies of achievement is that they measure the performance of minority ethnic school students by comparing it to the performance in examinations of 'white' students. This devalues the achievements of minority ethnic pupils by implying that their success can only be measured in terms of whether it equals that of 'white' students.

List those aspects of educational experience, other than examination performance, which might show patterns of achievement by ethnic origin.
   What would be the advantages and disadvantages of using these indicators instead of examination performance?
   What potential research problems might there be in using such indicators?

There are other measures of achievement which need not rely on a comparison with a 'white' norm. One example is the statistics on admissions to universities. Jones' 1993 analysis of them shows that:

South Asians now form a higher proportion of admissions to universities and polytechnics than they do of the population in the relevant age group, while Afro-Caribbeans form about the same proportion of admissions as of the population.

(Jones 1993)

So, the overwhelming concentration on performance in national school examinations probably produces a 'lop-sided' picture of achievement and underachievement among minority ethnic groups. However, we need to remember that many people, including students themselves, continue to see examination success as the route into work and high status professions. It is not surprising then, that researchers have seen patterns of examination success as socially relevant indicators of equality of opportunity.

Until quite recently few research studies had tried comparing different types of school to see if the school type influences patterns of success in examinations for minority ethnic students. The studies of Smith and Tomlinson and Nuttall and Goldstein in the late 1980s provide some information on these matters. Smith and Tomlinson conclude 'Some schools are much better than others and the ones that are good for white pupils tended to be about equally good for black pupils.'

Nuttall and Goldstein's 1989 study of over 30,000 pupils in 140 ILEA secondary schools found that there could be a difference between schools of as much as one high grade 'O' level pass in respect of African-Caribbean students with the same level of previous educational attainment. However, these studies do not provide a clear or full picture of how different schools, and their policies, might affect the performance of ethnic groups in schools.

Also of significance is the issue of how research subjects are assigned to the ethnic categories used in research into achievement. This is not about whether the particular categories used are valid, but about their reliability. For example, some studies have relied upon teacher judgements about the ethnic origin of pupils. This technique relies on highly subjective judgements and is likely to be unreliable. The introduction of systematic ethnic monitoring for schools, colleges and universities since 1991, using self-assignment, now provides a more (though not completely) reliable database for research.

The issue of gender

David: Teachers had different stereotypes for Asians and West Indians. Basically, the Asians were seen as good and we were seen as bad.

Deborah: That's true. At our school there was a further division between Asian girls and black girls. There's no way that a black girl would be encouraged to do the good subjects. It was music and sport for us.

Hameeda: But it's like we said before, that probably happens when there's a lot of West Indians but at my school, the Asians were the main group and the teachers had all the usual stereotypes, the bad stereotypes. The men teachers were very sexist. But the women teachers as well thought, 'an Asian, it must be an arranged marriage'. That's all they ever think of.

Maureen: I was the only black girl with about twenty-five boys in physics and they sat together and talked about what they were doing and wouldn't talk to you as a mate.

Parmjit: It was the same for me but mainly the problems came from the teachers. There was a lot of pressure on me. The science teacher, a man of course, always gave me as an example of neatness. My Mum or friends wouldn't agree. But when he gave examples of other things, like one day he was talking about lime on the soccer pitch and he said he was surprised I knew anything about it. He actually said it, how would you, an Asian girl, know about male knowledge.

(Mac an Ghaill 1989)

 At school, did you encounter anything similar to these experiences?

According to Mirza, a leading researcher in this field, none of the studies of ethnicity and education in the late 1970s is particularly significant:

for while they did acknowledge gender differences they failed to use their findings to explore new and enlightened directions in the race and education debate. The reason for this, it seems, is that none of these studies set out to address specifically the issue of black female academic achievement.

(Mirza 1992)

From the early 1980s, however, some research began to appear which did focus purposefully on the achievement of black girls in school. The most influential of these were those by Driver, Fuller, and Rutter *et al.*

Driver, the author of a highly controversial report *Beyond Underachievement*, investigated the GCE 'O' level and CSE results of over 2,000 16-year-old school leavers in five inner city schools between 1975 and 1977. Of particular importance was his finding that Caribbean girls did better than their white peers.

This confirmed Rutter's finding that black pupils, especially the girls, were more likely to stay on at school after 15. Fuller's study of black girls in a London comprehensive school found that the black girls obtained an average of 7.6 passes at GCE 'O' level and CSE compared to an average of 5.6 for the black boys.

Since these studies, others have focused even more closely upon gender differences both between and within ethnic groups. A good example is the ILEA study of examination results of over 17,000 and 15,000 school pupils in 1985 and 1986 respectively. The study calculated 'performance scores' for each group. Reporting on this study, Skellington notes:

In 1985 the average score for Bangladeshi girls, 15.1, was twice that of Bangladeshi boys, 7.6. The score for Bangladeshi girls was also four points higher than that for Caribbean boys and two points higher than for ESWI (English, Scottish, Welsh and Irish) boys.

(Skellington 1992)

It is clear, then, that just as ethnicity and social class combine in complex ways to affect the examination results of different pupils, so too do gender and ethnicity.

This activity could be completed in pairs. Using the information and arguments above, design your own research study into 'Educational achievement and ethnicity'.

Outline the research design: where and with whom it would be conducted, how key concepts and variables would be defined (e.g. class, ethnic origin), which instruments would be used to collect the data (e.g. questionnaire, secondary data), size of sample, and so on.

It may be useful to consult Chapter 2 (on research methodology) as well as the arguments above, before starting this exercise.

Explaining underachievement

Explanations of underachievement can be grouped under the following headings:

- pathology and culture;

- subcultures and resistance;

- school processes.

We examine each of these in turn.

Pathology and culture

Pathological explanations suggest that social problems are caused by the deficiencies within the individuals, groups or communities with which these problems are associated – essentially they 'blame the victim'. In the case of black (specifically African-Caribbean) 'underachievement', such explanations have focused upon below average intelligence, poor self-concept and low self-esteem, 'culture shock', family disorganization, linguistic deprivation, and 'underpreparedness' for English education.

The common thread throughout these explanations is that 'the problem' lies in the culture or background of the black child which leads to low motivation, disruptive behaviour and ultimate failure at school. These accounts have often stressed the supposed inadequacy of the home environment as a preparation for school success.

Rutter *et al.*'s comment that 'West Indian parents are just as warm and loving as other parents but it may be that they more often fail to appreciate the importance of play and conversation in children's learning and development' is an example of a pathological explanation.

Another example is the Rampton Report when it claimed 'West Indian parents may not recognize the importance to a child of an unstrained, patient and quiet individual dialogue with an adult'.

Rutter *et al.* provide another, more subtle example. They emphasize 'structural' factors contributing to the poor school performance of 'West Indian' children. They point to the fact that many 'West Indian' mothers work outside the home and are forced to use childminders through the absence of affordable state-provided nursery provision. However, the pathological part of the explanation lies in their stress on the lack of extended support networks; often the mother is a lone parent and there is no extended family to rely on.

 Compare these types of explanation for black underachievement with those given for working-class underachievement by researchers such as Sugarman.

However, it need not be the case that explanations of educational performance which look to family background pathologize the black family and culture. For example, Driver found that black girls are more academically successful than black boys and white girls. He explains this by reference to the matriarchal structure of the 'West Indian' family and the place occupied by women in 'West Indian culture'. He says that the patriarchal structure of white society leads to women having a lower status than men and, generally, being socialized into subordinate economic and social roles. In contrast, 'West Indian' girls are socialized to gain high status positions and thereby acquire those values which are more likely to guarantee educational success.

And even if such an analysis does not pathologize black culture and family life, it still runs the risk of stereotyping them.

Such accounts are not reserved for African-Caribbean school performance, nor are they without internal contradictions. Rattansi points out:

> The 'tightly knit' Asian culture and its cultural agent, the 'tightly knit' Asian family, are regarded in the Swann Report and elsewhere as the key influences producing high educational achievements. But this same culture and family system is held responsible for a widespread pathology supposedly afflicting 'Asian' girls and thus also their education: the malaise of being 'caught between two cultures', an identity crisis.
>
> (Rattansi 1992)

These explanations want to 'have it both ways': Asian cultures provide the right background and values for educational success but they also create problems (especially for Asian girls) relating to self-identity – which we are told should have a negative influence on school performance.

These types of explanation for ethnic differences in educational outcomes share certain assumptions with functionalist sociology (see p. 10). For example, they emphasize early childhood experiences and socialization. They argue that a failure to achieve is the result of low achievement motivation which itself results from inadequate socialization. This inadequacy is said to lie primarily in the culture of the family, which is perhaps also influenced by the process of migration and settlement.

However, as Burtonwood has noted:

> it is one thing to make a link between a cultural characteristic and an educational outcome but it is quite another to make a causal connection between the two let alone expose the processes involved.
>
> (Burtonwood 1986)

Explanations like these reproduce stereotypes of minority ethnic communities, cultures and family life. They assume that difference equals deficiency. It can be argued that if cultural differences between the minority ethnic child and the school do exist, then perhaps it is the school that is underprepared for the child as much (or more than?) the child being inadequately prepared for the school.

 Summarize, in your own words, the main weaknesses in pathological explanations of minority ethnic educational achievement and underachievement.

Compare these explanations with those of a similar kind offered in relation to social class and gender (see chapters 5 and 6).

Subcultures and resistance

Classical models of subcultural influences on educational achievement among working-class students (such as Sugarman's various studies in the late 1960s) described these cultures as homogeneous, all-embracing, and a problem for school success. They used the notion of cultural deprivation to explain underachievement: it is the student's culture that is the problem. There is a strong link here with pathological explanations. However, the idea that culture has something to do with educational achievement need not be based upon these questionable assumptions.

Recognizing the inadequacies of these explanations, many researchers turned to the idea of cultures of resistance. This rejects the view that a person passively receives cultural values and that cultures and subcultures are static – luggage which we carry around with us from early childhood. Instead, the cultures of resistance idea stresses that people actively and creatively engage with their culture, using it in a variety of ways in an ever-changing adaptation to their circumstances: from class to class, teacher to teacher and so on. There is a clear link here with the work of Willis in his studies of working-class youth.

We will now look at some examples of this approach related specifically to the education of black and other minority ethnic students.

Mac an Ghaill's ethnographic study of the school experiences of African-Caribbean and Asian male and female 'A' level students in a sixth form college stresses how students respond actively to situations both related and unrelated to racism. For example:

> Like pro-school students, they conformed to the technical demands made upon them, such as working in class, completing projects, doing home-work and preparing for examinations. But like anti-school students they did not automatically conform to their schools' social demands, in terms of appropriate dress and hair-style, keeping silent in class, being on time for lessons, showing teachers respect and appearing interested and stud-ious in lessons.
>
> (Mac an Ghaill 1988)

This finding tended to confirm earlier research in which Mac an Ghaill describes a group of young Asian and African-Caribbean women (the Black Sisters) who developed a 'mode of resistance within accommodation, which involved a pro-education/antischool perspective'. In explaining this perspective Mac an Ghaill emphasizes that the pupils' responses to immediate and structural conditions are not predetermined. They are, rather, 'consciously creating their own material culture' and, thereby, 'resisting institutional incorporation into white cultural identities'.

Fuller's study of black girls in a London comprehensive school in the late 1970s supports the picture painted by Mac an Ghaill. In class the girls often appeared disinterested yet, outside the classroom, discussing school, it was clear that for them schooling was important. Fuller's explanation for this is that the girls were adopting strategies for both maintaining their position in relation to boys and succeeding academically as a way of gaining control over their lives.

The girls did not, according to Fuller, suffer from low self-esteem. Instead they had a clear sense of self-worth but believed (with some justification) that this was largely unrecognized by parents and teachers. Academic success was a way of their self-worth being given wider recognition.

Other researchers show how contemporary forms of resistance and struggle are the latest in a long line of black struggle against oppression. Gundara, for example, locates contemporary black resistance to dominant culture in the UK in the wider context of the history of black resistance. This resistance took place during slavery in the Americas, by Aborigines in Australia, by Muslims and Hindus against the British 'Raj' in the 1857 uprising, and by African peoples during the late nineteenth/early twentieth century 'scramble for Africa' by European colonizers. He says 'Through the consciousness of historical resistance to this destructive colonization, black people in Britain are as aware of this form of oppression as their cousins in the Third World.'

Resistance takes many forms and is found in all aspects of life. Gundara argues that in relation to the younger generations it is found in schools and classrooms in the form of 'distinctive linguistic and cultural modes which reject the standard norms expected by society'.

These ideas are similar to the work of the Centre for Contemporary Cultural Studies (CCCS) in the 1970s which also emphasized cultures of resistance. However, a strength of the CCCS's approach was its stress on the importance of structural conditions (such as unemployment, low pay and dead-end jobs) in influencing the 'resistance through rituals' they described. Many studies fail to show clearly the link between school behaviour, resistance and structural conditions, and this undermines their analysis.

An additional problem for these explanations of underachievement is their tendency to romanticize the lives of the students and to suggest that the resistance is planned as a deliberate and, as Mirza puts it, 'defiant gesture to the world'. Her own research did not confirm this interpretation even though she did find similar strategies being employed by the students in her study to those found by other researchers. Mirza believes that teacher expectations are much more important. Also, students' lack of appropriate information, educational resources and the lack of job opportunities help to explain the students' strategies in school. For Mirza, these are not so much a form of resistance, as 'a strategy that rationalized in their interests the various educational and labour-market constraints that they encountered'.

 As a class, discuss which approach you find most valid: that which sees cultural resistance in school or college as 'a defiant gesture to the world' or that which sees it more as a rational adaptation to circumstances? Give reasons for your answer.

How do these explanations relate to your own school experiences?

School processes

The studies we referred to in the last section are concerned with 'what goes on in school' as a way of explaining the achievement and underachievement of black and other minority ethnic students. However, they have tended to focus upon the students and the ways in which they deal with school life. In this section, we turn our attention to those explanations which, without ignoring pupils' perceptions and interpretations, focus more closely on the interaction between students, teachers and the school itself.

Many studies have found that teachers hold stereotypical views of black pupils. The key issue, however, is how these views come to affect the educational opportunities, experiences and outcomes of minority ethnic pupils.

Figueroa argues that there are clear pointers to what might be happening in many schools.

1 Misassessment of minority pupils. This refers to the use of assessment procedures which are culturally biased or which tend to confirm stereotypes already held by teachers.

2 Misplacement. This is placement in bands or streams on the basis of teacher assessment of a pupil's ability which are lower than would be justified on the grounds of performance in tests.

3 Channelling: for example, the over-representation of African-Caribbean students in school sports teams as a result of teachers encouraging them into sports rather than the academic mainstream.

Wright's study of classroom interactions between teachers and African-Caribbean students described a catalogue of stereotypes which were translated into classroom teaching practice, for example, jokes about appearance or physical characteristics. One teacher told a black student that if she was not careful he would 'send her back to the chocolate factory'.

Stereotypes of Asian children were also common. For example, the Asian girls' desire for some privacy when changing for PE was often ridiculed by teachers and thought to be over-sensitivity. In another case a teacher questioned the girls on whether it was worth giving them a letter for their parents about a school trip, 'because your parents don't allow you to be away from home overnight'.

Wright also found that African-Caribbean students were more likely to be 'told off', blamed and 'picked on' by teachers, than Asian or white students, and to be placed in bands or sets well below their actual academic ability. She concludes that the interaction between teachers and black students is best described as one of conflict and confrontation. She argues that, overall, the educational experiences of these pupils are best explained by the concept of 'educational disadvantage or inequality' rather than 'underachievement'.

Wright's findings and conclusions fit with those of Smith and Tomlinson in their study of the effect of school processes, structures and policies on the performance and experiences of minority ethnic (and other) pupils. They found that the school attended has a very real effect on examination performance. This school effect is far more important, they say, than the effect of a child's ethnicity.

Some of the factors in school life, organization and teaching practices which appear to influence the educational performance of minority ethnic pupils in particular are:

- the amount of attention the child gets;

- whether that is positive and reinforcing or negative and distressing;

- the way the school is organized (especially as this affects friendship patterns);

- the approaches to language teaching and especially bi-lingualism.

David Gillborn's study of life in 'City Road Comprehensive' revealed that many teachers felt that African-Caribbean pupils in particular challenged their authority. Teachers interpreted their dress or aspects of behaviour (the way they talked, for example) as a deliberate challenge. Teachers seemed to recognize, however, that Asian pupils' failure to conform to some of the rules of the school (e.g. dress) was a reflection of the cultural importance attached to these things. Gillborn comments:

> the vast majority of City Road staff genuinely believed that treating every-one the same was the best way to deal with an ethnically mixed pupil population. Yet the result of their actions was that in the day-to-day life of the school, almost any display of Afro-Caribbean culture and identity was seen as inappropriate and therefore needed to be controlled.

> (Gillborn 1990)

One of the consequences of this was that African-Caribbean pupils were disciplined (e.g. by detention) more than other groups. The reasons given by teachers for placing pupils in detention demonstrated that they were interpreting behaviour as requiring discipline rather than the pupil actually having broken clearly defined school rules. For example, attitudes interpreted as 'arrogance' could easily lead to a detention for an African-Caribbean pupil. Gillborn's analysis highlights the way in which these processes are often inadvertent: reflecting the dominant white culture of the school even though the school was ethnically mixed.

Safe Sets?

by Mike Kivi

Every morning in assembly
Judith Jones is by my side,
Far away from weeping Wendy
Ever since the day she cried.

Then in Science I'm with Susan,
Down in Art I paint with Paul,
Mike and I make lovely music
When we're singing in the hall.

Peter is my little partner
When we're paired off in PE,
Craig and me go well together
Cutting card in CDT.

No one sits by me in Reading
(Miss says I can't settle down)
I prefer it best in Drama,
When the whole class runs around.

Fay's my friend when we are writing —
Just because we can't do double,
Usually we end up fighting,
then we get in awful trouble.

All our sets are in a folder
By the infant coats and hats,
So, that when we get older
We'll know where to sit our SATs.

Everybody's very pally
No one has a chance to moan:
Well there's one, his name is Ali –
He draws pictures on his own.

   Multicultural Teaching 11.2, Spring 1993, Trentham Books.

   What do you think is the message that Mike Kivi is trying to convey in his poem 'Safe Sets'?
   In what ways might a focus upon school processes such as that in the work of Gillborn or Wright help us to understand the situation described in Kivi's poem?

Beyond underachievement

Many of the studies described so far have had the rather narrow aim of identifying factors which might specifically explain patterns of achievement and underachievement. However, the studies by Gillborn, Mac an Ghaill, Wright, and Mirza see the research problem more broadly in terms of describing and interpreting 'the experience of schooling'.

To put this another way, many educational researchers now reject the overwhelming focus on underachievement of the past. Instead, they favour a much broader concern with the ways in which racism (and other dimensions of inequality) are produced and reproduced by and in schools, and how students experience these processes.

Some of these writers even reject the concept of underachievement altogether because it reinforces stereotypes and racism. They are not suggesting that differences in patterns of examination performance between ethnic groups are a myth or that they should be ignored. However, they are arguing that a continued concern with this diverts attention away from other aspects of schooling and contributes to the view that minority ethnic pupils are a problem for the school system, rather than seeing the system itself as the problem.

Racism, schooling and inequality

In this perspective, the key to understanding the educational experiences and outcomes of minority ethnic students will be found in an analysis of inequality. Whatever else may separate the theories of individual authors, those working within this perspective share a belief in the need to expose the workings of structures of power in society.

Brandt argues that the 'achievement/under-achievement formulation generates not simply a point of view but a way of thinking and a... vocabulary which locks one into a particular way of seeing'. This 'way of seeing' removes racism from the debate and so helps strengthen it. The debate comes to be about underachievement rather than racism. Brandt prefers instead a focus upon the processes through which schools perpetuate racism. These are:

- marginalization;
- production;
- reproduction;
- repression;
- regeneration.

These processes operate through:

1 the curriculum: that is, what counts as knowledge, from what perspective the teaching takes place, what images are used in teaching, and the material selected;

2 the pedagogy: how the teaching is done, trainer expectations, and teacher–pupil relationships;

3 the social and cultural environment of the school.

Brandt therefore focuses on the link between the nature of schooling and how it reinforces wider social, economic, political and ideological structures. The work of Troyna and Hatcher on racist incidents in schools, though different to Brandt's, also demonstrates this shift of focus.

Troyna and Hatcher attempt to develop a model for analysing racist incidents in schools, including harassment, bullying, abuse and physical violence. In it they contrast 'Grand Theorists' and 'Ostriches'. Grand Theorists have explained outbreaks of racial violence as expressions of the wider contest about control over jobs, houses and other resources (see Rex's approach on p. 128). Ostriches are those researchers whose focus is upon the detail of school and classroom life to the exclusion of any concern with what is happening 'outside the school gates'. This is equivalent to the micro/macro distinction in sociological research generally.

Troyna and Hatcher's model attempts to breach this divide. As they put it:

> It is, then, the fusion and interaction of the various levels that produces a combustible mixture leading on this occasion (the murder of Ahmed Iqbal Ullah at Burnage High School in September 1986) to an 'explosion' in the playground.

> (Troyna and Hatcher 1991)

They go on to highlight the importance of this type of analysis when they write:

> Without this understanding, racist harassment is dislocated from the broader context in which children live and make sense of their lives. Policies which stem from this impoverished and superficial understanding. . . are unlikely to operate effectively. The murder of Ahmed Iqbal Ullah was spectacular and extraordinary, but the intensity of conflict over apparently mundane matters such as friendship groupings provide the impetus for the mobilization of racism. The potential for this process resides in every school.
>
> (Troyna and Hatcher 1991)

Figure 4.4

Racism and racist violence in schools

Castles and Kosack's study of immigrant workers in Western Europe is a good example of the 'Grand Theorist' at work. Their comparative study of five countries concluded that migrant workers constitute a 'reserve army of labour' which is used by capitalism to keep wages low and maximize profit even during recession. In order to fulfil this function, migrant workers, and their families need to be located at the bottom of society. They come to form the lowest stratum: 'the most under-privileged and exploited group of society'.

Within this framework, (though in a later study), Castles explains the patterns of educational achievement and underachievement as resulting from the need of the capitalist state to encourage maximum economic activity among the second, third (etc.) generations of immigrant workers, but to ensure that this is mainly at the 'lower end' of the labour market (semi-/unskilled) for which few, and/or only 'lower-level' qualifications are needed. Castles argues that the state has only partially achieved these aims and that it is sitting on top of a 'social time-bomb'. Alienated, young, black and other minority ethnic members of the population demand rights to equal treatment and opportunity but are denied them. The 'riots' of the 1980s could be seen to demonstrate the validity of Castles' analysis.

What evidence exists to support or reject the view that the 'riots' of the early 1980s were a result of alienation among black youth?

Research the topic using media reports from that period and secondary sources in your library.

Castles' analysis is a Marxist one. This is shown, for example, by his emphasis on the role of the capitalist state and the needs of capital. John Rex's work, on the other hand, draws more upon a Weberian model of class structure.

Rex rejects the idea that racism is produced primarily by a capitalist class in order to maintain its position of economic dominance. Rather, colonial history and heritage have left a legacy of racism specific to black migrants from the ex-colonies. This racism is found within the white working class who mobilize it against the 'colonial immigrants' in their competition for scarce resources such as housing, jobs and education.

The result is that the 'colonial immigrants' end up as an underclass: systematically excluded from the opportunities to compete for the scarce resources on the same terms as the white working class. In his study of Handsworth in Birmingham with Tomlinson, Rex concluded:

> The relative satisfaction of parents with the educational system suggests that immigrants have been assimilated into the working class. But the segregation of the children, the attitudes of the authorities and the teachers, which have the effect of defining immigrant children as part of the problematic disadvantaged, and the development of new belief systems, especially amongst the young, all point to the development of a distinct class formation amongst the immigrants.
>
> (Rex and Tomlinson 1979)

In this analysis, schools play a decisive structural role in the development of the class structure and they will significantly influence the position of black and other minority ethnic communities in that structure.

Critically evaluate structural explanations of ethnic inequality in education.

White feminism and black feminism

We saw earlier how gender has often been ignored in studies of minority ethnic achievement in schools. However, even those studies which have focused upon Caribbean and/or Asian girls in school (e.g. Wright; Fuller; and Mirza) or have drawn comparisons between boys and girls' performance (e.g. Drew and Gray; Driver; Craft and Craft) are not necessarily feminist research. Just taking gender into account when designing research does not make it feminist.

For many years, feminism in Europe and the USA ignored the specific situations and experiences of black and other minority ethnic women. Research and political campaigns recognized that women's experiences were influenced by social class, but they did not seem able to recognize how racism and ethnicity influenced women's experiences.

Some of the first attempts to do this used the notion of triple oppression.

> The so-called **triple oppression** thesis states that inequalities related to 'race', class and sex 'add together', so much so that black working-class women are found 'at the bottom' of the social hierarchy. More recently, feminist writers have rejected this analysis on the grounds that it treats the various forms of inequality and oppression as too distinct. Instead, they argue, these dimensions are interconnected in complex ways.

Most recent analyses of the interconnection between class, ethnicity and gender have been heavily influenced by black feminist writings. Even here, though, there is not necessarily any agreement on the precise nature of them. The example of separate schooling for Muslim girls illustrates this point.

Nira Yuval-Davis analyses religious fundamentalism and women in Britain. She notes that the issue of separate schooling for Muslim girls is intimately linked to issues of racism. It also illustrates the divisions which exist within feminism over the issue of 'race'. She describes how, for example, the feminist novelist Fay Weldon has argued for a return to assimilationist policies in state schools whilst other feminists have argued that single-sex schooling enhances girls' academic achievement and, presumably, would do the same for Muslim girls in Islamic schools.

The position adopted by the campaign group Women Against Fundamentalism, which Yuval-Davis supports, is that setting up single sex and Islamic schools would be a mistake. These schools would actually have a different curriculum, one which could disadvantage its students. Yuval-Davis claims that it is racism itself which fuels the demands for such schools. This demand stems from racial discrimination and harassment, inadequate resourcing and teacher shortages in state schools in inner city areas.

Yuval-Davis also highlights the point that many Asian women are actively campaigning against single-sex Islamic schools. The answer to the issue of separate schools, she argues, is to end the problems in state schools, to end state support for all religious schools, and to make state schooling secular.

 Organize a debate with those in favour putting their arguments and evidence 'for the motion that separate schools for Muslim girls are a good idea' and those against putting their evidence and arguments afterwards.
Prepare for the debate by using your school/college and/or local library. Research the arguments for and against separate schools. The time allowed for each side during the debate should be the same. Take a vote on the motion at the end.

Black feminists have also commented upon the relationship between gender and 'race' in relation to a wide range of other educational issues. For example, the following extract from *Talking Back: Thinking Feminist – Thinking Black*, by the black American literary critic bell hooks, highlights some important questions about classroom practices, assumptions about academic study and the 'race'-gender dimensions of student and teacher experience.

On the first day of my class on Contemporary Black Women Novelists, a class in which all the students were white, some students expressed discomfort that there were no black women in the class, and then other students expressed similar feelings. When I asked them to explain why this disturbed them, they responded by saying that it seemed a bit ludicrous for them to be listening to one another talk about black women's fiction, that they would probably say stupid, racist things, and that they wanted to hear from black women. While I think it a meaningful gesture for young white women in a white supremacist culture to seek to hear from black women, to wish to listen and learn from black women, I cautioned them against turning the spheres of discussion on racial topics (or in this case, black women's writing) into yet another arena where we as black people are called upon to take primary responsibility for sharing experiences, ideas and information. Such a gesture places black people once again in a service position, meeting the needs of whites.

(hooks 1989)

bell hooks' perspective on this situation can be applied to other issues, for example, the ethics and validity of research into racism and education undertaken by white male and female researchers compared to that undertaken by black male and female researchers, or the ethics and validity of white teachers teaching about ethnic relations and racism. Feminism has been a major stimulus in raising these complex, but significant issues.

What are the arguments for and against bell hooks' perspective on this issue?

Should only black researchers do research into racism, ethnicity and education?

Can only black or Asian women provide valid comments about the relationship between racism and sexism?

Are the only valid views about racism to be found within black minority communities?

Discuss these issues with the other members of your class and draw up a list of the arguments for and against.

Ethnic inequality and participation in post-compulsory education

So far, we have been mainly concerned with the compulsory education sector – our discussion has deliberately reflected the history of research and debate on 'race' and education in Britain over the last thirty years. It is only very recently that issues around minority ethnic participation and experiences in further, adult and higher education (HE) have come onto either the policy or research agenda.

Undertake a survey of the books, journal articles, etc., in your library which are concerned with issues to do with 'race' and ethnicity. Note their dates of publication and whether they deal with education. Of those that do, identify whether they focus upon schooling or include some reference to post-school education and training.

Do the results confirm or deny the statement at the start of this section?
If they do, why do you think this situation has occurred?

Participation in the 16–19 sector

As we saw earlier in our discussion of achievement, several studies have reported that minority ethnic students are more likely to stay in full-time education after 16 than white students are (see Craft and Craft; Drew and Gray). The most recent data from the *Labour Force Surveys*, reviewed by Jones, confirm this earlier research.

The surveys show that 56 per cent of minority ethnic people in the 16–19 year old age range remain in full-time education compared to 37 per cent of the white population. There are gender differences between the minority ethnic populations: South Asian men are more likely to remain in full-time education than women, but the opposite holds true for African-Caribbean and white populations in this age range.

There are also differences between minority ethnic groups in terms of where they study after 16. The *Labour Force Surveys* reveal that 41 per cent of minority ethnic 16–18 year olds stay at school compared to 35 per cent of white 16–18 year olds. However, people of African-Caribbean origin are less likely to stay at school although a high proportion (25 per cent) are in some other sector of post-16 education (FE college, training programmes, etc.).

FE colleges are required by the DfEE to produce data on the ethnic composition of their student body. Go to your college and ask for the statistical breakdown of the student body for the college as a whole. If possible, ask for it to show the breakdown by gender for each ethnic category.
How does the picture painted by the local college data compare with the national picture summarized here? Are minority ethnic students concentrated in particular types of course? How might you explain this and any differences between your college and the national picture we have just outlined?

The ethnic monitoring of applications and enrolments in both FE and HE has significantly improved our knowledge about access to post-compulsory education for members of minority ethnic communities. However, the issue of monitoring has been fraught with problems. These include: disagreements over the ethnic categories to be used; fears within the minority communities about the use to which such data would (or could) be put; issues about storing the data confidentially yet allowing access to it for research and for guiding policy decisions (e.g. about admissions criteria and recruitment and selection procedures in colleges and universities). Despite these problems, ethnic monitoring is now required by the DfEE.

Discuss with other students and/or friends the pros and cons of monitoring the ethnic origin of students in education.
How can these data be used by educational researchers?
What are their limitations for research purposes?

Education and training in colleges is, of course, not the only form of training now available. Since the early 1980s there has been a marked growth in government training schemes, particularly those targeted at young people. One such scheme is Employment Training (ET). The proportion of minority ethnic people in ET in 1990–91 was 11 per cent. However, this figure conceals some significant variations relating to ethnic origin and gender.

Figure 4.5

Ethnic minorities in ET

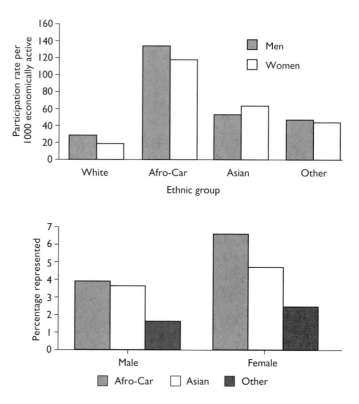

Figure 4.6

Distribution of ethnic minorities in ET

It is clear from these data that African-Caribbeans are heavily represented in these schemes compared to others, and that this is particularly so among women. Cross analysed this in relation to other data (e.g. staying-on rates for FE; labour market trends; participation rates in HE; unemployment rates) and concludes that 'ethnic minorities are likely to be disproportionately good customers for vocational training'.

The link between educational qualifications, employment and employment-training opportunities has been explored by R. Jenkins, formerly of the SSRC Research Unit on Ethnic Relations. He posed the important question 'To what degree is their labour-market position related to their levels of formal educational achievement?'

Lee and Wrench's study of this issue in the field of apprenticeships compared Asian and West Indian young people with the same job aspirations and level of educational attainment to a similar white group. They found the white group were much more successful in gaining apprenticeships. In the case of employment training, Cross concluded that despite having similar qualifications, black young people have been placed disproportionately onto government employment schemes which have 'a tenuous or non-existent connection with the labour market'. To summarize this, Jenkins says:

There is a wide body of research which demonstrates that black people, regardless of educational suitability, find it more difficult to obtain training, particularly at higher levels or in vocationally relevant areas.

(Jenkins 1988)

One of the factors affecting the placement of school leavers is the advice they get about job opportunities. Wrench's study of nine careers services in the North, South and Midlands in the mid-1980s throws some light on this. The study was based on case histories of nearly 3,000 young people on careers service files and involved interviews with eighty-eight careers staff about their work with minority ethnic young people.

About half of the careers staff believed that there was discrimination in the labour market against minority ethnic school leavers. Almost a quarter of those interviewed quoted examples of the way in which racial discrimination operated, for example in work placements. Employers often said that 'they only wanted a white trainee, or would refuse to interview a youngster with an Asian name'. Wrench also uncovered a degree of fatalism among careers staff in the face of this situation. For example, a Midlands careers officer said:

> It might be that this place has got a history of taking whites only. Rather than disappoint the kid – going for an interview that's a waste of time – you don't send him to that scheme.

(Wrench 1990)

Many felt powerless to challenge the discrimination especially when training vacancies were scarce. Others said that getting proof of discrimination was very difficult. Many staff appeared unfamiliar with the correct procedures to follow in the case of suspected racial discrimination by employers or other training providers.

It is also important to recognize that employment-related training does take place 'within work' or 'on the job'. Are there different patterns of participation here between majority and minority ethnic workers? Jones' study of *Labour Force Survey* data provides evidence on this. His analysis reveals that 'people in all ethnic groups from the younger age bands were more likely to have received some recent (on-the-job) training'. However, there were some significant variations between job levels and between ethnic groups.

Consider the following extract from Jones' study:

Training is more likely to be offered to those people working in the higher job levels. . . In the professional, managerial, and employer category, Afro-Caribbeans were relatively more likely than employees of other origins to have received training. . . South Asian employees in this group had a lower likelihood of having received some training. . . Within the skilled manual category, Afro-Caribbean and white male employees had similar probabilities of having received some training. . . South Asians were slightly less likely to have received training. . . In general, female employees in all job levels and from all ethnic origins were less likely than males to report job-related training in the last four weeks. The exception to this was in the top category. . . Afro-Caribbean women in this group were the most likely to have received some recent job-related training. . . In all job levels, Afro-Caribbean women were relatively more likely than women of other ethnic origins to report some recent job-related training.

(Jones 1993)

How might these patterns be explained?
How do they compare to findings about other training such as government schemes?

Participation in HE

In his study of student ethnic monitoring data Taylor suggests that '. . . minority ethnic students are well represented among those entering HE relative to the general population'.

For example, 6 per cent of all 18–24 year olds in the UK (the overwhelming age-range of HE applicants) are from minority ethnic backgrounds but of all admissions to HE in this age range in 1990, 9.6 per cent were of minority ethnic origin. Some groups are over-represented: for example, in the former polytechnics Indian students made up nearly 5.5 per cent of admissions compared to just under 2 per cent of the population. The data also reveal differences between types of HE institution. In 1990, 6.4 per cent of students accepted by universities were of minority ethnic origin compared to 14.5 per cent in the former polytechnics.

Figure 4.7

Acceptance rates (national entry 1990)

Figure 4.8

Acceptance by gender UCCA (1990)

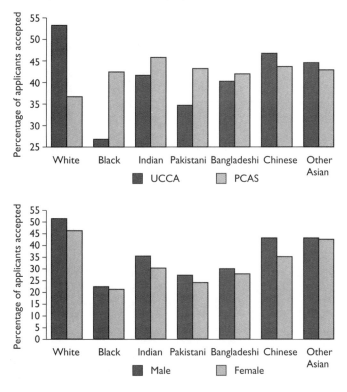

Figure 4.9

Acceptance by gender
PCAS (1990)

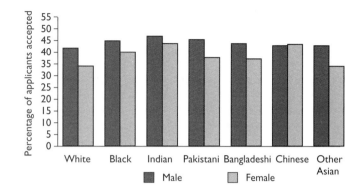

Attempting to explain the gender differences within and between ethnic groups shown in these data, Taylor examines the influence that differences in 'A' level points and types of qualification have upon acceptance into university. He concludes:

> acceptance rates were higher for virtually all men with more than eleven 'A' level points compared to equivalently qualified women from the same ethnic group. . . Women scoring fewer than five points or with less than two 'A' levels were more likely to be accepted than equivalently qualified men from the same ethnic group; among those with other qualifications (Scottish, BTEC and other) there was no consistent pattern of gender differences.

> (Taylor 1993)

Taylor sees these findings as a clear indication of the 'double disadvantage' for female minority ethnic applicants when compared to white applicants (of both sexes) and men of the same ethnic origin.

Part of the explanation for these patterns can be found in differences of subject choice between ethnic groups and between men and women. The data on this show that members of minority ethnic groups are more likely to apply for subjects which are either very popular or have traditionally high entry requirements. Asian women are more concentrated in pure science and social science compared to Asian men, whilst African-Caribbean women tend to concentrate upon the social sciences.

So far, we have treated 'participation' solely in terms of 'access': that is, in terms of getting into college or university or onto training programmes. Participation also refers, however, to the quality of the experience once in college or on a study/training programme. There is some evidence to suggest that the quality of the experience of post-compulsory education among minority ethnic students may be far from what they expected.

Such evidence and cases suggest that universities and colleges are not necessarily pursuing policies and practices which will enhance the learning experiences and chances of success for minority ethnic students. Is there any more systematic evidence for this?

Leicester and Lovell's two-year questionnaire, telephone and face-to-face interview study of the extent and nature of university departments' equal opportunities practice reveals a very patchy and inconsistent approach. In relation to ethnicity, they say:

Our research data on ethnicity revealed a patchwork of good practice. There are instances of good practice initiated by individuals, but on the whole antiracist practice is not built into departmental routines.

(Leicester and Lovell 1992)

One of their key findings was that although staff recognized racism and sexism as forms of oppression, there was little understanding 'of the functioning of indirect forms of racial and sexual discrimination'. Leicester and Lovell call for more staff development to promote this awareness and to integrate non-discriminatory procedures into every university department.

One of the areas in which we might expect there to be a major emphasis upon anti-discriminatory and even antiracist practice in HE is in teacher education. After all, we have seen evidence of the extent, and potentially very damaging effects upon pupils, of low teacher expectations and stereotyping. However, even though multiculturalism must inform all teacher education programmes, the picture painted by research into this area is not very promising.

Siraj-Blatchford's study of teacher education in seventy institutions revealed that 40 per cent of minority ethnic trainee teachers reported some form of racism among their lecturers. Over 60 per cent reported racist incidents involving other students on the course, and 60 per cent reported experiencing racism whilst on teaching practice in school.

At the same time, the research noted how multicultural issues are being included in the curriculum for student teachers. The study reveals a clear gap between what student teachers are taught and the ways in which many institutions and individual lecturers appear to understand their responsibilities and roles in promoting multicultural/antidiscriminatory/antiracist principles and practice through their own actions. We might be tempted to conclude that in many teacher education institutions the philosophy in relation to these issues seems to be 'do as I say not as I do'.

Suggestions for further reading

Sources specific to this chapter
Some organizations working in this field which you could contact for further information are:

Adult Literacy and Basic Skills Unit (ALBSU)
Kingsbourne House
229–231 High
Holborn
London
WC1V 7DA

Afro-Caribbean Education Resource Centre (ACER)
Wyvil Road
London
SW8 2TJ

Access to Information on Multicultural Education (AIMER)
Faculty of Education & Community Studies
University of Reading
Bulmershe Court
Earley
Reading
RG6 1HY

Centre for Multicultural Education
Institute of Education
University of London,
20 Bedford Way
London
WC1H 0AL
Commission for Racial Equality (CRE)

Elliot House
10–12 Allington Street
London
SW1 5EH

Early Years Trainers Antiracist Network (EYTARN)
1 The Lyndens
51 Granville Road
London
N12 OJH

Further Education Unit (FEU)
Information Centre
Citadel Place
Tinworth Street
London
SE11 5EH

Institute of Race Relations (IRR)
2–4 Leeke Street
London
WC1X 9HS

National Antiracist Movement in Education (NAME)
41 Strawberry Lane
Carshalton
Surrey
SM5 2NG

National Association of Teachers of English and
    Community Languages (NATECLA)
Hall Green College
520–24 Stratford Road
Birmingham
B11 4AJ

National Institute of Adult Continuing Education
    (NIACE)
19B De Montfort Street
Leicester
LE1 7GE

Runnymede Trust
11 Princelet Street
London
E1 6QH

Unit for the Development of Adult Continuing
    Education (UDACE)
94B London Road
Leicester
LE2 OQS

Your local Training and Enterprise Council (TEC), local
    Racial Equality Council (REC), and local community
    organizations may also provide useful information.

Recommended books for further study are:

Gill, D. and Mayor, B. and Blair, M. (eds) (1992),
    Racism and Education, London: Sage/Open
    University Press.
Mirza, H.S. (1992) *Young, Female and Black*, London:
    Routledge.
Skellington, R. (1992) *'Race' in Britain Today*, London:
    Sage/Open University Press.

Useful journals and newspapers include:

The Asian Times
Hansib Publishing Ltd.
Floor 3, Tower House
139–49 Fonthill Road
London
N4 3HF

European Journal of Intercultural Studies
Multicultural Teaching (journal published by NAME)
New Community (journal published by CRE)
The Runnymede Bulletin (published by Runnymede
    Trust)
The Voice
370 Coldharbour Lane
London
SW9 8PL

5

Social class and educational opportunity

Ken Foster

Figure 5.1

A satirical view of the class structure in 1960s Britain

In this chapter we examine definitions of social class and then go on to look at the evidence connecting social class and educational underachievement. We analyse the different sectors of education in turn: first schools, then post-compulsory education. We consider the main explanations that have been put forward to explain this underachievement and examine the suggested policy solutions. We then consider the relationship between education and social mobility.

Defining class

Does social class exist?

The term social class is often used to refer to the origins and characteristics of distinct groups of people. Class has different meanings in everyday conversation, in the media and in the world of entertainment.

These differences may be exploited for their humour as in the television comedy *Keeping up Appearances* where values, attitudes and ways of life are deliberately

Figure 5.2

A social climber

contrasted in a series of comic situations. Although class is not explicitly referred to, Hyacinth Bucket (pronounced 'Bouquet') finds it difficult to accept her social origins and struggles to keep the 'lowly' side of her family out of sight. She aspires to the lifestyle of those with high status in the community and beyond, symbolized, in particular, by her dream world of candlelit suppers.

1 Can you recall any other television series that feature social class differences in this way?
How are these differences turned into humour?
Is the portrayal of different class groups convincing?

2 Review a recorded programme of a popular series. With other students discuss your views on the way social class is portrayed. Your discussion could include reference to gender and race, for example, with a consideration of how these social dimensions relate to class.

Politicians also make references to the idea of 'class'. In October 1991 John Major, the Prime Minister, made the claim that we now live in a 'classless' society. However such statements are designed to persuade people that ideal conditions already exist, rather than being based on any evidence. Much of this chapter is designed to test out claims of this kind and to consider what a more detailed assessment of the evidence might reveal.

Social class groups

Social class is used to describe how different segments of the population may be grouped together. These groups are considered to share roughly the same levels of resources and similar styles of living. Class membership is generally indicated by the use of the Registrar Generals' (RG) scale of five social or occupational

Figure 5.3

Eton schoolboys

categories, though other systems of classification of socio-economic groups are also used.

Most standard textbooks on sociology also refer to 'working class', 'middle class' and 'upper class'. The distinctive nature of these groups and their relationship to each other are often questioned but the terms serve to introduce the idea that social classes still exist and may exercise a strong influence on life chances, particularly in relation to education.

Class and occupation

The main dividing line is between manual (working class) and non-manual (middle class) occupations, although it should be noted that the range of lifestyles and material wealth within these two groups can vary considerably. In manual occupations we would include those who do unskilled work, requiring little, if any, training, and skilled workers who have advanced technical skills, such as in the motor trade. In non-manual occupations there is a similar range including white-collar workers such as secretaries and shop assistants, and members of the professions, such as doctors, lawyers and teachers.

Between these two main groups, or social classes, there are marked differences in relation to earnings or income, living standards and health, with those in working-class, manual occupations having generally inferior life chances to those in the non-manual, middle-class occupations.

In Haralambos' introductory text on sociology, the chapter on social stratification defines social class in terms of the four main groups:

I Upper class - made up of between 5 and 10 per cent of the population, including company directors, financiers and senior civil servants. As a group the upper class own a substantial part of the nation's wealth.

2 Upper middle class – made up of 25–30 per cent of the population, including professionals, senior managers and those running small businesses. The group is sometimes referred to as the professional-managerial class.

3 Lower middle class – made up of 35–40 per cent of the population, including white-collar workers who are employed in shops and offices. This group may be referred to as the personal service class.

4 Working class – made up of 35–40 per cent of the population, including manual workers who may be skilled or unskilled, working in heavy industry, manufacturing, transport or agriculture.

The percentages given in the above outline of social class categories are approximate, based on data reviewed by Haralambos, Reid, Sarre, and Statham and MacKinnon. These authors acknowledge changes in class composition during recent times, with a decline in jobs associated with manufacturing and heavy industry and an increase in non-manual, service-class occupations. In addition there has been a substantial increase in the number of people unemployed, to such an extent that some might claim this represents the emergence of a new social class category.

Schemes for identifying class position

It is important to be aware of the way researchers may group occupations for the purpose of surveying social trends based on class. In Table 5.1 John Goldthorpe of Oxford University defined seven main groups for the purposes of his pioneering study of social mobility. His aim was to consider the extent of movement between these groups and the extent to which, for example, people moved out of the working-class (manual) into the middle-class (non-manual) occupations.

Table 5.1		John Goldthorpe's classification of social classes
Classes	*No.*	*Description*
Service Class	1	Higher professionals, higher grade administrators, managers in large industrial concerns and large properietors
	2	Lower professionals, higher grade technicians, lower grade administrators, managers in small businesses and supervisors of non-manual employees
Intermediate Class	3	Routine non-manual – mainly clerical and sales personnel.
	4	Small proprietors and self-employed artisans
	5	Lower grade technicians and supervisors of manual workers
Working Class	6	Skilled manual workers
	7	Semi-skilled and unskilled manual workers

Many researchers use the official classification of occupations used by the Office of Population Censuses and Surveys (OPCS) which are shown in Table 5.2.

Subjective or objective social class?

Wearing overalls on weekdays, painting someone else's house to earn money? You're working class. Wearing overalls at

weekends, painting your own house to save money? You're middle class.

(Prizewinning entry for a definition of class from the Sunday Correspondent 14 October 1990)

Financial Times *readers rule the country, while* Guardian *readers wished they ruled the country and Sun readers don't care who rules the country.*

(Jasper Carrot quoted in Ainley 1993)

What's your definition of social class?

Table 5.2	The OPCS classification of occupations
I	Professional (this includes university teachers)
II	Intermediate (this includes school teachers)
III (N)	Skilled non-manual
III (M)	Skilled manual
IV	Partly skilled
V	Skilled

Social class and educational underachievement

At all levels in the British education system, there is a continuing link between social class and underachievement. In the past this has been addressed as a matter of 'wastage of talent' where those from particular social origins, such as working-class children, have been unable to achieve their full potential in education.

Politicians have frequently sought to remedy this situation through educational reforms, including, for example, the introduction of comprehensive schooling in the 1960s. It was hoped that such a change in the education system would result in a social mixing of class groups and an equalization of educational opportunity.

Education and privilege

The national debate concerning equality of opportunity has often focused on the differences between state schools and public schools in the private sector. The historical legacy of this issue is featured in Figure 5.4.

The cartoon in Figure 5.4 was published shortly after the appearance of the Labour Government's *Public Schools Commission Report* (1968). There was concern about the relationship between public schools and social privilege and it was proposed to end this 'divisive influence', making half the places available in independent schools open to pupils from maintained state schools. However, these recommendations were never implemented.

 What are your views on the continuing division of schools into public (or private) and state schools?

Figure 5.4

State schools – a privilege to attend?

The Minister of Education, urging that ALL children from five to eleven should be sent to State schools, said: "Children of that age learning and playing together are not inhibited by any sense of differences."

Divide into groups holding opposing views. Prepare the arguments for and against private education and hold a debate.

City technology colleges – a new educated elite?

In recent times Conservative governments have attempted to increase the different types of school on offer by introducing city technology colleges (CTCs). There are fifteen such CTCs established in urban areas, each promoted as 'a new choice of school' and a 'beacon of excellence'. They were intended to specialize in science and technology and to offer children from deprived, inner city areas an opportunity to succeed.

Critics of these new schools have suggested that they may encourage the selection of a new educated elite. Access to such schools is to be based on pupils' commitment and the support of parents, and it is considered that this may favour children from middle-class backgrounds. Putting this idea to the test, three educational research experts Whitty, Edwards and Gerwitz (1993) found that the first year intakes of two CTCs showed no sign of middle-class bias. The social class composition of the intakes corresponded closely to that of the local population and the local comprehensive schools.

Examine Table 5.3 adapted from the research by Whitty, Edwards and Gurwitz.

Describe the social class distribution for each of the schools. Are there any major differences?

What are the differences in terms of the social class of mothers and fathers? Why were both mothers' and fathers' class included in the data?

What other data might be useful in considering the nature of equal access to these two CTCs?

The study by Whitty et al. *also involved interviews with pupils and parents to obtain their reasons for choosing a CTC. Below are some extracts from these interviews.*

	I	*II*	*IIIN*	*IIIM*	*IV*	*V*	*Unemployed*	*Homeworker*
Table 5.3 Social class of parents of first year intake students at two CTCs (rounded percentages)								
Kingshurst (1988 intake)								
Fathers	1	9	12	49	21	2	6	0
Mothers	0	9	45	4	16	3	7	16
Harris (1990 intake)								
Fathers	9	17	17	23	20	3	11	0
Mothers	0	26	20	6	9	11	6	15

Source: Based on a sample of pupil interviews and questionnaires (N = 155) and classified according to OPCS social class classification (Office of Population Censuses and Surveys 1980)

Pupils

1 'Yes, because I'd be able to know more about technology and have a better future.'

2 'Well, there isn't any other school that is as good as this, and I just wanted to see if I could get into it.'

3 ''Cos I thought it had a good education so I'd get a good job afterwards.'

4 'It was just that it was different to other schools that I wanted to come here.'

5 'It was more that the other schools that I've seen are nearly falling down, and this place is all new.'

Parents

1 'He's going to need a good education to get anywhere in this world and he's interested in computers.'

2 'We looked at all the other schools. The elder one was at —— and it didn't stretch him really. —— is really run-down. So it was really a lack of choice in the vicinity.'

3 'Grammar schools – I think that was the next best thing to the CTC. I think you can class the CTC just like that, as a grammar school.'

4 'There's not many people like our families that get in unless they are extremely clever.'

5 'I weren't going to send her in the beginning because I didn't agree with it . . . I think it should be available in every school. I thought they was being choosy . . . I think they should all be as good as the CTC but they're not.'

(Whitty et al.)

List the main reasons given for choosing this type of school.
Do parents seem in favour of the selection of pupils?
Do they – or the pupils – appear conscious of social disadvantage in education?
Are they critical of the idea of CTCs in any way?

Send for information from The CTC Trust (see address on p. 172) to learn more about these types of school. Devise a questionnaire or interview schedule to investigate how people in the local area respond to the idea of specialized education. Your questions should focus on social class and equality of opportunity. You should also select evidence which is linked to social class groups for purposes of comparison to find out, for example, if there are differences in opinion between working-class and middle-class respondents.

Social class and educational attainment – primary and secondary schools

A 1991 study by the National Foundation for Educational Research (NFER) found that reading standards in primary education had declined. Out of the twenty-four schools surveyed, fifteen had declining standards; of these schools, seven were in urban areas. This evidence suggests that reading performance is linked with social disadvantage.

Certainly Mortimore and Blackstone's well-known 1982 review of a wide range of research studies confirmed the link between social class and attainment in primary schools. More recently in a report for the National Children's Bureau, Kumar has reviewed data from the *National Child Development Study* and concludes that 'the gap between children from different social class and ethnic backgrounds tends to widen as they progress through primary schools'.

In secondary schools there seems to be good news. Comparison of the earlier GCE 'O' level passes with current GCSE results shows that there is a general pattern of improvement. There has been an increase in the numbers of young people gaining five or more GCSE passes at grade 'G' or above and also in the numbers gaining five or more grades 'A' to 'C'. Girls especially have done well recently.

Unfortunately these results are not true for all areas. In a 1992 study of deprivation and education for the Policy Studies Institute, Willmott and Hutchinson reported that in some LEAs results have actually declined. In LEAs such as Knowsley, Coventry and Bradford, little progress has been made. More strikingly, in Knowsley, Liverpool and Manchester, during the 1980s there was an increase in the proportion of pupils leaving with no graded GCSEs at all. It seems that in these areas social class, coupled with poor standards of living, is very strongly linked to failure in school.

This link was confirmed by a 1991 study by Jesson and Gray. They conducted research in secondary schools in Nottinghamshire. They found that pupils from deprived backgrounds (defined in terms of a combination of low income, large family size and other factors) suffered poor performance in GCSE examinations. More dated research such as psychologist Michael Rutter's 1979 study or information from the Inner London Education Authority in 1981 had also demonstrated that those from social classes IV and V perform less well in public examinations.

On the basis of such evidence, it is clear that social class is a significant factor in underachievement but, even so, it is important to note that not all children from such backgrounds have their education marred in this way. Kumar, for example, identifies factors which can offset social disadvantage:

> At a general level, research indicates that the relatively greater progress of children who do well at school, despite their deprivation, is related to ability, will-power, achievement-oriented attitudes and values; and circumstances such as emotional support and security at home, other favourable life experiences of various kinds and, above all, the availability of opportunities.
>
> (Kumar 1993)

Social class and urban schools

Finally in this section we consider the findings of a report by the Office for Standards in Education (OFSTED 1993). The inspectors responsible for this report visited schools in areas on the edges of towns and cities in England, including Bristol, Derby, Hull, Manchester, Slough, Tilbury in Essex and Thamesmead in southeast London. They concluded that standards were 'inadequate' and 'disturbing' in more than a hundred schools, colleges, and youth and adult education centres in seven predominantly working-class districts. In particular they recorded that children's learning in reading, writing and numeracy was often poor.

The report emphasizes the responsibility of schools and is critical of poor levels of attainment in primary and secondary schools. We look more closely at school influences later in this chapter. Importantly, though, this report identifies widespread social deprivation, acknowledging that some schools were drawing their intake of pupils from 'pockets of severe disadvantage'. Similar surveys in the past have used such information as a basis for major reforms in urban education.

Some of the main identified characteristics of the areas and schools surveyed are:

- social class: Census data for 1991 indicates that the areas have higher than average proportions of families from lower socio-economic groups; many children were in families where the head was classified as partly skilled or unskilled;

- families: there were high proportions of pre-school and school-age children; there was also a large number of families with three or more children and a high proportion of children from lone-parent families (one in five children under 16 years came from a lone parent family);

- housing: a high proportion of accommodation was rented and there were high levels of overcrowding in some homes;

- car ownership: in some areas 37 per cent of children were living in households without access to a car;

- unemployment: the rate of unemployment was higher than the national figures (14 per cent compared with 9 per cent in 1991); 24 per cent of economically active 16–19 year olds were unemployed.

The OFSTED report describes the local community environment like this:

In some areas the quality of flats has deteriorated since their construction; neighbouring shopping centres offer a limited range of services or are sometimes closed and boarded up. Litter, graffiti and the effects of vandalism are readily apparent in these dismal environments. The level of crime – drug abuse, theft and sometimes violent attacks against the person – is relatively high, although according to police reports it is often undertaken by a small number of persistent offenders. Especially where minority ethnic groups are a small proportion of the population, racially motivated abuse and attack are frequently reported.

(OFSTED 1993)

Creating an underclass

Figure 5.5

'I am social scum'

Underclass describes a sub-category of the poor. This group comes from a lower social class background, has a high rate of unemployment, is in receipt of welfare support from the state and is prone to high rates of crime and delinquency. The idea of an underclass is also linked with the idea of a dependency culture or culture of poverty. The term has been criticized for its implication that the victim is to blame. Wider issues like government policy on employment need to be taken into account when discussing the very poor.

Researchers like C. Murray or D. Smith believe that an underclass is emerging in Britain. This view is partly a result of reports like OFSTED's. The idea has also caught on in the popular imagination as a result of media reporting of riots and crime in some areas of large cities. Relative geographical and social isolation has become a feature of some urban estates constructed in the late 1950s and 1960s. This, combined with the conditions we have just described, has reinforced disaffection and the growth of crime and violence.

 Can you name three areas in Britain which are reported in this way in the mass media?

Social class – a major determinant of success?

We could summarize the results of studies like those we have outlined by saying that there is a clear correlation between social class and educational success. Attainment levels and progress through the education system favours those from middle-class and professional family backgrounds.

Statham and Mackinnon comment on the absence of recent sample surveys investigating this relationship. One reason for this, they suggest, is that earlier surveys gave such very clear results that 'at virtually every stage of education, by virtually every criterion of achievement, middle-class children had higher levels of achievement than working-class children'.

Bates and Riseborough also consider the present situation to be one of 'deepening divisions' and 'fading solutions'. These authors dispute the Majorite thesis of a classless society in the making. Their studies of youth and inequality demonstrate that social class remains a major determinant of educational success and social mobility.

We end this section with some telling statements from Statham and Mackinnon which are based on OPCS data from 1989.

> Roughly speaking, the lower the socio-economic group of someone's father, the more likely it is that his or her full-time education ended in school, rather than college or university . . . The likelihood that a person enters higher education continues to be strongly related to his or her family's social class. In Great Britain in 1987, 62 per cent of students in universities and polytechnics had fathers in non-manual occupations, and 38 per cent had fathers in manual occupations.
>
> (Statham and Mackinnon 1992)

This quote highlights the issue of progress to higher education (HE), which we consider later in this chapter.

 Allocate to individuals or pairs within the group the following factors which affect progress in education:
- *low income;*
- *unemployment;*
- *health;*
- *housing;*
- *environment;*
- *homelessness.*

Each member of the group should research one of these topics using sources listed at the end of chapter. They should seek information which shows how their chosen aspect of deprivation may affect educational opportunity. Finally, each person should make a presentation to the rest of the group.

Explaining underachievement

The history of mass education in Britain can arguably be viewed as a history of the legitimation and institutionalization of the 'failure' of the working classes.

(Lee 1989)

Figure 5.6

It's all in the genes

'Some people would blame your genes, others your home environment, but I blame you, Wimpole, plain and simple.'

Early explanations of the links between social class and educational underachievement included poverty, housing, family size, language and socialization. We look at some of these explanations next.

 Jan Lee, and many other researchers, now dismiss these sorts of explanations. She sees them as merely providing socially and politically acceptable reasons for a very deep-rooted, historical problem. Such explanations ignore the problem and instead blame the victims. As you read through the next few pages, decide who is right.

Family and language use

Linguistic deprivation means that particular groups of children have inadequate language skills, both verbal and written, because they are not exposed to rich and diverse language use in the home. In other words, linguistic deprivation is a result of poor socialization.

Most researchers today reject this idea. They say the emphasis should be on language difference, not deprivation. They argue that varying types of language used by children from a range of social backgrounds should be seen as different but equally efficient for communication.

Family background is critical in providing support for children and young people in school. It has been argued that poor socialization experiences in the home can lead to educational underachievement and failure. Studies in the 1960s and early 1970s concluded that working-class children received poor language-learning experiences and so were linguistically deprived when they reached school. The most famous of these was by the pioneering educational researcher Basil Bernstein (though he now says that his studies were misinterpreted).

In his early work Bernstein suggests that the working class speak a restricted code or public language. The characteristics of this are:

- shorter sentences;
- fewer qualifications (e.g. 'however', 'although');
- narrower vocabulary;
- predictability;
- repetitiveness;
- frequent use of question tags ('isn't it', 'didn't I');
- less subtle use of grammar;
- less discriminating use of adjectives;
- greater use of gesture;
- few abstract nouns (e.g. 'equality', 'democracy');
- frequent repetitions of conjunctions and phrases.

Elaborated code, or formal language, is spoken by the middle class, who also have access to restricted code when its use is appropriate, according to Bernstein's early work. Supporters of Bernstein are now few, but at the time the idea of linguistic deprivation was widely accepted. For example, Bernstein's co-researchers Brandis and Henderson said 'Middle class families more often use language to express thoughts and concepts and they do so in a way which is precise and takes less for granted.'

Since then, studies like that of the American ethnographer Brice-Heath have observed that social class differences in language use are certainly critical, but they also suggest that the cultural and procedural rules of classrooms may inhibit intellectual development for some groups of children. Such studies recommend that the focus should be on differences *between* groups rather than the 'deficit' of one group, and that approaches to teaching and learning should not assume middle-class language styles and procedures are natural, universal or superior.

Write down as many school rules as you can recall from your own experience. Then make a note of your response to the following questions.

1) *Do any of these rules prevent pupils from talking and communicating in order to learn?*
2) *What do you think a middle-class language style amounts to?*
3) *Do teachers use such a style exclusively, or do they communicate with pupils on their own level, using, for example, local vernacular or dialect and 'street-wise' vocabulary?*
4) *How critical is the teacher's style in relation to encouraging pupils' learning?*

The quotes from pupils in Dubberley's 1988 study may help with this task. Dubberley's research concerned the experience of working-class boys and girls in a comprehensive school in a mining village in the Yorkshire coalfield. Dubberley's main concern was with the extent to which teachers understood working-class culture.

> *Carl - Teachers sometimes contradict yer - like if you say summat, they say 'no this is the proper way to say it' and they tell you the proper way.*
>
> *Girl 1 - They expect yer to talk posh when yer from round 'ere and yer can't - cos yer talk like people from round 'ere, don't yer?*
>
> *Jane - Yeah, Mrs Shea, she called mi a tart cos I were brushin' me hair.*
>
> *Janet - He were teaching our Maureen and she were talking to 'er mates and he called 'er a set of sluts, just for talkin'.*

(Dubberley 1988)

Compare your lists of school rules and your views about language with those of your partner.
1) How important is language for learning?
2) In what ways could pupils be encouraged to learn through the use of their own language style?

Language for learning

Studies of children's socialization and language use by linguistics specialist Gordon Wells, and Tizard and Hughes (1986) have challenged the idea of working-class linguistic deprivation. Tizard and Hughes studied pre-school children: fifteen girls from middle-class families and fifteen from working-class families. They were interested in mother–daughter interaction and the relationship between talking and learning. Overall it was concluded that there were no major differences between the two social class groups as far as linguistic skills and competence were concerned. Tizard and Hughes believe we need to distinguish between language competence and the style, or mode, of communication. Many differences between groups of children are more about values and lifestyle, than the capacity to use language for learning.

Language terms used by Tizard and Hughes include: **'Why'** questions asked by children. These took several forms, including questions concerned with **curiosity** to find out more about the topic ('Why does snow melt in the sun?') and questions which were used as a **challenge** ('Why do I have to go to bed?').

Intellectual search is defined by Tizard and Hughes as the child 'actively seeking new information or explanations, or puzzling over something she does not understand, or trying to make sense of an anomaly in her limited knowledge of the world'.

 We have listed below some of Tizard and Hughes' findings. Use them to discuss the role of language in learning.

Middle-class

- *Mothers used a wider range of vocabulary.*
- *Mothers paid attention to 'why' questions.*
- *Girls asked more 'curiosity' questions.*
- *Girls were more persistent in asking questions, matching answers to their existing knowledge (intellectual search).*

Working-class

- *Mothers often played exciting, physical 'fun' games with their children.*
- *Mothers gave more information on family and domestic topics.*
- *Girls asked fewer 'why' questions but more 'challenge' questions.*
- *Girls spent more time playing in the afternoon in the nursery school.*

You could consider the following questions during your discussion:
1) How critical is mother-child interaction?
2) How might it influence learning?
3) Are differences in style of communication important?
4) Do you agree that the differences between working-class and middle-class language use are not very great?

Tizard and Hughes did find class differences in mother–child interaction, in mother–child conversation and in the views of mothers about education and play. However the authors stress:

> By no means all our measures showed social class differences. There was no social class difference in the amount of mother-child talk, the length of conversations, the frequency and nature of mothers' questions and controlling remarks, or the amount that mothers played with their children . . . There was a wide range of behaviour within each social class group, with some working-class mothers using language in the same way as middle-class mothers, and vice versa.

(Tizard and Hughes 1986)

Empty words?

An interesting debate took place between the American linguistics researcher William Labov and Basil Bernstein about middle-class language. In *The Logic of Non-standard English*, on the basis of an extract from a respondent 'Charles M', Labov argues that so-called 'good speakers' often produce verbose but empty sentences. They sound good but don't say much. In arguing this, Labov was criticizing Bernstein's early idea of elaborated code. Meanwhile Labov considers a younger respondent, 'Larry', who speaks a form of black non-standard English, to be producing a clear and logical argument (albeit in 'bad' English).

Bernstein replied (1990), arguing that 'Charles M' is not redundant or verbose, but using a particular set of rules of argument while 'Larry' is using the same argument 'endlessly recycled'.

 If you can, look at the debate. Labov's article is in Keddie (1973). The reply is in Bernstein (1990). See page 172 for references.

Cultural capital and family climate

Cultural capital refers to the educational advantages that some families may have in terms of knowledge of the education system, and the way they use such knowledge to ensure success for their children. Such an advantage is reinforced by a broader range of cultural resources that are valuable in achieving educational success. These include intellectual pastimes, selective reading, political awareness and facility with language use.

Looking at class differences in language and education, it is clear that in all cases the family provides an important context for learning. What takes place in the family may well influence future life chances and, in particular, provide support (or not) for doing well at school.

It has been suggested that families may possess their own culture, shared with others from similar social backgrounds. Depending on the nature of this culture and the values and attitudes it promotes, children may be given favourable conditions for facing the challenges of school, particularly passing exams.

Some families may possess what the French sociologist Pierre Bourdieu calls cultural capital. Children learn from their family how to use the formal language that is required by teachers and others and they learn what counts as an 'intelligent' or 'knowledgeable' activity. They know how to progress through the system, how to make informed judgements about good schools, and how to choose the courses that will get them a good job or into higher education. The family support these children receive gives them a great advantage throughout the education system. The following extract gives a flavour of what this means:

> Parents and teachers are preparing to drill seven-year olds for the new national reading tests . . . Booksellers and publishers were deluged by inquiries last week after the Department of Education issued a list of 51 books that will be used for the tests . . . At Blackwell's in Oxford and Heffers in Cambridge, ambitious parents, carrying the Government's list, scoured the shelves hoping to ensure top marks for their children . . . In Bath Julia Harrison of Waterstones thought that, at between £6 and £7, some of the hardbacks were too expensive for most parents.
>
> (Judd and Borrill 1991)

In their well-known study of education and social mobility, Halsey, Heath and Ridge (1980) have taken this argument a stage further by suggesting that family climate may be crucial. A favourable climate involves the combination of having cultural capital and good material circumstances.

Halsey *et al.* found that cultural capital influenced the selection of secondary schools but that material circumstances were more important in influencing staying on at school and future academic success. They suggested that low-income families have problems in supporting children after the school-leaving age and this makes it difficult for their children to stay in education. Halsey *et al.* saw the lack of maintenance grants for the 16–18 age group as a major obstacle to equality of opportunity in the school system. There are still no such grants.

More recently, the *Youth Cohort Study* (Gray *et al.* 1989) found that young people from manual backgrounds were less likely to continue their education beyond 16 years of age. A possible reason for this is identified in the report of the National Commission on Education (1993) which notes that 'real difficulties' may be encountered by low-income and single-parent families and those drawing Income Support and Family Credit, if they wish their children to stay at school beyond the age of 16.

Schools 'failing pupils'

> Many young people do not stay on beyond compulsory schooling because they are not qualified to do so. The education system instead of rewarding achievements is a process of failure. How deeply depressing it must be to go through school knowing that at the end you will have little to show for it. Is it surprising then that so many youngsters should . . . leave at the first opportunity when allowed to do so?
>
> (Smithers and Robinson 1989)

This quote is from a study by Smithers and Robinson who argue that the school system and particularly its examination system, is largely responsible for educational failure. From this point of view, it is not the young people but rather the schools who fail by not preparing their pupils adequately for the future. This argument was also presented by HMI in the 1993 OFSTED report we referred to earlier in this chapter. The authors of this report considered that teachers in primary and secondary schools had low expectations of pupils and were inclined to blame poor performance and failure on pupils' social disadvantages. Similar criticisms can be applied to FE colleges, and the lack of support in the youth service and adult education.

From this point of view, schools in general and teachers in particular are blamed for working-class educational underachievement.

The 'good' pupil

Many studies have focused on teacher–pupil interaction, pupil subcultures and school organization as possible key factors in determining educational success and failure. Those by educational research experts such as Ball (1981) and Woods (1979) are well known. Many similar studies have also been brought together in edited form by Hammersley and Woods (1984) and Hargreaves and Woods (1984).

Taken collectively, this research supports the idea that school processes associated with teaching, learning and assessment are biased in favour of the 'good' pupil. The teacher's idea of a 'good' pupil is that s/he:

- works hard;
- follows school rules;
- behaves 'well' in the classroom;
- wants to, and can, answer teachers' questions;
- produces written work in standard English.

'Good' pupils also identify with the broader cultural aspects of a school, including its requirements for mode of dress, extra-curricular activities and taking on extra responsibilities, like playing for a school team, taking part in a drama production or being a prefect.

These kinds of academic and cultural expectations permeate the school and become institutionalized. Pupils who do not conform to them often become alienated from the school over time and eventually have little prospect of identifying with what the school represents. It is possible that in these circumstances such alienated pupils will be more often from working-class, rather than middle class, backgrounds.

Look closely at the data summarized in Table 5.4, adapted from the study of Stephen Ball's Beachside Comprehensive. Compare the two groups of pupils in different bands in relation to the different aspects of schooling identified.

1) What are the main differences between the two bands of pupils?

2) What do the data tell us about the nature of school organization and its relationship to the social class background of pupils?

3) Are some of these pupils failing the school, or is the school failing its pupils?

The hidden curriculum and the idea of 'fair' testing

The hidden curriculum describes the way schools shape pupils' behaviour through the range of 'official' and 'unofficial' experiences. These may include both teacher–pupil interaction and peer group influence. Such activity conveys messages concerning approved forms of behaviour, definitions of what is acceptable in terms of school work and what counts as success. There may be a conflict of interest between formal (teacher-directed) and informal (pupil-directed) expectations.

All of this suggests we should challenge the supposed 'objectivity' or 'neutrality' of the school system, especially regarding the fairness of assessment and testing. It also raises important questions about the compulsory publication of school examination results. These do not take into account the social disadvantages that their pupils have to cope with. One way of doing this is to devise a value-added formula. This means that there would be a measure of the abilities the pupils had when they entered the school and what they left with. Schools would publish, and be rewarded for, the value they had added to the pupils during their time there.

Unfortunately even such a proposal, though concerned to promote equality in terms of measured outcomes, may not have much impact on the hidden curriculum of schools. Authors such as John Urry argue that present forms of assessment embody the values and attributes of the middle and upper classes and favour the 'cultural competence possessed by the minority'. The only way to change this is to change the forms of assessment (or the class system!).

Identify and list concrete examples of the hidden curriculum that you have experienced. Think about how the classroom was organized, the way teachers treated different pupils, the sorts of tests you had, and whether they were fair to everyone.

Table 5.4	Different bands, different worlds. A comparison of top band and middle band, second year cohort at Beachside Comprehensive	
	Top band	*Middle band*
Teacher's stereotype of each band	Academic potential Neat workers Bright, alert and enthusiastic Want to get on Rewarding	Not up to much Rowdy and lazy Cannot take part in discussions Not interested Unrewarding
Proportion of pupils from working-class homes	36%	78%
Proportion of teachers' time in class devoted to maintaining order	1.5%	12.5%
Average number of detentions, per pupil per year	0.4	3.8
Average number of absences per pupil in term 1	8.1	12.6
Average number of minutes spent on homework per pupil	47	16
Proportion of end-of-year subject tests graded at 50% or higher	58%	11%
Number of extra-curricular activities or club memberships, per class	43	10
Proportion of pupils who dislike school	13%	48%
Views held about each band by pupils in the other band	Brainy Unfriendly Stuck-up Arrogant	Thick Rough Boring Simple

Source: Compiled from Stephen Ball (1981) *Beachside Comprehensive*, Cambridge, Cambridge University Press, ch. 2

Greater equality of opportunity?

Schools are clearly important in influencing the educational success or failure of pupils. We will now look at how far the comprehensive school system, in particular, has equalized the opportunities for pupils of all social classes. In their 1987 survey of the Scottish comprehensive school system, McPherson and Willms found that there had been a rise in educational attainment for all pupils. The effect of social class difference had actually fallen over time. They suggest that in England and Wales too there are signs of equalization of opportunity. Gray and Jesson got similar results for pupils up to the age of 16 from their 1989 review of a large number of research studies.

Beyond 16 there is less room for optimism: the British system has low staying-on rates compared to others. Halpin's work shows that although two-thirds of all 16 year olds in the UK are involved in some form of further education, in most cases this is on a part-time basis. Of the 20 per cent who do stay on full-time, most are pupils from the independent schools sector. In addition there is a class bias in relation to staying on, with those from non-manual backgrounds being most likely to progress to FE, including sixth form, and then on to HE. We will examine this in more detail in the section on social mobility (see p. 163).

The impact of recent educational reforms

Since the Education Reform Act (ERA) 1988, there have been substantial changes in the organization of the education system of England and Wales. Examples include the introduction of a National Curriculum for primary and secondary schools, formal testing of pupils at key stages in their schooling, and attempts to diversify the types of schools through the setting up of CTCs and awarding grant-maintained status (GMS) to some primary and secondary schools. Schools have also been encouraged to specialize in areas such as technology or the performing arts, and to market their services, backed up by an open enrolment policy.

In assessing the significance of these reforms in relation to equality of opportunity, members of the radical Hillcole Group such as Davies *et al.* are far from optimistic. They conclude that the changes being implemented are more likely to reinforce inequalities of class, gender, race and special needs, rather than promote greater awareness of disadvantage and a widening of horizons for all social groups. Many of the adverse processes of schooling acknowledged in the earlier sections of this chapter, will be likely to continue, and there are various limitations to the reforms. These include:

- limited entitlement to the National Curriculum for some pupils through the disapplication ruling (including those with behavioural problems and ESN categories);

- the increased emphasis on formal testing may result in children being labelled as failures from an early age, reinforced by negative teacher expectations;

- the possible re-emergence of victim-blaming explanations such as working-class underachievement, laying the blame on the home, the family and cultural deprivation;

- the influence of market values on education, persuading schools to be selective, competing for the 'brightest', most able and highly motivated pupils.

Disapplication refers to a set of official procedures to be followed by schools when they wish to make special provision for some pupils. If granted, this means that certain pupils do not need to follow the National Curriculum but follow their own separate programme. Some would consider this to be a form of exclusion from mainstream schooling and a possible social disadvantage.

Figure 5.7

'Back to basics'

There has also been controversy over the content of subjects in the National Curriculum. Some politicians and political interest groups want a return to traditional values and a British emphasis in subjects such as English, history and religion. Critics argue, though, that this will result in an exclusive and selective curriculum which favours the interests of white, middle-class groups. Jones, for example, notes how the teaching of English had become quite broad before the 1988 Act. It took into account the needs of working-class children, recognizing the place of non-standard dialects, the importance of non-printed media and valuing students' own creative writing. Jones describes the outcome of the National Curriculum proposals for English like this:

> To read the anthology of literature on which 14-year-old students will be tested this year is to take a journey into the pastoral dream lands of a certain kind of English imagination, where winter is a 'red huntsman', where spring means 'golden daffodils', where steam trains hiss in Edwardian summer afternoons, and where autumn, of course, is a close bosom friend of the maturing sun.
>
> (Jones 1993)

The emphasis is now placed on 'standard English' rather than recognizing the variety of dialects in the UK. As Jones puts it:

> a particular version of 'heritage' and 'excellence' takes absolute priority over the language and experience of pupils . . . a curriculum designed in this way contains its own implicit systems of inclusion and exclusion, based on pupils' familiarity with the dominant cultural forms, its own predictions of who will succeed and who will fail. These systems, deriving

from a particular model of culture, will be strengthened by what the new English contains by way of a model of learning.

(Jones 1993)

How does the idea of cultural capital (p. 153), apply here?
What about Michael Young's ideas (p. 14)?

Specialization and selection in schools

The increased specialization of schools is equally controversial. Some concentrate on academic subjects, such as languages, maths or science, while others may specialize in technically based subjects or the performing arts. Critics such as Chitty (1993) and Davies *et al.* argue that this is simply another strategy for introducing selection. Schools may opt to pick the 'brightest' pupils on the basis of interviews, for example, and may favour the selection of those whose parents are more knowledgeable and influential in the schools' marketplace. This will mean that those without this cultural capital will be left with those schools offering a lower status curriculum leading to reduced life chances.

A number of authors (Chitty 1993; Coulby 1989; Davies 1992; HMI 1990; Whitty and Menter 1991) have concluded that the effects of the sum total of these recent changes to the education system will disadvantage working-class and black young people, particularly those in inner cities. The 1988 Reform Act and subsequent changes to the system are seen as likely to increase inequalities, rather than serve the needs of the least advantaged members of society.

Chitty (1993), for example, cites the case of a grant-maintained school in Barnet, north London, which is intent on removing 'difficult' pupils. These pupils would have to be taken by other schools in the area. In this situation parents are not choosing schools but schools are choosing pupils. In time this will lead to the creation of unpopular 'sink' schools containing a group of disadvantaged working-class pupils.

Whitty and Menter predict the emergence of an educational underclass in Britain's inner cities, with little chance of improving their educational prospects or life chances. There will be, in other words, a cycle of deprivation or poverty trap partly caused by educational policy.

There is much academic criticism of contemporary educational policy. Concern for equality of opportunity is still on the agenda, though, and educational authors, commentators, teachers and HMI are actively seeking ways to promote this. Recent studies which consider alternative futures and possible reforms for a more equitable education system include those by expert professional commentators such as Hopkin, Newman-Turner, Taylor, Thompson, and Wragg and Jarvis. Many of them argue that solutions are still to be grasped within the schools, and are dependent on the willingness of teachers to recognize and work towards a fairer system for all their pupils.

Read the extract from Curriculum Guidance.

(. . .)recognition that preparation for life in a multicultural society is relevant to all pupils should permeate every aspect of the curriculum

schools need to take account of and challenge attitudes present in society which consider that subjects such as mathematics, science and technology are less relevant for girls than for boys

schools need to foster a climate in which equality of opportunity is supported by a policy to which the whole school subscribes and in which some positive attitudes to gender equality, cultural diversity and special needs of all kinds are actively promoted

preparing young people for adult life; this means life in a multicultural, multilingual Europe . . . in a world in which the roles of men and women are changing and both sexes are likely to have dual responsibility for home and work.

The ethos of a school should support the school's policy on equality of opportunity by countering stereotypes and prejudice, reducing the effects of discrimination and helping pupils to accept and understand social diversity. Teaching materials should not be stereotyped or discriminatory. Where evaluation shows materials to be inappropriate, plans for its replacement or adaptation should be established.

National Curriculum Council 1991

 Try to agree a 'whole school' policy on equality of opportunity with the rest of your group. After you have completed your plan, discuss the problems you might face in putting it into practice.

Imagine you are a headteacher who wants to rephrase this to become a statement of goals for the school. Rewrite it so that it is understandable to parents and pupils.

This part of the activity should be completed in pairs. You are jointly the same headteacher. Write a list of possible ways to achieve these aims in your school. Try to focus on social class where possible, though you may find that you need to link this with other aspects of inequality, including, gender, race and special needs.

Areas to consider in your proposal could include:
- *the culture and ethos of the school;*
- *the curriculum content and the use of textbooks and materials;*
- *teacher–pupil relations;*
- *pupil–pupil relations;*
- *home–school links.*

Social class and further education and training

We saw in Chapter 3 that participation rates in vocational education and training in the UK are much lower than in other countries. Social inequalities are also apparent for those who do participate, with more pronounced class differences in VET than in education in general. The shift in control of further education away from the DfE to the DoE and to employers that we examined in Chapter 3 may further limit opportunities by making the prospects of the 16–19 age group dependent on the strength or weakness of the local labour market.

The critical commentator on educational reforms Leslie Bash (1989) and, more recently, the National Commission on Education have highlighted inequalities among students in terms of the material support they receive. Lack of Income Support or grants for FE for the 16–19 age group, for example, may prompt an increased number of lower working-class youth to opt for YT schemes, leaving established FE courses, such as BTEC/GNVQ, to those from the upper working-class and middle-class groups who can rely on financial backing from their parents. Experience of YT indicates that there is a shortage of job placements in deprived areas and that some young people experience discrimination at work on employer-based schemes.

'Care girls' and fashion designers

Two research projects undertaken by the ethnographic researcher Bates (1993) give a vivid indication of the importance of social class in vocational training and how this interlinks with gender issues.

One project concerned the experience of 'care girls' on a Youth Training Scheme (YTS – now YT) programme. The girls were training mainly as care assistants in homes for the elderly and working towards a City & Guilds qualification. Bates wanted to answer the question: 'Why do working-class girls continue to enter working-class, gender-stereotyped jobs?' He looked for the answer in the interaction between the labour market, family background and vocational training.

Bates describes the situation as follows:

> The basic parameters of choice were set by the labour market. In the context of high unemployment and job scarcity, the evidence of this study suggests that class gendered divisions of labour may be reinforced. The intensified competition for jobs and courses brings both qualifications and underlying social and cultural attributes more forcibly into play in selection processes, with the consequence that the barriers of class and gender are more difficult to overcome.
>
> (Bates 1993)

Bates observes that the girls' socialization in the family had involved them in considerable domestic work, caring for babies and other relatives, particularly when the mother was working. Bates describes the ideal YTS candidate for the care course in the following terms:

> Working-class girls, particularly those whose family life has exposed them to experiences such as care of the young or elderly, crowded conditions, demanding physical work, verbal and physical aggression and related psychological stress, would appear to be ideal candidates.
>
> (Bates 1993)

Selection and screening of the girls for the course, and subsequently for employment, effectively pulled 'tougher' working-class girls through the system 'as Oxbridge pulls public schoolboys'.

The second research project contrasted sharply with the 'care girls'. Here Bates researched the experiences of a group of students (mainly young women) on a BTEC National Diploma course in fashion design. Many of the students wanted to be fashion designers, which they hoped would give them a good income, independence, mobility and freedom from domesticity and childcare. They were probably influenced by media representations of the fashion industry and Bates notes that they had little understanding of the limited number of top jobs in the design industry.

The fashion design students and the 'care girls' came from quite different social backgrounds. The fashion students came from 'upper' working-class and 'lower' middle-class homes and all had the benefit of both psychological and financial support from their families. This support enabled them to stay on the course, and parents gave it without concern for future career prospects.

On the fashion course there was a conflict between the students and the tutors. The students wanted the emphasis to be on creativity and fashion design. The course tutors wanted the students to concentrate on marketable skills relating to employment as pattern cutters or assistant designers. During the course the aspirations of the students were lowered, partly as a result of these tensions, and most headed towards low level occupations.

It was noticeable that the few who came from more privileged family backgrounds were able to progress to higher education, while others had to seek employment. Given the general contraction in the garment industry at the time, many ended up in routine jobs in shops or factories. Such a trend was shaped by the interaction between the state of the labour market, family background and the expectations of course tutors. Bates considers that the life chances of this group were 'mediated through BTEC curricula' acting as a screening process to direct most of them to low level occupations.

Bates contrasts this situation to the one experienced by the 'care girls'. For the 'care girls' the problem the tutors faced was persuading them to accept a job which they disliked (initially at least). In the case of the fashion design students, it was a matter of 'cooling out' an over-supply of would-be fashion designers.

Note down the similarities and differences between the two groups of students. Address the following issues in particular:
- *the importance of the family;*
- *the course organization and the attitudes of the tutors;*
- *the adjustment students make to the demands of their programmes of study;*
- *the expectations students have of the job market.*

In a group, investigate the attitudes and experiences of other young people who are undergoing some form of training for work. Aim to select a representative sample, if possible, with people from different types of social class background.

Each member of the group should interview two people. The interviews could revolve around the trainees':

- *hopes for the future;*
- *job prospects;*
- *support from home;*
- *how helpful the course is for acquiring the right kinds of skills;*
- *how they came to join the course in the first place.*

Before starting to collect the data, the group should agree a common format and series of questions for the interviews.

When the interviews have been completed, compare results across the group, noting similarities and differences. Draw up conclusions about the nature of vocational training based on your findings and compare the results with those reported by Bates on p. 161.

Social mobility

Social mobility refers to movement 'upward' or 'downward' through the social stratification system. When such movement takes place within a person's working life this is referred to as intra-generational mobility. If the movement takes place between one generation and the next then it is referred to as inter-generational mobility. Social mobility may result in changes in income, material circumstances, working conditions and lifestyle. Debate centres on how far mobility is due to individual effort, family support and connections, a good education or just the luck of the draw.

Complete Table 5.5.
Compare your answers and discuss them.

Table 5.5 Social mobility	Strongly agree	Agree	Disagree	Strongly disagree
Education is important in gaining a better job				
School-based qualifications, such as GCSE, BTEC or 'A' levels, are important in getting started on a mobile career				
Education provides an opportunity for young people from working class families to advance into better paid, non-manual occupations				
I am socially mobile				
I will be socially mobile				

Early studies of social mobility

Glass's survey in England and Wales in the early 1940s found a fairly high level of inter-generational mobility. However this was rarely movement from low status to high status categories. For those moving 'upwards' from unskilled manual backgrounds (based on father's occupation):

- 36.4 per cent moved to skilled manual occupations;

- 12.7 per cent moved to non-manual occupations;

- 0.8 per cent moved to managerial positions;

- none moved to higher professional and administrative groups.

So, there was little long-range mobility between the extremes of the social stratification system.

 Patterns of social mobility have changed since Glass's study. Before reading on, what do you think the changes are and what social or economic factors might have caused the changes?

In a later survey, usually referred to as the *Oxford Mobility Study* and summarized by Halsey *et al.*, it was noted that long-range mobility had increased. There was now more opportunity for those from working-class backgrounds to reach higher social class categories. This study showed, however, that those who were born into social class 1 and 2 had the best chance of staying there, and those born into social class 5 the least chance of reaching class 1. Family background still gives an advantage or handicap to occupational advancement.

Are we now more socially mobile?

The *Oxford Mobility Study* (see summary of findings in Figure 5.8) showed that there was an increase in social mobility after the war and into the 1970s. This was largely due to the changing shape of the occupational structure, roughly from a triangle to a balloon. More middle-class jobs were created by the expansion of the welfare state and jobs were lost in heavy industry as Britain moved away from manufacturing. This created space for people (or their children) to move 'up': for the children of shipbuilders to become teachers, for example. For women in particular there were numerous new jobs in the lower middle classes such as secretarial, teaching and nursing positions. As a result women especially experienced more social mobility than ever before.

> The sons of foremen and technicians are spread across the class structure in an apparently random manner.
>
> The 1:2:4 Rule: Whatever the chance of a working class boy reaching the service (upper middle) class, a boy from the intermediate class has twice that chance and a boy from that background already has four times the chance.
>
> (Halsey, Heath and Ridge 1980)

Figure 5.8

Summary of findings from the *Oxford Mobility Study*

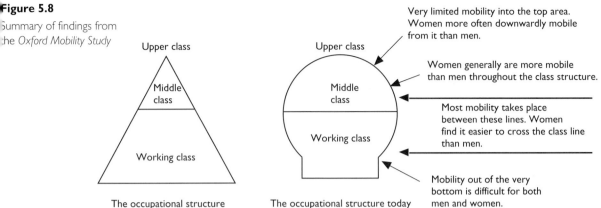

Upper class

Middle class

Working class

The occupational structure earlier this century

Upper class

Middle class

Working class

The occupational structure today

Very limited mobility into the top area. Women more often downwardly mobile from it than men.

Women generally are more mobile than men throughout the class structure.

Most mobility takes place between these lines. Women find it easier to cross the class line than men.

Mobility out of the very bottom is difficult for both men and women.

However, the story is not all good news. Researchers like Ivan Reid and John Urry show us that:

- institutionalized racism or sexism within the working class and elsewhere limits the social mobility of women and those from minority ethnic groups;

- the decade of the 1980s has increased social inequalities which have (as John Urry says) 'increased the difference between the "have-nots" and the "have-lots"';

- social class background still affects how far women can benefit from the increased educational opportunities and greater social mobility that women generally have had recently;

- there continues to be only limited movement into the elite occupations (in law, the civil service, the military and in industry). Silver spoons still seem important here;

- women who leave work to have and care for children often suffer downward mobility. For example, in their 1984 study Martin and Roberts found that 37 per cent of women returning to work changed social class and were downwardly mobile.

Starting out on the mobility trail

We look now at the prospects for young people who are seeking a better education and enhanced job opportunities.

In a 1993 study of youth and the labour market, Roberts reminded us that Margaret Thatcher was a grocer's daughter and John Major the son of a circus artist. Both prime ministers promoted the idea of an open, classless society where success and advancement came from individual effort and enterprise. In contrast, Roberts' study of the 16–19 Initiative, shows that actually Britain is 'still a land of unequal opportunities'.

On the positive side, the study found that qualifications made a difference to those seeking jobs at the age of 16. Those with higher qualifications got higher pay and were encouraged to do more training. Less qualified teenagers, though, were confined to the local labour market, not being able to afford to move to other parts of the country.

In this situation social class has a very important influence. The school process we looked at earlier meant that those from lower social classes had less chance of gaining qualifications and getting a good job. Schools can work against the interests of some pupils from working-class homes. In Roberts' research group such pupils were poorly qualified at 16 and found themselves limited to unskilled employment. This was still the case even if they stayed on in education or entered the YTS programme.

Young people from middle-class families were twice as likely to progress to higher education or obtain skilled manual or white-collar jobs. In the extract below, Roberts describes how this may come about. This provides us with a further example of the way in which access to cultural capital works out.

> The parents not only wanted but expected their children to succeed, and by the age sixteen the young people had internalized these aspirations. Also, the parents could advise their children knowledgeably and confidently, and could use their own contacts if necessary, in order to ensure that the young people were given the opportunities that they wanted and were deemed to deserve.
>
> (Roberts 1993)

Not all young people from the working-class homes in Roberts' study were failures. Only 12 per cent had below average qualifications and experience of unemployment or poor quality jobs. Nevertheless two-thirds of those from working-class backgrounds found it difficult to make progress in the labour market between the ages of 16 and 18. They were more likely than their middle-class peers to experience lack of material and moral support, and to encounter setbacks and failures.

Further education and training and social mobility prospects

More optimistically Roberts reports that just over a third of those in his research sample from working-class homes found success in their further education or training and moved on to higher education or good jobs. This was a higher proportion than was found in earlier surveys in the 1950s and 1960s.

There was evidence of increased mobility overall for those from working-class backgrounds but, even so, there are still relative inequalities in life chances. In the 1980s 'just over a third of young people from working class homes, but over two thirds from middle-class homes were experiencing continuous success'. Roberts cites the reason for this relative success of the working-class groups as being the expansion of high level jobs, the contraction of manual employment and increased opportunities in higher education.

The vocational and academic divide – 'A' level versus GNVQ

Although inequalities based on social class persist in education, this is not due to a lack of concern from successive governments and policy makers. Much time and energy has been devoted in recent years to making courses more vocationally relevant and to raising standards in education overall. These policies aim to

Figure 5.9

GNVQs beat path to degrees

encourage all young people to succeed by diversifying opportunities and exploring ways to match education and training to the needs of industry and the job market.

A recent initiative designed to bridge the academic-vocational divide has been the introduction of a General National Vocational Qualification (GNVQ). GNVQ, level 3, is aimed at 'A' level standard, providing equal status and the same prospects for those who take it.

A report in the *Times Educational Supplement* (1994) was optimistic that this new award would open up access to higher education in 1994. Of 900 GNVQ students who applied for higher education in 1994, 85 per cent were offered places, compared to three-quarters of all applicants, most of whom were 'A' level candidates. The government's intention is for 60–70 per cent of the school population to achieve two 'A' levels or their equivalent in GNVQ awards at level 3 by the year 2000. Such developments could help open up the system and provide greater opportunity across the range of social backgrounds.

 Working with a partner, find out as much as you can about the series of GNVQ awards, levels 1–3, and how they differ from GCSE or 'A' levels. Then discuss the following issues.
  1) *Do they assess different skills?*
  2) *Will GNVQs help students to gain entry to good jobs – or improve access to higher education?*
  3) *Do you think the academic–vocational divide should disappear?*
  4) *Might there be a social class bias in relation to students taking either 'A' levels or GNVQs?*

Higher education

We see in Chapter 6 that higher education in the 1980s was the 'decade of the women' (see p. 177). Table 5.6 compares enrolments in higher education between 1980–81 and 1990–91 in the UK. Full-time enrolment of women students in the 'old' universities has increased by 40 per cent since 1980–81, while in the 'new' universities (former polytechnics) the increase is 85 per cent.

Unfortunately that good news is tempered by the fact that there are still social class

Table 5.6 Enrolments in HE by type of establishment, mode of attendance and gender, 1980-81 to 1990-91, UK.

	Men		Women		All	
	1990–1 (000s)	% increase since 1980–1	1990–1 ('000s)	% increase since 1980–1	1990–1 ('000s)	% increase since 1980–1
Old universities						
Full-time	208	9	162	40	370	21
Part-time	82	37	72	76	154	52
Total	290	16	234	50	524	28
New universities						
Full-time	190	50	187	85	378	66
Part-time	161	10	112	143	274	43
Total	351	29	299	103	652	55
All HE Total	641	22	533	76	1,176	42

inequalities in the system. This was shown in a survey by OPCS published in 1989, showing an uneven distribution of the percentages obtaining a university degree in each of the five major class divisions.

Table 5.7 Percentages obtaining a degree in each of the five major class divisions

	Social class category	% with a degree
I	Professional	65%
II	Employers and Managers	16%
III	Intermediate and Junior Non-Manual	13%
IV	Skilled Manual and Self-Employed Non-Professional	1%
V	Semi-skilled and Un-skilled	1%

Adapted from OPCS, 1989, Table 10.11a)

Compare Tables 5.6 and 5.7.

What do they each tell us?

Can we say whether the influence of social class revealed by the OPCS data will be greater or lesser for women than men?

What might be the limitations to comparing the two sets of results?

What information would we need to provide a more complete picture of the situation regarding social class and higher education success?

It is clear from the OPCS data in Table 5.7 that there are still social class inequalities in entry to HE. A 1993 study by Egerton and Halsey confirms this. They reported that the service class (that is the top of the middle class) has an advantage over the intermediate and working classes in all types of HE institution. In the same study it was noted that those from the service class were more likely to attend the established universities, while those from an intermediate or working-class background were more likely to obtain their degrees from polytechnics ('new' universities or colleges).

Egerton and Halsey point out that the widening of access to HE, through the encouragement of mature students as late entrants, has benefited those from the intermediate and working classes. Noticeably this opportunity has been greatest in the 'new' universities and the colleges. Women in particular were gaining access through late entry and Egerton and Halsey believe that 'women's education will soon be on a par with that of men'. Even so, in terms of social class and equality of opportunity, it is still concluded that:

> The overall picture for social class is of unchanging service class advantage. The children of managerial or professional families are more likely to gain access to university, more likely to have obtained the most prestigious qualification, a degree, at a university and more likely to have qualified earlier in life than people from an intermediate or manual class background.
>
> (Egerton and Halsey 1993)

Credentialism

Credentialism is the spread of the need to have higher and higher levels of paper qualifications for entry to jobs for which no such qualifications were previously required.

This state of affairs is confirmed by Blackburn and Jarman's 1993 study of the relationship between the demand for HE and the job market. They point out the dangers of credentialism. The increasing numbers of well-qualified people (e.g. graduates) leads to a demand for yet more higher qualifications for entry to particular jobs. This will set in motion a vicious circle, further disadvantaging those from the working class who are already disadvantaged in the educational system and job market. Blackburn and Jarman conclude:

> As the number of graduates has grown the degree has become an increasingly common entry qualification for a growing number of high-level occupations. Thus, higher education has played a progressively greater part in the reproduction of the occupationally based class structure. So it is not surprising that class inequalities have persisted. Nor is it surprising that class differentials among women are just as marked as they are among men.
>
> (Blackburn and Jarman 1993)

Access courses

Access courses are specially designed for late entrants to HE. Often such people do not possess standard entry qualifications, such as 'A' levels or GNVQs, but are keen to progress as mature students. Usually mature entrants are over the age of 21 and many left school at 16 to enter the job market. It is government policy to encourage

Figure 5.10

Educating Rita

these non-traditional entrants and many access courses aim to attract students from working-class and ethnic minority groups.

Table 5.8 is taken from an article by Wakeford (1993) and provides information on the social class of access students to HE. This is based on two sets of figures: one giving the numbers of access students in each social class category in a 1991 survey, the other the total number of graduates in the population as a whole from the 1992 British Election Survey (BES).

Do these figures support the case that there is widening access for

Table 5.8		Social class of Access course students by gender.				
	Male Access students (%)	*Male BES excl. graduates (%)*	*Male BES graduates (%)*	*Female Access students (%)*	*Female BES excl. graduates (%)*	*Female BES graduates (%)*
Class						
I	10	15	24	5	3	27
II	12	12	22	18	15	18
III	25	8	15	52	41	10
IV	3	12	13	1	4	10
V	5	9	7	2	2	8
VI	21	19	15	6	5	14
VII	24	26	5	17	28	13
	n = 134	*n* = 1174	*n* = 125	*n* = 250	*n* = 1355	*n* = 80

students from all types of social background?
How do women compare with men?
Are some social groups more advantaged than others?
Are there differences between the access groups and the numbers of those who are graduates according to the survey?

Conclusion

In this review of social class and educational opportunity we have attempted to present an objective and realistic assessment of the current situation. It is important for you to follow up some of the recommended reading and to seek out further information presented in published research or official reports. Education is high on the agenda for policy makers and of considerable importance for parents and young people alike.

A significant point to note is that some pupils from working-class backgrounds are entirely successful within the system and may move on to obtain higher level qualifications and well-paid, high status jobs. Similarly it is possible for some pupils from the middle class to encounter failure and to experience difficulty in making the grade.

The aim, of course, is to improve the standards attained by all pupils, whatever their social background, and to encourage more to stay on to further and higher education. Pursuing this ideal means continued research and discussion aimed at seeking explanations for underachievement of particular groups, coupled with reforms in education to bring about greater equalization of opportunities to succeed.

Suggestions for further reading

Woods (1979), Corrigan (1979), Ball (1981) and Pollard (1985) provide good examples of research in schools with a focus on the effects of teacher-pupil interaction and school organization on pupils' progress. A useful summary of these and other similar studies is provided by Woods (1990).

Bates and Riseborough (1993) provide a useful update on social class and education with a review of studies which focus on post-16 education and the issue of equality, while Booth and Coulby (1987) provide a series of edited readings on the problem of disaffection in the school system, many of which have relevance in terms of considering social class differences.

We have referred to two official reports in this chapter and both are worth careful study. They are the report of the National Commission on Education *Learning to Succeed* (1993) and *Access and Achievement in Urban Education*, produced by the Office for Standards in Education (OFSTED) (1993).

Other sources, which, from time to time, will provide you with relevant discussion of equality issues in education, include the *Times Educational Supplement* and the *Education Guardian*.

You could also delve into some entertaining fiction which is based on the experiences of working-class youth in schools. Edward Blishen, for example, has written about his early days as a teacher in deprived, inner city London schools, in a book entitled *Roaring Boys*. Another writer, Barry Hines, describes the experiences of a working-class boy, *Kes* (the book's title) who does not fit into official school life but is an expert on falconry and as a result learns more outside school than in it.

There are also many films available on video featuring aspects of education. An example is based on Willy Russell's play *Educating Rita*. This is about a married hairdresser from a working-class background who gains non-traditional access to a university to do a degree. The story reveals the social pressures involved in such a move in relation to the expectations of others who remain entrenched in a different culture and more 'narrow' view of life.

Rogers (1980) and Statham and Mackinnon (1993) give details of reports on deprivation and its link to educational underachievement.

Suggested sources for the exercise on p. 164 are:

Bradshaw, J. (1990) *Child Poverty and Deprivation in the UK,* London: National Children's Bureau.

Central Statistical Office, *Social Trends 1991, 1992, 1993,* London: HMSO.

Cohen, R. *et al.* (1992) *Hardship in Britain: Being Poor in the 1990s,* London: Child Poverty Action Group.

Hill, J. (1991) *The State of Welfare: The Welfare State in Britain since 1974,* Oxford: Clarendon Press.

Kumar, V. (1993) *Poverty and Inequality in the UK: The Effects on Children,* London: National Children's Bureau.

OPCS (March 1993) *Population Trends,* no. 71, London: HMSO.

Roll, J. (1990) *Young People: Growing up in the Welfare State,* London: Family Policy Studies Centre.

Changes resulting from the National Curriculum are reviewed by Bash and Coulby (1989), Chitty (1993), Coulby and Bash (1991), Davies *et al.* (1992) and Moon (1990).

The references for the exercise on page 152 are Keddie, N. (1973) *Tinker, Tailor . . . .* Harmondsworth: Penguin and Bernstein, B. (1990) *The Structuring of Pedagogic Discourse,* London: Routledge.

Finally, you will find a useful summary of social mobility patterns for women in Reid (1989).

The address of the City Technology College Trust (for the exercise on p. 145) is:

15 Young Street
London

6 / Gender in education and training

Paul Trowler

Think back over your experience of formal education. Are there any gender-related incidents that you recall particularly vividly (such as the behaviour of male or female students or teachers, or the materials you were studying)? Make a note of one or two of them.

Compare the experiences you noted down with a partner. Did you share similar sorts of experiences or were they unique?

Swap experiences with other pairs and discuss them. Make a note of any significant points (e.g. similarities/differences, general points, qualifications, categories of experience).

Each small group should discuss their notes with the larger group.

The debate around gender issues in education came to prominence in the mid-1970s. Before that, gender questions were largely ignored by the (predominantly male) researchers in the sociology of education. For example, of the well-known observational studies of the 1970s – Nash (1973), Sharp and Green (1975) and King (1978) – only King's refers to gender issues.

Before reading any further, brainstorm the main issues around 'gender and education and training', either individually or with another member of the group. Note them down. When you have finished the chapter, compare them to the areas you discussed here.

In this chapter we first examine gender differences in achievement in education and then go on to look at differences in student participation across the curriculum and in education in general. We present the evidence and then review some of the explanations given by different authors to explain it.

Read from p. 174 to p. 178, then:

Prepare one or two overheads to summarize in a few sentences the important points about gender differences in achievement in education and differences in participation.

Brainstorm (as a group) the reasons for these two sets of differences. Prepare to give a short presentation to the whole group.

Each small group should give its presentation and the others should respond with questions and comments using the material they have read.

Gender differences in achievement in education

The evidence

In looking at the evidence we concentrate on quantitative data; qualitative data will be used when looking at explanations for the evidence presented.

In the past it was true to say that females, on average, outperformed males from the earliest years of schooling right up to 'A' levels, where they took and passed fewer than boys. Now, though, girls have started to do as well as boys at the 'A' level stage too, while continuing to outperform boys in most subjects lower down the school. In 1991 29 per cent of girls and 25 per cent of boys got at least one 'A' level pass.

Getting firm quantitative evidence about the different performance of boys and girls before they take public examinations was difficult before the introduction of the National Curriculum. J.W.B. Douglas' early study of primary schools was based on a longitudinal study of 4,195 children born in Britain during the same week. It followed them to their eleventh year and so provided extensive, but now dated, information. Data were collected by interviewing teachers, examining health and attendance records, interviewing parents, obtaining data from LEAs and administering tests of mental ability and school performance. Douglas concluded that:

> In primary schools boys and girls are for the most part taught together in the same class-rooms and their measured ability and attainment are similar. The girls, on the average, make rather higher scores than the boys in all tests, except for vocabulary at eight and eleven years. Their advantage was however slightly less at the older age... The primary school teachers assessed the girls as a having a more serious attitude to their work.
>
> (Douglas 1964)

In English in particular it has always been clear that girls perform better than boys. Surveys carried out by the Assessment of Performance Unit in the mid and late 1980s showed that between the age of 11 to 15 girls do better at writing and reading comprehension. This is reflected in the fact that when classes are organized by ability, there are more girls in the upper classes. A 1993 OFSTED report tells us that in National Curriculum assessments of 7 year olds (Key Stage 1) in 1991 and 1992, girls, on average, did better than boys in reading, writing and spelling. It also shows that GCSEs, with their continuous assessment requirements, seem to have worked to girls' advantage rather than boys', compared to the old 'O' levels.

The 1992 National Curriculum test results for 7 year olds made it clear that girls were, on average, outperforming boys even in science, technology and maths at that age. Again, they did even better in English.

Evidence on male and female achievements at the stage of public examinations is widely available as Figure 6.3 demonstrates.

In the light of all this evidence that girls perform better than boys at school, it is strange that this is often ignored by commentators. For example, Roland Meighan writes about 'the case of girls in general, whose "failure" in school is now well documented'. In his chapter on gender he skips over the superior performance of

Figure 6.1

Results of tests for 7 year olds: by sex and subject, 1993, percentages. Level 2 is average, level 3 would be average for a 9 year old.

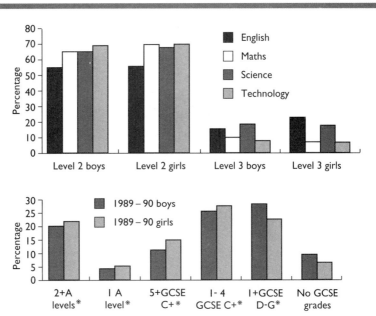

Figure 6.2

Highest qualification of school-leavers: percentages

females up to the age of 16, concentrating instead on the limited range of subjects they have access to. As Valerie Walkerdine says, 'There is a widespread myth that girls and women perform poorly in school.'

On the other hand males' lower achievements in, say, English, or the difficulties they have in dealing with poetry and other areas involving the emotions have received far less attention than the limitations there are on the opportunities for females in education and training. The Equal Opportunities Commission notes that:

> the consequences of sex-stereotyping on young men are. . . a matter for concern. The effect on the individual, and on society, of those who leave school lacking communication skills, social skills and skills for personal independence should not be under-estimated.

Certainly teachers at primary level agree that girls, in general, are more able than boys, as Clarricoates reports:

> 'The boys aren't as academic as girls'. . . 'In this primary school. . . there's simply more girls at the top of the class than boys'. . . 'I think in the past five years I've been here. . . [girls have] always been my brightest pupils.'

> (Clarricoates 1987)

However, Walker and Barton suggest many teachers find boys more interesting and rewarding to teach. Girls are seen by them as simply conforming to institutional expectations and thus presenting no challenge. Walkerdine refers to the 'just or only phenomenon' in relation to girls' success in mathematics particularly:

> Whenever a positive remark was made about girls' performance. . . a remark would be brought in which suggested that the performance was to be accounted for by 'something which amounted to nothing'.

> (Walkerdine 1993)

For example, one teacher in Walkerdine's study of thirty-nine classrooms said this about a female pupil: 'Very, very hard worker. Not a particularly bright girl. . . her hard work gets her to her standards. . . ' but this about a male pupil '. . . can just about write his own name. . . not because he's not clever, because he's not capable, but because he can't sit still, he's got no concentration. . . very disruptive. . . but quite bright'.

It is only in post-school education that females are underachieving. For example the *University Statistical Record* of 1991 tells us that in 1990 10 per cent of men got first class degrees compared to 6 per cent of women. The inequality persisted even in subjects where women predominate.

Think back over your own educational experiences.
Were the 'high fliers' boys or girls?
What about the lower achievers?
Did this vary by subject?
Was this different when you were, say, 14 compared to when you were 9?

Gender differences in participation

The evidence

In schools girls have traditionally outnumbered boys in some subjects, with boys outnumbering girls in others. The advent of the National Curriculum has reduced

Figure 6.3

Percentage of pupils leaving school obtaining GCSE/GCE/SCE (grades A–C) and CSE grade 1 in the following subjects, Great Britain, 1990-91.

Figure 6.4

Pupils leaving school with two or more GCE 'A' levels or equivalent, in the following subjects, Great Britain, 1990–91.

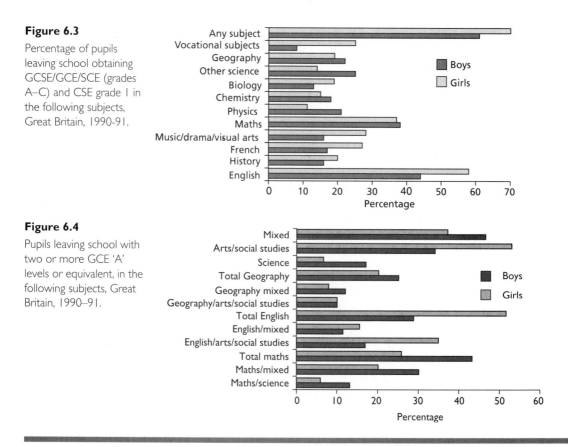

pupils' abilities to choose (or opt out of) subjects, but these differences are still reflected at GCSE and 'A' level.

With the introduction of the National Curriculum, intended to make ten subjects compulsory for both boys and girls to the age of 16, there was a move towards legislated equality by gender across the curriculum. The ten subjects were: English, maths, science, art, geography, history, modern language (secondary school only), music, physical education and technology. Thus girls were to be required to study areas previously dominated by males to that age, and vice versa – technology and maths would be studied by all girls to 16, and a modern language by all males.

However, this plan was fraught with problems from the beginning. Duncan Graham (the chair and chief executive of the National Curriculum Council from 1988 to 1991) talks about the 'nightmare of Key Stage 4', that is the teaching and testing of these subjects at ages 14 to 16, because of the clash at 16 with GCSEs and the fact that the National Curriculum subjects would displace all others. Pupils would have no time to study anything else and this would impoverish study beyond 16.

Sir Ron Dearing's review of the National Curriculum (DfE 1993), however, recommended a severe paring down of the National Curriculum, more room in the school timetable for optional subjects outside of it and more choice within it. The recommendations were immediately accepted by the government. This once again allowed pupil and teacher 'choice', and so allowed room for that choice to be conditioned by gender.

What subjects did you do at school and how did you 'choose' them?
What are the arguments for and against a substantial proportion of school subjects to be compulsory for both sexes?
Sir Ron Dearing recommends work outside the National Curriculum to be given between 10 and 15 per cent of the time available in primary schools, and between 20 and 25 per cent of the time available in secondary schools. Are these the right percentages?

In the past there were fewer women than men continuing their education beyond compulsory schooling, but now women have caught up and passed men in both full and part-time FE and are rapidly catching up in HE. In 1991–92 there were over two million students on FE courses, 25 per cent more than in 1981, and women students accounted for 84 per cent of the increase. In HE by 1991 women outnumbered men in the oldest age group of students and constituted 47 per cent of all HE students compared to 41 per cent in 1981. Oliver Fulton rightly says that 'the 1980s has truly been the decade of the woman student'. (See Table 6.1.)

Information on the intended destinations of school-leavers shows that the trend of increasing numbers of women in further and higher education is set to continue. (See Figure 6.5.)

The problem now concerns not so much the numbers of women in post-compulsory education, as the subjects they study. We can summarize the evidence by saying that with regard to any sector of education and training, where a choice of subject area for study is available, particular subject areas tend to be dominated by one or other of the sexes, with women participating to a more limited extent overall in HE.

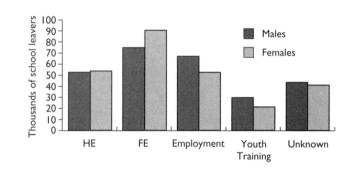

Table 6.1   Full and part-time students in HE in 1991–2 (thousands)

Type	Male	Female
Undergraduates Full-Time	385	361
Undergraduates Part-Time	201	163
Postgraduates Full-Time	57	40
Postgraduates Part-Time	52	40
Total Higher Education	695	604
Full Time Further Education	250	291
Part Time Further Education	666	883
Total Further Education	916	1174

Figure 6.5

Intended destination of school-leavers 1992 (thousands)

Figure 6.6

Students obtaining first degrees by subject and sex, 1989-90 (thousands)

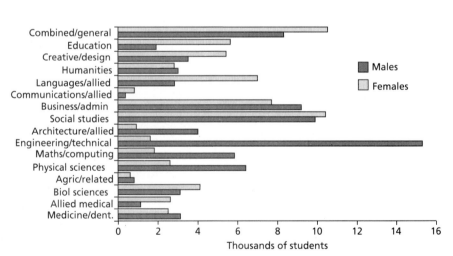

Collect the statistics on the distribution of the sexes across the subjects where there is a choice in your own educational institution. How could you explain the patterns you identify?

The explanations

Each group should select one from the following list and prepare to:
- *explain it to the whole group (and add anything you can);*
- *give your group's views on its quality as an explanation of the evidence on gender differences in achievement and student participation;*
- *say what else you would like to know about your area and how you could find out.*

The list

The main cause accounting for gender differences in achievement and student participation in education could be seen as:
- *sex differences – i.e. biological differences between boys and girls (pp. 179–81);*
- *the home (pp. 182–7);*
- *the school (pp. 187–95);*
- *society (pp. 195–201).*

In the following sections we explore a number of approaches to explaining gender differences in achievement and student participation in education. In each case the arguments are put forward and explained. These approaches are not necessarily mutually exclusive. In some cases they can provide complementary explanations.

Sex differences

Sex is used to mean the physical characteristics which distinguish males and females (genitals, hormones, gonads, internal reproductive organs and chromosomes).

Gender refers to the social guidelines for sex-appropriate appearance, interests, skills, behaviours and self-perceptions.

The earliest and easiest approach to explain these differences in achievement and participation in education and training is to point to biological or genetic differences. According to this first approach, it is sex differences rather than gender roles which are the causative factors.

Girls mature more quickly than boys, so that a girl of 11 is, in many ways, more advanced than a boy of that age. This may well explain why at younger ages girls frequently do better than boys. In the days of the national 11+ examination (which largely decided whether a child would go to selective grammar schools or to less prestigious secondary moderns) many LEAs demanded higher pass marks for girls than for boys. If they had not done this grammar school populations would have been dominated by girls. A court case in the late 1980s concerning differential educational provision for boys and girls in selective schools in Northern Ireland established the illegality of this practice.

Tests show that neither sex is more intelligent than the other: average IQ scores are the same for males and females at all ages, though girls under the age of 7 do slightly better than boys of the same age (possibly because of their more advanced maturity). Dr E. Rudd of the University of Essex suggests that 'there might be a difference in the distribution of intelligence between men and women, with the women clustering in the middle'. However there is no firm evidence for this and it seems at least as likely that it is teachers' beliefs that this is the case that causes any lower levels of outstanding performance among females (e.g. the smaller number of first class degrees achieved by women).

There may, though, be a difference in the type of intelligence between the sexes. On average females seem to do better at tests which measure verbal ability. Males on average seem to do better at tests which measure visual-spatial ability (i.e. the ability to visualize and manipulate objects in space). This difference is found by the majority of (but not all) tests of ability, though one interesting finding is that the difference in verbal ability seems to be less pronounced now than it was, suggesting that it is at least partly a social product. This social construction argument is indicated by some experiments conducted by clinical psychologist Lisa Serbin:

> We found that preschool children who play primarily with 'boy' toys such as blocks, trucks, and climbing apparatus showed stronger visual-spatial problem solving abilities than children who play primarily with 'girls' toys including dolls, housekeeping materials, and fine motor activities. Sex differences in visual-spatial ability are not yet present during the preschool period, but these data suggest that sex-typed activity patterns may contribute to later sex differences in problem solving ability and achievement.
>
> (Serbin 1984)

There seems to be no difference between girls and boys in primary school in how much or what sort of information they can take in. By the age of 11, however, the slightly greater verbal skills of the average female and the slightly greater visual-spatial skills of the average male become apparent. Again, though, we need to beware of interpreting what is possibly a social product as the result of biological causes, particularly as merely spreading the idea that girls 'naturally' have different abilities than boys can lead to a self-fulfilling prophecy.

 Do males solve this puzzle faster than females on average?

Figure 6.7

These plans can be folded to make cubes. Which plan makes a cube different from that made by the other four?

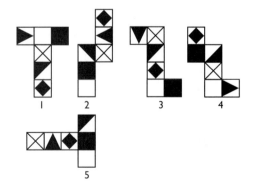

Biological explanations for sex differences in educational achievement are fraught with a number of problems, however. One is that sex differences in examination performance are averages, meaning that while on the whole men do better in, for instance, physics, a number of women will do better than most men in that subject while the reverse is true in, say, English. Yet one would expect all women, or all men, to under-perform compared to the opposite sex if the difficulty they experienced was intrinsic to their sex.

Another problem for the biological explanation of gender differences in education is that the list of common attributes found in the sexes around the world is a short one. They are as follows:

- boys indulge more in rough-and-tumble play than girls;

- girls demonstrate more caring attitudes and behaviour;

- boys generally are better at mathematical/logical problems;

- girls generally are better at linguistic problems.

 Think about your brothers and sisters, if you have them. Compare them with yourself when you were younger. Were these patterns true of your family?

Even this list is highly disputable. Discussing it, Gerda Siann notes that:

- studies rarely define clearly what they mean by 'rough and tumble';

- any differences identified in this list can be explained by socialization differences;

- differences in maths spatial abilities are decreasing over time.

These points lead us to question these findings and the conclusion that there is a biological explanation.

Obviously there are differences between males and females – physical, hormonal, genetic and so on. Even the less obvious ones can be established in a scientific way. The problem comes when trying to establish a link between social behaviour (e.g. women being better at languages) and these scientifically validated physical characteristics. It is very difficult, if not impossible, to say for sure that they are causally linked.

> If two phenomena, A and B, occur together there may be a **causative** link or only a **correlation**. If they are causally linked then one (A) gives rise to the other (B) which is dependent upon it. If they are merely correlated then they occur together but A does not cause B, there may be a third agent, C, which causes them both. **Correlation** is often mistaken for **causation**. The rise in crime rates and decline in church attendance may be correlated over time but not causally linked, though some people claim they are.

Psychological and sociological explanations

Researchers have focused on a number of alternative 'sites' as the source of the gender-related differences in educational achievement and participation that we have been examining. These are:

- the home: the site of primary socialization, where self-concepts and gender roles become firmly established and where girls may be materially deprived compared to boys;

- the school: where teachers' behaviour, the institutional organization and culture, the behaviour of boys and material deprivation may again have important influences;

- society: where secondary socialization and other subtle influences will affect males and females in important ways.

We deal with each of these in turn.

The home

For many writers the foundation for later educational outcomes is laid before boys and girls set foot through the school gates. A popular theory in the early 1970s was that young girls learn a 'fear of success', that is, are socialized in the early years against being achievement oriented. A famous study was conducted by the American researcher Matina Horner in which college students were asked to complete a story beginning 'After the first-term examinations, Anne/John finds her/himself top of her/his medical school class' (the sex of the main character being matched to the sex of the student asked to do the writing). The findings were that most of the female students described Anne as ugly and unloved, lonely and possibly having a nervous breakdown or committing suicide. The male students, meanwhile, predicted a glittering future for John.

Results such as these were hailed as confirming the fear of success hypothesis, but attempts to replicate them later found conflicting, even contradictory results. Generally studies of motivation differences in males and females have given inconclusive results.

Another suggested explanation for differences in achievement was that females learn to have lower self-esteem than males do, which results in lower educational performance. Psychologist David Fontana, for example, is quite categorical: 'Turning now to the position of girls, we find that they generally. . . have lower levels of self-esteem than boys.' This widely held theory has led to educational programmes designed to improve women's self-esteem, notably in Australia. However, like the fear of success hypothesis, the evidence seems shaky. Jane Kenway and Sue Willis have edited a collection of studies which question the factual and ideological foundations of this theory. They note that, despite Australian government funding and policy aimed at this 'problem' and teachers' support for improving girls' self-esteem, 'some hesitation [about the idea] seemed long overdue'. In a useful summary of the research evidence on differences between the levels of self-esteem of males and females, psychologist John Nicholson says:

> individual women do not seem to value themselves less highly than individual men, whatever they may think about their own and the other sex generally. In childhood, any difference between the sexes in self-esteem actually tends to be weighted towards the girls: a few studies have found that they value themselves more highly than boys do, despite the fact that they are more willing to admit to their own failings. . . Later in life, it is no easier to show that men and women differ in self-esteem.
>
> (Nicholson 1984)

Self-esteem is usually thought of in terms of the gap between the characteristics a person would like to have – their 'ideal self' – and their perception of the characteristics they actually have. The larger the gap, the lower the self-esteem.

Despite this, and seemingly paradoxically, there is considerable evidence that women are less confident than men in their own ability to achieve particular things. So, though women value themselves as highly as men, are equally motivated to succeed and have the same capabilities as men, they have less confidence in their own abilities. This is sometimes referred to as learned helplessness. Walkerdine quotes an example of this sort of attitude (though in fact she rejects the learned helplessness explanation for it):

> A woman teacher, one of my students, received a well-deserved distinction for her Master's degree. She received more or less straight 'As' for all her work, but still she cannot believe that the distinction belongs to her. It is as though the person with her name exists somewhere else, outside her body: this powerful person that she cannot recognize as herself. Instead, she feels that she is hopeless, consistently panics about her performance and appears to have little confidence in herself.
>
> (Walkerdine 1993)

 Is this true of people you know, men or women?

The reasons for this lack of self-confidence in women (on average) as compared to men (on average) are not hard to find, at least according to feminists. From a very early age females are socialized into lacking control of their lives. The female characters in children's stories tend to have things happen to them while the male characters take an active role and are the doers. The same is true of television fiction.

This is likely to lead females on average to adopt an external locus of control (i.e. see themselves as in the hands of luck or fate) while males are more likely to adopt an internal locus of control (they take the credit for their own success). This is the product of both primary and secondary socialization, processes which begin early and are reinforced as girls grow older.

Education research shows that students are more likely to be successful learners if they believe that they are in control of the learning process; if they ascribe their successes and failures directly to their own abilities and the effort they put in. Students who take a fatalistic attitude, saying that outcomes will depend on 'the quality of the lectures' or some other factor not to do with them, tend to be unsuccessful. G. Brown and M. Atkins argue:

> Students are likely to initiate learning, sustain it, direct it, and actively involve themselves in it when they believe that success or failure is caused by their own effort or lack of it, rather than by factors outside their control such as ability, luck, or the quality of teaching. Similarly praise, reward, or other positive (teacher) reinforcements are likely to enhance motivation only if students perceive them to be related to factors over which they have control.
>
> (Brown and Atkins 1988)

If it is true that women are more likely to have an external locus of control, this could be a very useful piece of evidence in explaining poorer performance amongst females than males. As we have seen, however, females tend to do better than males, at least at school. It could be that this is an achievement they manage in the face of this extra difficulty.

Kim Thomas builds on the notion of self-perception, suggesting that what prevents women taking science in higher education is something she calls gender identity.

> Women in science. . . are faced with a particular set of problems. The chief problem is that of the dual identity: trying to be a scientist on the one hand – which means proving one is 'as good as a man'- and being a woman on the other – which, in its social definition, entails being uncompetitive. Further, while men were able to build their identity through commitment to the coursework, to studying and pursuing a career in science, and through a self-definition as 'physicist' or 'physical scientist', women often saw science as being only one part of their lives: they had other interests which were as important to them as physics. Science was simply something they enjoyed and were good at, not an all-consuming interest, and in looking for jobs, many were keen to broaden their lives as much as possible. The conflict of identity was strengthened when women thought about their long-term futures; whereas men saw themselves as climbing the ladder of success, women were only too aware of having to make a choice between following a career and raising a family: being a physicist or being a woman.
>
> (Thomas 1990)

Gender identity refers to the beliefs people have about both their own selves and about school and academic 'subjects' in terms of how they relate to generally accepted notions of gender roles.

According to Thomas, subjects of study are believed to hold qualities which have close connections to beliefs about 'masculinity' and 'femininity'. People choose which subjects to study partly on this basis. For a woman to take a subject like physics, she essentially has to rebel against the widely available ideas of gender. Despite claims of egalitarianism, universities also subscribe to these ideas in their subject offerings, which are usually presented in terms of traditional discipline areas (which themselves are social constructions according to Thomas). However, Thomas hopes that by offering interdisciplinary areas for study, such as physical sciences and communications, the newer universities will be able to break the links between gender and subject in HE.

 Quickly write down ten separate adjectives which you associate with each of the following subjects:
- *physics;*
- *sociology;*
- *chemistry;*
- *psychology;*
- *engineering;*
- *biology;*
- *computing.*

Compare your list with that of a partner. Do they suggest that the subjects have a particular gender identity in your minds?

Gender roles

Early sex stereotyping will affect educational and career aspirations of males and females differently. The idea of a 'caring' role for girls will be stimulated and reinforced by giving them dolls, nurses' uniforms and so on. Similarly they may come to believe that gaining qualifications through education is secondary to goals of love, marriage and having children of their own. Feminist Sue Sharpe quotes a 14-year-old girl in a social studies lesson talking about the causes of these attitudes:

> In most families the girl learns from a very young age that she must behave in a very different manner from her brother, from the day she is given her first doll and is told she cannot go outside and play because it is raining and yet her brother can. Children learn how they are different from one another by the way the parents and their friends talk about them. Example – 'Oh what a sweet little girl you have and so pretty, does she help you around the house?' 'What a rascal of a son you have, always getting into mischief. Oh well I'd worry and think there was something wrong with him if he didn't.'

> (Sharpe 1976)

The results of this socialization in the home are seen later in the school, as reported by Measor who carried out a non-participant observation, ethnographic study of pupils in classrooms. The research was conducted on 11–13 year olds during 18 months' observation of middle and upper schools. It found that gender and school subject identities were firmly fixed in pupils' minds and were articulated in the school. Pupils were following the integrated Nuffield scheme:

> Girls would be slightly late for science lessons, and they would try to edge a little time off the end of them, packing up their things early for example. They would wander around the room and chat to people on the way. If they were challenged they would claim that they were looking for equipment and again avoid trouble... Girls could avoid answering questions and keep out of class discussions if asked a question directly. They displayed a quality of shy quietness during verbal exchanges in class, it seemed that this shy quietness was in evidence especially in interactions between female pupils and male teachers. Girls could answer questions so quietly that they could barely be heard. On such occasions the teacher would usually sigh and pass on: the girls had answered after all... Girls repeatedly engaged in acts that were known to be deviant, albeit subtly and surreptitiously.

> Pamela: We just suck polos in science lessons.

> Sheila: We do, or the end of our pens – we all suck pens on our table, and don't take no notice.

> (Measor 1984)

According to this account, then, the pupils are the main problem or, rather, the norms and values they bring with them from the home which are further amplified in the classroom. However, teachers are not entirely absolved of blame:

> Of course I would not want to suggest that gender differentiation in schools is simply a pupil-initiated phenomenon. Teachers no doubt also influence pupils through their attitudes, expectations and interactions. In a sense they finish off and reinforce the messages that pupils have already learned through primary socialization. . . There were some clear examples of bias. The Headmaster would welcome his class with 'Come in my merry men'. One teacher, the head of the science department, always stood directly in front of the boys and talked to them almost exclusively.
>
> (Measor 1984)

We will deal with these aspects later.

 From what you already know about early socialization, how might these attitudes about boys, girls and education be learned in the home? Give specific examples.

Material differences

Though on the face of it any material deprivation in the home would seem to affect sons and daughters to an equal extent, some writers have argued that females are likely to suffer greater material deprivation than males from a very early age because of their lower status. The very first instance of this in a girl's life may be at her mother's breast. The psychotherapist Christiane Olivier claims that female babies are given less time at the mother's breast than males. Many feminist writers have noted that boys will have more money spent on them than girls by their families. There is little hard evidence available on this, but anecdotal (and certainly historical) evidence indicates that sons rather than daughters are likely, for example, to be sent to a private school if a choice has to be made.

This differential allocation of resources by the family may be reproduced in the world of formal education. Eileen Byrne, a Senior Education Officer with Lincolnshire County Council writes that:

> the allocation of resources in education shows that proportionately more, better, and different types were generally held to be automatically necessary for respectively able, and less able pupils; urban and rural pupils; older and younger pupils; and boys and girls. Thus a less able girl in a rural school has a triple chance of resource deprivation. The declining number of women in senior posts make future change still doubtful.
>
> (Byrne 1975)

Another example of differential allocation of resources between the sexes is the fact that building plans for post-war single sex schools clearly show the different resources allocated to the two sexes: boys' schools were relatively well provided for with science laboratories – girls' schools were not. More recently the Equal Opportunities Commission (1989) notes that some schools spend more on boys' curricular, sporting and extra-curricular activities than girls'. Teachers in FE report, for example, that safety equipment like reinforced shoes is not available in the smaller sizes that tend to fit women.

Just as material deprivation in the working class can lead to educational underachievement, then, so it may with females.

 Do you have any examples of boys getting more resources than girls in the home, for example, comparing brothers and sisters?

The school

Teachers' attitudes

Work on teachers' labelling of individual and categories of pupils such as that of American psychologists Rosenthal and Jacobson (see p. 55) tended to reinforce the view that teachers' attitudes can unconsciously influence pupils' self-images and hence their achievements. The study itself is not without its critics: Colin Rogers' book reports numerous studies which cast doubt on Rosenthal and Jacobson's results. However, the basic point seems valid: many teachers do interact differently with pupils according to images they have of them. They seem to behave differently with girls than boys, though the effects of this are not easy to establish.

For example, research by psychologist Carol Dweck shows that there are differences in the way teachers reward and reprimand boys compared to girls. Rewards generally are given to girls for appearance or conduct; to boys for their work. Reprimands generally are given to girls for their work; to boys for untidiness or misbehaviour. To oversimplify and generalize the effect of this: the girl learns that what she is good at is being ladylike, while her academic work only brings her criticism. Neither sex may notice that it's happening, but the message may still get through. Less subtly, an HMI (schools) report quotes one biology teacher as saying 'Now which of you boys will do the cutting?' and 'Girls, let me know if you feel sick.' Martin Hammersley (1990) reports one of the teachers at 'Downtown' school saying: 'Now will you stop being so silly, the next boy who laughs in that stupid manner like a little girl I shall drop on quickly.'

Sally Cline, an ex-journalist, and Dale Spender, an Australian feminist, note the same kind of comment:

> Then the teacher said he was pleased to see so many girls in the class because there would be such a lot of washing up to do. I thought he was joking, but he meant it.
>
> (Cline and Spender 1987)

Research also shows that teachers are less likely to encourage girls to try again when they make mistakes in masculinized subjects like maths; they are more inclined to tell them not to worry about it. Learned helplessness is being taught in school too – 'don't worry, it's not your fault, no one expects you to be able to do sums'. All the women interviewed by Sally Cline and Dale Spender for *Reflecting Men* thought that the school had caused them to doubt their own ability. This confirms the research findings about women's confidence in their own abilities we discussed earlier, and supports the idea that though the cause of this may begin in the home, it is perpetuated and reinforced in school.

In *Invisible Women* Dale Spender argues that males get more attention from teachers, even female ones, because they are more troublesome and therefore need attention to prevent them from disrupting work. Conversely girls are socialized into being passive and obedient and as a result do not present a problem which the teachers feel they have got to attend to. The 1993 OFSTED report on *Boys and English* notes that in many observed lessons boys dominated the physical space, the teachers' attention and class discussions, while girls were sometimes more reticent about taking part in discussions. Because society sees men as more important than women, teachers unconsciously give males more time. According to Spender:

> Because we take it so much for granted that boys are more important and deserve more of our time and attention, giving the girls 35 per cent of our time can feel as if we are being unfair to the boys.

> (Spender 1983)

Spender even quotes the example of taped lessons she gave and found to her surprise that she had given the girls 42 per cent and the boys 58 per cent of her time, despite deliberately trying to be fair. Other teachers were similarly surprised to find they had only given the girls around 34 per cent of their time, even though the girls often outnumbered the boys in the classroom. Sadker and Sadker (1985) confirm this: they showed teachers in the USA a video of classroom talk in which boys made three times as many contributions as girls – but teachers believed the girls had talked more.

 Adapt Powell's methodology (see p. 53) to determine how much time a teacher spends in a lesson interacting with males and with females. (Obtain their permission first.)

Spender and others suggest that many teachers often have a negative view of girls: they can frequently name all the boys in the class but see the girls as an undifferentiated mass. The girls are 'invisible' in the classroom as individuals, being treated merely as a group and an inferior one at that. Where male teachers are concerned it is often the case, according to Spender, that the only females to be individually recognized are the ones who are attractive to them. (Spender quotes the comments of female pupils in support of this.) If girls do distinguish themselves from the group, they run the risk of being labelled unladylike for being too pushy and, anyway, their questions will be interpreted by the teacher as simply an attempt to fulfil the requirements of what is expected rather than a real sign of intelligence or interest.

Spender quotes teachers as saying of girls' work: 'I think she could have spent more time on getting some facts than on making it look pretty', or 'Typical, isn't it? All that effort just to make it look nice – you can't beat girls for being concerned with appearances.' But of course the girl has learned to be concerned with appearances from the agencies of socialization all around her, while the teachers' perceptions are likewise being coloured by the way they have been taught to perceive girls. Females adopt the male definitions of how they should behave, what they are good at and so on. In the end female behaviour confirms the stereotype. Spender quotes a study which found that young girls tend to say that girls are just as good at mathematics as boys, while boys tend to say that girls can't do maths. By the time they are older, the girls tend to agree that boys are better at maths.

Spender's methodology is not fully explained in *Invisible Women*, leading to doubts about the validity and reliability of her findings. However, a larger scale study was conducted by John Pratt and a colleague for the Equal Opportunities Commission, completed in 1982. It consisted of a survey of the attitudes of over 850 teachers in fifty secondary schools in England and Wales. Roughly equal numbers of men and women covering twenty-nine different subjects were sampled. The survey offered teachers a series of twenty-eight statements about equal opportunities to which they were invited to indicate their degree of agreement or disagreement.

The findings are reported in *The Attitudes of Teachers*. They are that the majority of teachers were sympathetic to equal opportunities issues (just under 60 per cent). However, males were more likely to be opposed, with 27 per cent strongly opposed. Teachers of maths, physical sciences and technical crafts (mainly male) and languages were most opposed. John Pratt writes:

> While it is perhaps unsurprising that teachers of traditionally stereotyped subjects such as the physical sciences and crafts show least sympathy to equal opportunity, the lack of sympathy of teachers of 'core' subjects such as maths and PE is a matter of concern since practically every pupil follows these subjects until leaving age. The attitudes of maths teachers suggest that girls' reluctance to study that subject, and by association, physical sciences, is unlikely to be recognized as a matter of concern by these teachers. . . While it is clear that a majority of teachers are in favour of equal opportunities in principle, they show a markedly lower commitment to practices which positively encourage equality.
>
> (Pratt 1985)

Michelle Stanworth, who conducted a more limited survey, also points to the teachers as the cause of selective participation and underachievement by females. She conducted individual interviews with teachers and pupils in seven 'A' level classes in the humanities department of an FE college. She found that:

> though it need not be the case that teachers grade girls more harshly than their present performance warrants, female pupils are less likely to be challenged and stretched academically, with serious implications for their future performance. Second, girls are less likely than boys to be singled out as worthy recipients of the teacher's attention; this. . . makes the girls feel less valued in the classroom, and reinforces other pressures urging them to take a back seat in classroom activity.
>
> (Stanworth 1984)

 How far did your experience of school confirm these findings about teacher–pupil interaction? The exercise on p. 188 asks you to conduct research into this issue in your current institution.

Two other questionnaire studies conducted in the 1980s by Judith Whyte and Alison

Kelly also tend to confirm these results. (Kelly's methodology is discussed on p. 41.) These found that:

- most teachers were broadly sympathetic to equal opportunities in school;

- many were unhappy about the dissonance between their beliefs and their practices;

- attitudes on these issues are highly correlated to the subject taught. Specifically maths, PE, physical sciences and crafts teachers were least sympathetic and least in favour of greater equality;

- female teachers were more likely than male teachers to favour greater equality;

- most teachers favour encouraging non-traditional subject choices for boys and girls but most are unsure or hadn't thought about how to accomplish this;

- many teachers were unhappy about advising non-traditional career choices.

Jane Gaskell suggests, however, that teachers' attitudes about equal opportunities specifically may not be that important. She studied vocational training in eight business teachers' classrooms in Vancouver for four months. The results suggested that vocational training has its own imperatives, at least in the minds of the teachers, which lead to the reinforcement of gender stereotypes and a blindness towards the socially constructed nature of social relations in the workplace. These relationships were reproduced in the business studies classroom, leading to the very direct correspondence between education and the workplace discussed by Bowles and Gintis, among others.

Business teachers, she notes, deal with technical issues: how to write a business letter, how to compute taxes. They are interested in instilling 'competence', even in courses which are not competence based. The fact that, for example, women's work experience is different to men's is assumed but not discussed. Where students raise such issues the teacher quickly returns the discussion to technical 'how to' questions. Teachers encourage students to identify with the employer's point of view, even though the employer is usually referred to as 'he' and the students are virtually all female, and even though the student could more easily identify with the interests and viewpoint of, for example, consumers. Thus students learn to be a good employee and value and define the world as the employer does – they are not led to question it. One teacher admitted: 'It's the world we live in [but] I guess we do indoctrinate.'

Teachers do this because they want to attract and motivate students. They believe that in order to recruit, retain and successfully place students in employment it is necessary to concentrate on undemanding, specific, low level skills and to instil the 'business point of view'. The teachers' justification for their decisions is very clearly the need to enhance the employability of their students, to keep them interested in the subject matter by making it undemanding and task-oriented, and hence to maintain a smooth orderly classroom where students get on with clearly defined tasks. Whatever the personal views of the teacher, what they believe to be the demands of the classroom take precedence.

Thus what is important, in Gaskell's account, is not the attitudes of teachers towards equal opportunities, but their taken-for-granted assumptions about the nature of training, its relation to work and to what employers want, as well as their assumptions about the abilities and interests of the students they teach. There are, of course, alternatives which could be implemented if teachers' assumptions were different:

> The notion of what employers want would need to be reconstructed to include a more analytic, problem-solving employee. The notion of employability would need to be reconstructed to include not just what the employer wants, but also what the employee wants – a safe, equitable work-place. Ideas about what students can achieve and be interested in would similarly need to be reconstructed to include a broader range of thought and content.
>
> (Gaskell 1992)

Many sociological studies have shown that what teachers see as educationally unavoidable in dealing with large numbers of students, such as streaming them according to 'ability' and routinizing behaviour, can have important consequences for disadvantaged groups of students. One example is Stephen Ball's study of 'Beachside Comprehensive' which showed how labelling and streaming in one school were closely tied up with social class. While the National Curriculum has stopped sex differentiation by subject so that, for example, both boys and girls study technology rather than woodwork and home economics respectively, the hidden curriculum still remains (see p. 155). Recently researchers have concentrated their attention on the influence of schools' ethos and practices (the school regime) in transmitting a hidden curriculum. Peter Woods reports the following:

> I was in a primary school recently observing a class of 7 year olds. The register was being called. After the teacher had called out the first six names, she suddenly lost her voice. But the answers went on, unprompt-ed. . . 'Yes, Miss Jackson. . . Yes, Miss Jackson. . . Yes, Miss Jackson. . .' all the way through without hesitation, in alphabetical order, boys first. The teacher looked across at me afterwards and said, 'I sometimes wonder why we bother to come.' I had a vision of a regulated school, wound up at the beginning of the day, and unfolding to precision.
>
> (Woods 1990)

 List and then discuss examples of practices that form part of the school or college regime in your institution.

Another important aspect of any school's regime is its gender regime.

> Kessler and others have developed the concept of **gender regimes** to describe the codes that operate in institutions about what is acceptable as masculinity and femininity. These might differ from institution to institution, but in each case they influence, and are in turn influenced by, for example, decisions about timetabling, option choices that are made available to students, the language that is used in the classroom and the materials available there.

Barrie Thorne quotes another example of the gender regime in operation:

Early in October, Miss Bailey introduced the maths game. She would write addition and subtraction problems on the board, and a member of each team would race to be the first to write the answer. She designated the teams with two score-keeping columns on the blackboard: 'Beastly Boys'. . . 'Gossipy Girls' Several boys yelled 'Noisy girls!' 'Gruesome girls!' and some of the girls laughed in response. . . By organizing girls into separate teams and by giving them names with (humorously) derogatory gender meanings, Miss Bailey set up a situation that invited gender antagonism.

(Thorne 1993)

Teachers operate and enforce such gender regimes, but they are also subject to them. This can work to the detriment of boys as well as girls. The 1993 OFSTED report on English notes:

Departmental schemes of work rarely paid specific attention to the under-achievement of boys in English or the need to ensure that boys benefited from the affective aspects of the English curriculum.

From this perspective, then, institutional culture is more important than the attitudes and values of individual teachers.

 List and then discuss examples of practices that form part of the gender regime in your institution. Consider, for example, its hidden curriculum, timetabling and its accepted but unofficial practices.

To conclude this section we should note that while it is easy to blame teachers, often their attitudes and behaviour are products of the system they find themselves in. Again, Woods notes:

Teachers often appear to be the villains in these scenarios with their racist [and sexist] taunts and selection injustices. But it is not easy for them. Developing an alternative definition of the situation requires time for reflection, which teachers do not have in great quantity. On the contrary, their working conditions are most alien to self-reflection.

(Woods 1990)

As we shall see in the next section, the implicit view that it is only teachers who have the power to control what goes on in the classroom is also mistaken.

Students' attitudes

Some authors have stressed that girls in schools do not want to be seen to do better than boys. Around adolescence particularly, girls may be caught between wanting to be popular at school and wanting to please their parents and teachers by excelling academically. The desire to be popular with boys and being seen to be more able than them may well appear to be a contradiction best resolved by deliberate under-performance: girls 'learn to lose' in Spender's phrase. This may be one reason why girls do significantly better at maths and science in single sex schools, while boys do equally well in single sex and mixed schools.

Another reason, as Spender argues in *Invisible Women*, is that the boys in the class make trouble if the teacher devotes too much time to the girls or tries to orientate the knowledge towards them. The children themselves are aware that being active, asking questions and demanding reasons and explanations is a male prerogative and that for a girls these are 'unladylike'. Thus social control comes from the students themselves, operating both on the teacher and the girls alike. Spender reports the following:

> why girls would withdraw from mathematics and science – en masse – was no puzzle for the women to whom we spoke. Most did not hesitate to declare that the woman who does well in these fields is found to be unfeminine. For many women, to be unfeminine is to be a failure. Furthermore, the women we talked to could tell tales of what happened to girls who would not go willingly: they were verbally and sometimes physically harassed. Older women talked of being 'teased' and taunted when they triumphed in traditionally male areas of expertise. Younger women (and mothers in relation to daughters) talked of being physically prevented from using the computer.
>
> (Spender 1983)

The behaviour of the boys in school classes strongly influences the behaviour of the teachers. Sally Cline and Dale Spender suggest: 'They have to plan their lessons for the boys, spend time with the boys, get the interest of the boys. Because if they don't – the boys riot.'

In HE, the 'boys' (now men) may have other influences on female achievement. According to Elizabeth Llewellyn-Smith, principal of St Hilda's College Oxford:

> It is possible that. . . women may be exploited by their boyfriends and asked to wash shirts more, the old difficulty of women being expected to do two jobs while men do only one.

A relatively recent sociological method called discourse analysis has given some interesting insights into the gendered nature of interaction in the classroom. This method involves the very detailed study of the language and behaviour used between people and in written texts or pictures (see p. 60). An example comes from Graddol and Swann's 1989 study of interaction turn exchange mechanisms. They showed how pupils can affect where teachers give their attention, though teachers' attitudes can also structure turn exchange in subtle as well as obvious ways. Boys, for example, are more likely to volunteer information, make heavier demands on teachers' time and ask more questions.

Similar findings were arrived at by Gay Randall, whose study of gender differences in pupil–teacher interaction in workshops and laboratories demonstrated that boys position themselves around the workbench in such a way as to be able to dominate interaction with the teacher while the girls may tacitly comply with this.

Interaction turn exchange mechanisms are the ways in which it is tacitly decided who speaks when and for how long. This is often done through non-verbal communication (particularly raising the hand) and making or avoiding eye contact; it might be a conscious or unconscious process.

Janet and Peter French demonstrate similar points on the basis of detailed discourse analysis of the interaction between a pupil, Tom, and his teacher. They show how Tom uses tactics to dominate the talking time and to structure the content of talk by, for example, giving answers to questions which he knows will elicit further interaction. The dialogue in the example they give is about what time pupils get up; Tom's answer is half past four, in order to feed his numerous pets. Table 6.2 shows how the number of talking turns divided between boys and girls in the class overall.

Table 6.2	Talking turns in a classroom discussion		
Male speakers	*Turns*	*Female speakers*	*Turns*
Tom	17	Marie	5
Mathew	10	Rachel	3
Andrew	10	Angela	2
Simon	5	Sharon	2
Peter	3	Anne	1
Wayne	3	Claire	1
Jason	1	Laura	1
Warren	1	Rowena	1
Thomas	0	Anna	0
Andrew C	0	Debbie	0
Allan	0	Gina	0
Martin	0	Helen	0
Paul	0	Jenny	0
		Joanne	0
		Linda	0
		Lorraine	0

Note that while as many girls as boys participated in the discussion, the boys took more turns overall and that these turns were concentrated in a small group. French and French argue that the best way to explain this sort of gender-related turn distribution (which they consider to be typical) is not to put responsibility just onto the teacher, as has traditionally been done. Rather the patterns of interaction which arise in the classroom are *collaborative*: Tom, the other boys, the teacher and the girls in the class behave according to well-understood rules of participation which they use to achieve their aims. Tom offers newsworthy claims which he knows will make the teacher ask for further information. Other pupils carefully time the point at which they put up their hands to answer so that they will not be asked to do so but will get the 'benefits' of having offered to answer and of being presumed to know what the answer is.

Important clues in influencing the turn exchange mechanism are the direction of the teacher's gaze, his or her body language and the point at which eye contact is established. These, combined with a sophisticated understanding of the goals of other participants, particularly the teacher, are used by pupils to achieve their goals in classroom discourse.

Discourse analysis can only take us so far at the moment, however. Some of the limitations on our understanding are:

- we have only limited information on how pupils'/students' strategies and behaviour change according to variables such as context, classroom organization, teaching style, teacher attitude, classroom activity;

- 'girls' and 'boys' are not homogeneous groups – class, ethnicity and personality play a large part in affecting how individuals behave in the classroom and how they are responded to by teachers. These influences need to be understood;

- we have to look at how all the participants behave – boys' dominance may be the outcome of strategies by boys and girls and teachers. This makes analysis complex;

- boys may have an advantage in terms of structuring the turn exchange mechanism because of the general social advantages they have and we need information about this. Tom was able to dominate the class analysed by French and French because he had a large number of interesting pets. The girls had little discourse capital so that Rachel answers the teacher's question of 'What time did you get up?' with 'Quarter to eight' which elicits no further dialogue.

Analyse the discourse patterns in a formal education group you belong to. After careful observation, try to answer these questions:
1) Who speaks most, who least?
2) How are the turn exchange mechanisms working?
3) Is anybody consciously using these mechanisms?
4) Who is structuring the nature of the discourse (what is talked about and for how long)?
5) How are they doing this and to what purpose?

In the light of all this, it is not surprising that many feminists argue in favour of single-sex schools. Rosemary Deem says, for example:

> Although girls in single sex schools may have less choice of subjects, they are likely to be freer to choose which ones they take than in a mixed school where they will be competing with boys for resources and also perhaps subtly encouraged to fulfil their traditional sex roles. In addition, the emphasis on academic learning in a single sex school is not likely to convey to girls the impression that it is unimportant whether girls do well at school or not, a message which may already be conveyed to girls by their socialization and culture and not always contradicted in mixed schools. Furthermore, girls in single sex schools are more likely than girls in mixed schools to be taught maths and science by women and hence are less likely to think of these subjects as 'masculine'.
>
> (Deem 1988)

Knowledge, education and schools

Read the next section (to the middle of p. 201). Then attempt the following questions.
1) Summarize the arguments in this section in a few sentences.

2) *Consider the group's views on these arguments and formulate a joint position statement.*

3) *Come up with as many arguments/pieces of evidence as you can to substantiate your point of view.*

4) *In a plenary session each group should put its case forward for general discussion.*

The following approach to explaining educational inequality focuses on the forms of knowledge taught in schools. It is sometimes referred to as the epistemological explanation.

> **Epistemology** is the branch of philosophy that is concerned with the theory of knowledge. It studies the relationship between the perceiving person and the world of objects around him or her. It addresses questions about the nature of 'reality', the status of knowledge and how different societies and subcultures create their own realities.

In the study of education questions about knowledge have come to be seen as of great importance since the publication of *Knowledge and Control*, edited by Michael Young. We discussed the general issues raised by this book, and the 'new sociology of education' in general, earlier. They have special significance in explaining gender disadvantages in education, however.

Figure 6.8

A woman's intuition

Young makes the point that the knowledge taught in classrooms is only one form of knowledge. It excludes other forms, discounting them as worthless. While Young and other contributors to *Knowledge and Control* are mainly concerned with school knowledge as the type of knowledge that is most easily assimilable by the middle class, Dale Spender in *Invisible Women* points out that it is also most easily assimilable by males; it is 'male knowledge'. Other authors have examined the knowledge transmitted in non-school settings. The 'authorities' on most subjects are men (even in such areas as childbirth): they write the books, they explain society and it is they who therefore provide a picture of the world from which women are missing or 'invisible'.

From the position of subordination women can see that men miss much of the evidence and can construct only poorly informed explanations. . . women know a great deal about the world that men do not, they know a great deal about men that men do not know about themselves, and until women's view of the world coexists with men's view of the world, our entire system of education will be limited, distorted, sexist.

(Spender 1983)

The female perspective and the contribution made by women in many fields is ignored (Spender mentions scientists like Mary Somerville, Hertha Ayrton and political journalists like Mary Manley and Harriet Martineau). This omission is not accidental but results from the fact that it is in men's interests to keep women invisible. Thus women's lack of progress in education is not the 'accidental' product of sex role socialization, but is the product of a male conspiracy, which uses male knowledge as its main weapon: 'Men have been saying [these kinds of things]. . . for centuries as a means of trying to scare women off, and as a means of protecting their own privilege.'

A feminist perspective

Feminism and feminist perspectives on education

Feminism is the combination of a view that women have been systematically disadvantaged throughout history and across cultures and the commitment to act to rectify this situation through the abolition of patriarchy (domination by men). Roughly speaking feminism can be divided into three perspectives, as shown in Table 6.3.

Table 6.3	Three feminist perspectives		
Issue	*Liberal Feminism*	*Radical Feminism*	*Marxist Feminism*
Main problem	Socialization of boys and girls in the family and school	Deliberate oppression by men throughout all aspects of social life	Capitalist system which oppressed women in particular (low wages, temporary work etc.)
Importance of education and training	Can act as a force for good if teachers are trained, textbooks improved etc.	Instrument of oppression: 'knowledge' is constructed and reproduced by and for men	Reproduces exploitation of women by preparing them for low paid insecure jobs
Strategy for abolition of patriarchy	Positive action for women (e.g. girls into science and technology changing attitudes, abolish stereotypes	Separatism: educate and train women apart from men and in their forms of knowledge	Attack capitalist system: oppression of women is a symptom of wider issues.
Example of authors	Alison Kelly	Sally Cline, Dale Spender	Simone de Beauvoir

Black feminism is not included in Table 6.3. Read pp. 128–30 then add another column for that perspective.

Spender is arguing from a radical feminist perspective. This says that, as a result of men's dominance in the academic world most knowledge will not only be approved by male experts, it will also be about males. Sandra Acker notes that of the publications in the field of the sociology of education between 1960 and 1979, 37 per cent were exclusively concerned with males while only 5 per cent were exclusively concerned with females.

Madelaine Arnot points out that studies of 'working-class culture' like those of Paul Willis and Dick Hebdige focused specifically on working-class boys and ignored the sexism inherent in their particular subcultural style.

Another example of the relative invisibility of females in this field is Paul Corrigan's work *Schooling the Smash Street Kids*. He argues that, as a male, he is 'unable to understand the multiple oppressions that females suffer' and so decides to exclude them from his study!

While there has been an increased consciousness of gender issues among academic writers in some areas, others have been slower to change. Burton Clark's 1988 study of American academics, for example, uses remarkably sexist language (e.g. 'academic man'), hardly refers to female academics at all even though they were included in his sample, and makes no linkage between gender issues and the lower status, pay, conditions and security of those lower on the academic ladder.

The fact that men control the dominant positions in the educational institutions which transmit this knowledge gives them the power they need to retain control over it. With limited representation in such positions, women cannot challenge this ideological hegemony. Spender says:

> Men are disproportionately the heads of all schools and colleges, even where men comprise a very small proportion of the staff. In a patriarchal society the rule is that the further up the hierarchy one goes, the more men and the fewer women are to be seen.

> (Spender 1983)

This is illustrated in Figures 6.9 and 6.10.

 Research and then draw up an organizational chart of your current educational institution. How does it compare with Figures 6.9 and 6.10?

Women find it very difficult to publish feminist points of view in textbooks and elsewhere, according to Spender, because men dominate the editorial boards, they are the reviewers and advisers and so can refuse to publish the knowledge that women have. The tradition of academic peer review in HE has the same effect, as this sector is so dominated by men, particularly in its upper reaches. This avenue of change or resistance is also a narrow one for women. Because of the dominance of males in defining knowledge and in overseeing its transmission, it is not surprising that females are disadvantaged.

Figure 6.9

Qualified teaching staff in primary and secondary education.

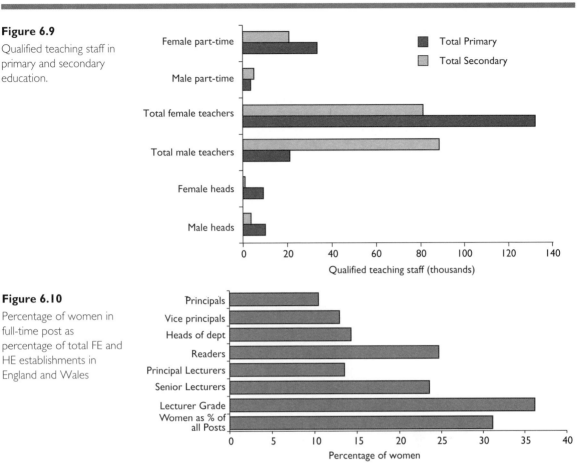

Figure 6.10

Percentage of women in full-time post as percentage of total FE and HE establishments in England and Wales

While Spender discusses the gendered nature of knowledge in the field of school education, Jane Gaskell makes a related point in the training area. She notes that as clerical and secretarial work changed from being a predominantly male occupation at the turn of the century to a predominantly female one today, so the status and rewards attached to it declined, despite the fact that today it is a highly technical and, objectively, 'skilled' occupation. She points out that whether we see a job as skilled or unskilled is not only the product of a neutral description of the nature of the work, but also a largely social construction. It serves to explain and justify the work's relative economic advantage or, in the case of secretarial work, disadvantage. Because of their lack of economic and political power and their relative lack of trade unionization, women have not been able to insist on the value of their work and so it has declined in rewards and status. Training for it, likewise, has come to be seen as undemanding, so that gaining a qualification does not mean increased reward as it does in, for example, the law.

Both Spender and Gaskell, then, make the point that the distribution of power between the sexes in society has important effects on what is seen as worth knowing, what is taught in education and training institutions, and what the rewards are for those who successfully complete their education or training.

A gendered language?

The Sapir-Whorf hypothesis was developed by two linguists, Edward Sapir and Benjamin Lee Whorf. It says that the language we learn as young children helps to structure the way we think because any language sets up a kind of grid through which we perceive the world. It forces our gaze on the world in certain directions, allows us to focus on some elements while seeing others only dimly, and structures the way we think about ideas.

Media observer Marshall McLuhan argued in the late 1960s that the medium of communication is as important as what is said: the medium is the message. Many authors note that the main medium of knowledge transmission in the UK, the English language, is itself important in delivering particular ideas about the world. Such ideas are informed by the Sapir-Whorf hypothesis and, more generally, by discourse analysis. Joan Swann, applying these ideas to gender issues, argues that the English language has a male-centred bias. There are three main aspects to this:

1   In its use of generics English favours the male form. This is true of individual words (e.g. 'postman', 'chairman', 'businessman', 'spokesman') and the use of 'he' and 'man' for both men and women and humanity in general. It is also true in phrases such as 'one upmanship', 'manmade', 'the man in the street'. Dale Spender (1985) agrees, quoting studies which show that this usage makes children think exclusively of males and thus renders females invisible. To illustrate, she points out that while we can accept the phrase 'man is an intelligent species', the phrase 'man, being a mammal, breastfeeds his young' appears humorous.

 If you can get a copy of the first edition of Haralambos Sociology: Themes and Perspectives analyse pp. 534–5 (the introduction to Marxism) for its sexist language. Compare this to pp. 781–3 on the same subject in the third edition.

2   English often involves semantic pejoration, that is the attribution of negative connotations to words. Examples associated with males and females specifically are 'master/mistress'; 'bachelor/spinster'; 'governor/governess'. Historically, Swann argues, previously neutral terms when applied to women begin to acquire negative connotations, which then stick. Words which were originally neutral were 'wench' (which simply meant 'young girl'), 'gossip' and 'hussy'.

3   English contains lexical gaps, that is omissions in the words available to say particular sorts of things. We have the word 'virility' for men for example, but no equivalent for women. Most verbs relating to sexual intercourse relate to the male perspective. There are, though, several words for the promiscuous woman.

These characteristics of the English language's syntax and semantics both reflect and reinforce the assumptions and perceptions of the culture concerning gender.

Common-sense assumptions about valuable knowledge and about the nature of reality tend to be reflected in the curriculum materials found in schools, which in turn serve to reproduce them. In *Patriarchy in School Textbooks* Marion Scott analysed numerous textbooks in a variety of subject areas in order to 'locate some of the sexist trends in curriculum materials'. She finds that one important trend is for texts to fall into three categories:

1. The derogation of women

In these texts women are relegated to a subordinate role or else portrayed through grotesque cartoons. They also present women serving primarily a 'decorative' function.

2. The invisible woman

These books do not focus on women at all.

3. The insignificance of women

These books treat women inadequately and are the most common genre.

(Scott 1988)

Some examples she quotes are geography books which ignore the crucial role women play in farming in the South, and history books which deal almost exclusively with the exploits of men and ignore, for example, women's contribution to the war effort during the First World War. Books on political and economic history were particularly prone to this: one book had a chapter entitled 'The home', which focused on the man relaxing after some do-it-yourself work.

Another tendency in such books is to trivialize women's role, one example being a discussion of their part in the labour market in the twentieth century which ends in 'an uninspired discussion of fashion'. Several of the social studies and history texts tended to assume that most of the problems of inequality in Britain have now been overcome, and where they still exist this is because (in the words of one text) 'women and girls have failed to make full use of the opportunity now open to them'. In maths, science, engineering and technology textbooks the world depicted is the male world. Men and boys are portrayed doing things involving mathematical calculations while, for example, a girl sips tea or stands decoratively in a phone booth. One section on flow charts directs girls to consider a chart of a knitting process while the boys study a flow chart of a cement-mixing operation.

Scott's argument, then, is that textbooks perform an ideological function, reproducing and reinforcing both patriarchal relations and assumptions about the nature of the subjects we study. In this way they set the stage for the problems of gender identity and the gendered nature of subjects explored by Kim Thomas in *Gender and Subject in Higher Education*, which we examined earlier.

Scott would like to see a full investigation and exposure of women's past – recorded and documented in special women's history books – and an integration of women and their contribution to history within existing accounts. She would like girls and women to be integrated into the world of engineering, maths and technology as it is depicted in these texts. The books also need, she argues, to use examples and questions which move away from football, cricket, men driving cars and traditional boys' hobbies, and to address the world of women as well as that of men. Similarly there would need to be an end to the practice, reported in the OFSTED report *Boys and English*, of schools stocking books that reflected a 'good read for boys' because it is easier to win girls over to 'male books' than boys to 'female' ones.

 Discuss Marion Scott's proposals for change. What is your view of them? Share your conclusions with the rest of the group. Conduct a similar analysis of any one item of curriculum material. Can

you find examples of any of the patterns she identifies? (You may wish to consider an item from the National Curriculum, an area which has not yet received much attention from researchers.)

 Alison Kelly has advocated what she calls a 'feminine science' which would involve, for example, designing chemistry projects which show how nylon stockings are made, or doing experiments in which perfume is mixed.

What is your view of this suggestion? Can you suggest any alternatives or modifications to it which might achieve the same end?

A new curriculum?

Finally in this section we should note that for some liberal feminists the National Curriculum, with its promise of 'a balanced and broadly based curriculum' for all pupils to the age of 16 holds out the promise of promoting girls' education, particularly in the possibility that it will give girls access to masculinized subject areas. Andy Green argues that, paradoxically, a reduction in subject choice may enhance the prospects of equal opportunities. The precise specification of content for each subject, the setting of attainment targets and a national system of testing may overcome teacher stereotyping and low expectations for girls and other groups. Duncan Graham, ex National Curriculum Council chair and chief executive, agrees with such views, concluding: 'The National Curriculum is a potent tool for change and for bringing about equality of opportunity [though its] potential is largely unrealised as yet.'

In this way the gendered nature of the curriculum may be overcome. However, Sheila Miles and Chris Middleton are sceptical of this view. They argue that the sorts of processes we have discussed above (classroom processes, teachers' and pupils' attitudes and behaviour, and so on) will still operate in the context of the National Curriculum and that 'it is implausible to suppose that the treatment of girls and boys as though they were already equal will result in the creation of genuine equality of opportunity'. They also note that there is a real danger that by forcing girls to study subjects for which they have an aversion, the National Curriculum could make the situation worse by turning disaffection from certain subjects, manifested for example in truanting from those specifically, to a rejection of schooling itself.

More choice, as recommended by the 1993 Dearing Report, is not the answer, however. Even changes such as the reorientation of subjects to make them 'girl friendly' in the manner advocated by Scott, Kelly, Thomas and others would be inadequate. At the root of the problem, according to Miles and Middleton, are the gender and other structured inequalities in society. Until these are changed, even the best 'reforms' (among which they do not count National Curriculum) will be doomed to failure.

Conclusion

To conclude this chapter, we should note that although we have concentrated on the question of the gendered nature of educational inequality, much of the discussion has demonstrated that what goes on in schools is closely linked to wider society. These include the ways in which boys and girls come to see themselves and each other, how the sexes interact both at school and outside its gates, and how knowledge and language are gendered.

It is possible that schools do, on the whole, act to counteract sex stereotyping and other inequalities. Even if this is so, however, it is unlikely that schools will have more than a marginal influence while parents, teachers and pupils themselves continue to be exposed to limited and sexist portrayals of women in the mass media, in video games and in advertising. Similarly, while there are a limited number of role models of women in senior positions in the wider society, it is unlikely that the different aspirations of boys and girls can be tackled.

Consultants and assessors

Divide into teams of about five people. The task of each team (the 'consultants') is to make four or five policy proposals to address the situation we have described in this chapter. After 10 minutes you will be asked to choose a member of your team to leave and become part of the Assessors' panel. You will then have an agreed period of time in which to formulate your proposal.

Consultants: You will be expected to present your proposals to the panel at the agreed time. You will have 5 minutes to present them. After the proposals have been heard there will be 3 minutes for a question and answer session with the Assessors' panel, which will then evaluate them.

Assessors: Your panel has three tasks:

1) to determine criteria for judging the merits of the presentation session;

2) to take full responsibility for the presentation session;

3) to make an open adjudication on the various proposals presented to you.

You should act as independent assessors, not for the teams from which you were elected. You should note that the teams will present their proposals in their own way and this should take no longer than 5 minutes. All the presentations should be complete before the question and answer session starts. You should not question each team for longer than 3 minutes. Once this is complete you should take no longer than 5 minutes to discuss your impressions and make the necessary decisions. This should be done openly so that all the teams can hear. You may decide to announce one of the teams as the winner.

Essay Question

Evaluate the major sociological explanations of why some social groups are disproportionately represented among the 'failures' of the education system.

Conceptual twenty questions

One person in the group chooses a concept from the field of education. The rest of the group can ask up to twenty questions – which must be answerable by yes or no – to try to guess what the concept is.

Suggestions for further reading

Sources specific to this chapter

Brooking, C. *et al.* (1987) *Teaching For Equality: Educational Resources on Race and Gender*, London: Runnymede Trust.

Guinness (1975) *The Guinness Encyclopaedia of Female Achievement*, Enfield: J & K Mackey Superlatives Ltd.

Measor, K. and Sike, P. (1992) *Gender and Schools* London: Cassell. Gives a readable overview of gender issues in schools in particular.

Ruddock, J. (1993) *Developing a Gender Policy in Primary Schools*, Milton Keynes: Open University Press.

Learners with disabilities and learning difficulties

Alan Hurst

Since the passing of the Education Act of 1981, some people consider that in the UK significant progress has been made both in the policy and the provision of education for learners with disabilities and learning difficulties. In this chapter we examine the evidence for making such claims. We look at the situation prior to 1981 and then go on to consider how the more recent developments in education might sustain or impede further improvements. We begin by looking at what happens at school level and then explore more briefly aspects of post-compulsory education.

Some indication of recent trends is given in tables using information provided by the government. If you want to explore what lies behind the statistics, the various experiences of children with special educational needs in schools today have been collected by two educational researchers, Barrie Wade and Maggie Moore, in a survey published in 1993. It is interesting to contrast what these children say with comments from people with disabilities and learning difficulties who were at school earlier this century; we include some of their comments later in this chapter.

Table 7.1 Special schools population

Year	1982	1987	1991
Special Schools	1469	1393	1333
Pupils in Special Schools	119,000	104,200	94,500
Teachers in Special Schools	16,900	16,900	16,000
Pupil-Teacher ratio in Special Schools	7.5	6.2	5.9

Source: Chapman, Niels 'Caught in the Crossfire: the future of special schools' in *British Journal of Special Education*, Vol. 21 No. 2, June 1994, p. 60.

Table 7.2 Percentage of pupils in special schools

Year	1984	1985	1986	1987	1988	1989	1990	1991
%	1.45	1.43	1.42	1.40	1.37	1.34	1.32	1.30

Try to arrange an interview with a person with a disability and ask her/him about experiences at school. You could talk about the attitudes of the other pupils, the responses of the teachers, and the subjects studied.

However, before we go any further, it is important to discuss issues relating to the use of terminology and language which is acceptable and preferable.

Definitions

'**Disabled**', '**handicapped**', '**impaired**', etc. are terms which are sometimes used indiscriminately and yet it is possible both to make distinctions between them and to indicate which term is the most appropriate in the contemporary context. In 1980 the World Health Organization (WHO) tried to give a clear starting point. Its suggestions are given at the end of the chapter, but before looking at them there is a task for you to complete.

Compose your own definition for each of the following terms:
- *impairment;*
- *disability;*
- *handicap;*
- *special educational needs.*

Having done this you can now compare your own answers with what the WHO suggested. Its definitions are listed on p.228.

Note that there is considerable sensitivity about the terms used. Some terms have become quite unacceptable and are not often found in late twentieth-century Britain. In contrast, the literature published at the turn of the century is likely to refer to 'cripples' and 'mental defectives'. However, even today people use language which causes offence, especially to those in the social group to which reference is being made. Thus we should never refer to *THE* disabled – it is much more preferable to say disabled people. Table 7.3 offers more examples and provides an opportunity to test out your own practices.

Table 7.3	Disability – the language we use
The issue of language with regard to disability is an important one.	
Look at the following words and ask yourself whether they imply a positive or negative image.	
wheelchair-bound	positive/negative/neither
the disabled	positive/negative/neither
people with disabilities	positive/negative/neither
disabled person	positive/negative/neither
cripple	positive/negative/neither
invalid	positive/negative/neither
integrated	positive/negative/neither
spastic	positive/negative/neither
handicapped	positive/negative/neither
people with learning difficulties	positive/negative/neither
spina bifida	positive/negative/neither
independent	positive/negative/neither
sufferer	positive/negative/neither
special	positive/negative/neither
mental patient	positive/negative/neither
Avoid	*Use*
Victim of	person who has/person with/person who experienced
Crippled by	person who has/person with
Suffering from	person who has/person with
Afflicted by	person who has/person with

Soc

Offensive	Preferred
Wheelchair bound	wheelchair user
Invalid (means *not* valid)	disabled person
Mental	disabled person

Offensive	Preferred
Handicap	Disability
Handicapped Person	DIsabled Person
Spastic	Cerebral Palsy
Deaf and Dumb, Deaf/Mute	Deaf or Partial Hearing
Mongoloid	Downs Syndrome
Cripple/Crippled	Disabled Person or Mobility Impaired ambulatory disabled
The Blind	Blind Person, Partially sighted
The Deaf	Deaf People
Mentally Handicapped, Backward/Dull Retarded, Idiot, Imbecile, Feeble Minded	Learning Difficulty Developmental Disability
Mute, Dummy	Speech Difficulty
Crazy, Maniac, Insane	Emotional Disability
Mentally ill	Mental Disturbance
Abnormal	Exceptional/Different

Perhaps the accompanying cartoon offers the best summary of what we need to do.

Figure 7.1

chair. She works as a clerical assistant for the Department of the Environment. She wants to travel to as many places as possible and in a few years would like to have children.

From the age of six years old I attended a residential school for disabled children. The school was very poor on education, so much so that at the age of sixteen I was only at the level of a nine-year-old. I used to go home at weekends and talk to the able-bodied kids about what they were doing at school. I had never even heard of some of the subjects they studied. I felt so ashamed that they knew more than I did and I was a lot older. I decided to ask my teacher why I did not do the same things as my friends did at their school. She told me that it was because I was disabled and that there wasn't much point in educating me to 'O' and 'A' level as I would never get a job. I told her that I was not prepared to spend my life in a workshop making baskets. I was going to improve my education and get a job in open employment no matter how long it took. Since the age of twelve I had been very bored with school life and started to become rebellious. I felt frustrated and couldn't explain why. Most of the other children were not very intelligent and this made me feel very alone. I could not talk to them as friends. I tried to talk to some of the staff about how I felt, but in their eyes we were all the same whatever disability we had. I was told to go and play and stop bothering them. This was quite common amongst the staff, never explaining what their ideas meant. One idea which most of the staff held was explained to me quite clearly. I was about fourteen years old and had just finished preparing a salad in the cookery class. The teacher came over and said, 'What a good job you have made of that. You would have made someone a good wife.' 'What do you mean, I would have?' I asked. 'Well,' she replied, 'What I meant to say was if you marry a disabled man, you would make him a good wife.' The school had really strange ideas on marriage and the disabled. They believed that if a disabled person got married it should be to another disabled person as it would not be fair on an able-bodied person to burden them with a handicapped partner. Anyway an able-bodied person would not fancy a disabled person. I didn't go along with this idea at all. I knew for a fact that able-bodied boys fancied me. I had proved that when I went home for weekends.

Campling, J. *Images of Ourselves*, RKP, 1981

This raises an important issue about the obviousness or otherwise of a disability. For some people there are few opportunities to meet others with disabilities and learning difficulties and therefore their views and attitudes are uninformed: they operate using stereotypes and as a consequence those at the receiving end are made to feel different. By including learners with disabilities and learning difficulties in mainstream schools, much of the current ignorance might be eliminated with particularly beneficial effects on individuals' self-concepts.

 Which sorts of disabilities are most likely to have an effect on how people act and react to us? Which least?

A further aspect of social life which provides knowledge and information are the mass media. Often our views of disabled people and those with learning difficulties are reinforced by images in books and newspapers, on television and in films. Consider the portrayal of disability in children's fiction – Clara in *Heidi*, or Long John Silver in *Treasure Island*.

There are many other examples of how disability is portrayed in both children's and adult fiction. Try to list some books and make a collection of articles from newspapers and magazines which are about disabled people. What kind of images of disability are being given? Are they positive or negative?

In pairs, compare your lists.

Another source of information is the publicity material produced by charities. Collect some of these, and then consider how disability is represented. If you feel that it is negative, design your own poster or information leaflet.

Educational provision for learners with disabilities and learning difficulties before 1981

Often it is easy to forget that state involvement in providing education for the majority of the population is a comparatively recent phenomenon. It was only with the passing of the Education Act 1870 that local school boards could provide schools in their area. Ten years later further legislation brought about compulsory free elementary education. However, given the attitudes at the time towards children and young disabled people and learning difficulties, it is hardly surprising that little progress was made in the provision of special education. In a very small number of places special schools developed, usually trying to cater for the needs of those whose disability was obvious. This supplemented the activities of a few charities who had been making some provision previously. The quality of the educational experience was poor – as was that experienced by most other people.

All the patients whose state of health permits attend school each day for periods proportioned to their respective capacities. Thus 34 of the lowest grade of intellect are instructed in the classroom daily for half an hour only: 38 others more intelligent but of tender years, form an infant class which meets each morning for one hour; a mixed school of about 80 selected boys and girls pleasantly spend the first hour of the afternoon in conjoined singing and kindergarten exercises; and for another hour and a half the 34 girls receive, in their own classroom, instructions in both matters of ordinary scholastic routine and in industrial employments suitable to their sex. In the boys school, which is attended by 97 of the older boys (the pupils attending school and work alternately morning and afternoon) much progress is evident as the result of the careful and patient teaching of the master. Eight boys are now able to read fluently, 10 write sufficiently well to correspond with friends, 40 use copy books, 12 work simple addition sums, and one boy is able to do compound multiplication, whilst another, of exceptional arithmetical talent, works problems in compound interest and is learning decimals. Six boys draw fairly on paper, one of them remarkably well: and two are making good progress, (under the tuition of the music master) in learning to play instruments from notes whilst a large number are able to sing creditably from ear. Increasingly useful work is done by the boys and girls, the former work as shoemakers, tailors, joiners, basketmakers, farm boys, boot cleaners, laundry boys, corridor cleaners, some are also employed as errand boys. The latter work as bedmakers, kitchen assistants, scrubbing, scullery, wardrobe (14 girls do needlework in school and 4 do plain knitting).

Alston, J. (ed.), *The Royal Albert: Chronicles of an Era*, Centre for North West Regional Studies, University of Lancaster

In the early years of the twentieth century the state was being increasingly drawn into providing education and progress was being made, albeit very slowly and inconsistently. Some important reforms were introduced by the Liberal Government between 1906 and 1914, but progress stopped when the First World War began. When war ended in 1918 the country faced a series of major economic problems and these took precedence over education. There were few developments even in mainstream education, and the situation for children with disabilities and learning difficulties was little different from that at the start of the century. To give you some impression of what it was like, here is an account written by someone who was at school during this period:

Teachers also often made the assumption that children with disabilities were lazy. In fact they were often working desperately hard all day simply trying to hear or see the teacher's instructions. The immense difficulty and strain of this made some so tired they would occasionally fall asleep in class. Marie Hagger:

One day I remember the teacher was going to read us a play. All the children got excited about it. And she said she was going to take the different characters herself from the play and she wanted us to guess what the characters were. And she starts and I think after about five minutes I came over terribly tired. To be able to hear was -strain, strain, strain – the whole time. In fact, it's true to say I didn't know how to relax. So this particular occasion she started – drone, drone, drone – because that's how it came through to me, just a drone. I could hear the voice but what she was saying was another matter, the actual gist of the story was totally lost. I gradually felt myself going to sleep, dozed right off. Suddenly, a bang on my desk. I was woken rudely. 'I've never come across such a lazy child in all my teaching history!' But I went along with that. Preferred her to think I was lazy or that I was not paying attention.

Very often on my school reports it would say, 'She's too lazy' or, 'She's very lazy' or, 'She could do better if she wasn't so lazy.'

Humphries, S. and Gordon, P. *Out of Sight: the experience of disability 1900–1950*, Northcote House Publishers Ltd, 1992

Before any major changes could occur the Second World War began. Remarkably, during these troubled times, some people had the foresight and imagination to plan for a world after the conflict had ceased. The results of their efforts appeared even before the war ended in the form of the momentous Education Act 1944, a piece of legislation that operated with some success almost unaltered until 1988.

The major change introduced by this Act was the provision of free secondary education for all, according to aptitude and ability. Thus came the idea of different types of schools to meet different needs.

The Act opened the debate about policy and provision for children with disabilities and learning difficulties. For example, did the government mean literally *everyone* when it talked of education for all? Also, if schools were to be created to meet the different needs of pupils, this could be extended to those with special needs too. Eventually a system of categories was introduced known as the Handicapped Pupils and Special Schools Regulations. Originally eleven categories were used but this was later modified to ten. The categories were as follows:

1 blind;

2 partially blind (later partially sighted – use of language!);

3 deaf;

4 partially deaf (later partially hearing);

5 physically handicapped;

6 speech-impaired;

7 delicate;

8 epileptic;

9 educationally subnormal;

10 maladjusted.

Look again at the list of categories and then suggest how the educational needs of children with the various kinds of disability could be met, paying particular attention to whether it would be possible to include them in mainstream schools.

Consider the order in which the list has been set out. Can you see anything about the sequence moving from blind children to those who are categorized as maladjusted?

The category system appeared to work effectively for a long period. A system of special schools was established and children were placed in them according to their disabling condition. In other words (and to return to the point we discussed earlier) a medical model of disability was being used.

As with any system there were problems. An obvious one is where to place children with multiple disabilities, such as a child who is both deaf and blind. Nevertheless it was only in the 1960s that people began to express concern.

One of the factors which prompted this was the policy supported by the Labour Government elected in 1964 to try to end selection for secondary education at age 11. By that date a lot of research had accumulated which claimed to demonstrate the unfairness and shortcomings of the 11+ examination. One strategy to overcome the problems was to send all pupils to the same school for their secondary education, the comprehensive school. One definition of 'comprehensive' is that it refers to something which is 'all embracing' and those in favour of mainstreaming took this opportunity to suggest that 'all' should include pupils with disabilities and learning difficulties. The focus on reforming secondary education presented an opportunity to draw attention to the debate about integration.

Further attention was drawn to issues about special schools with the passing of the Education Act 1970. This brought the children in long-stay hospitals into the responsibilities of the Education Service rather than the NHS. These children (whose measured IQ was less than 20) had not been included within the old category system. Because they spent their lives in hospitals, they were seen as the responsibility of the NHS. The 1970 Act changed this and the Education Service was faced with a new group of pupils of whom it had little experience of.

At the start of the 1970s many issues were arising on which the government was urged to take action. However the issues were complex and the government was uncertain about what changes should take place. To find out more and to buy time, a committee of enquiry was set up. A leading educationalist and philosopher, Mary Warnock was asked to convene the group, which produced its final report in Spring 1978. The findings and recommendations of the Warnock Committee were to have a profound impact on policy and provision for children with disabilities and learning difficulties.

The Warnock Report and special educational needs in 1978

The Warnock Report (1978) began by stating that it viewed the aims of education as being the same for all children:

> We hold that education has certain long-term goals, that it is has a general point or purpose, which can be definitely, though generally, stated. The goals are twofold, different from each other, but by no means incompatible. They are, first, to enlarge a child's knowledge, experience and imaginative understanding, and thus awareness of moral values and capacity for enjoyment; and, secondly, to enable him to enter the world after formal education is over as an active participant in society and a responsible contributor to it, capable of achieving as much independence as possible. The educational needs of every child are determined in relation to these goals. We are fully aware that for some children the first of these goals can be approached only by minute, though for them highly significant steps, while the second may never be achieved. But this does not entail that for these children the goals are different. The purpose of education for all children is the same; the goals are the same. But the help that individual children need in progressing towards them will be different. (. . .)
>
> From: *The Warnock Report*, 1978, p.5, 1.4, Department of Education and Science
> 1978

Having collected evidence on a wide scale both at home and abroad, the Committee suggested that the scope of special education should be widened. The term special educational needs should be used partly to embrace this broader range, and partly to try to eliminate some of the problems which had been created by the category system described earlier. It was estimated that one in six children would have a special educational need at some point during their school career.

The Report first discusses terminology and then sets the scene. The content of the

Report is organized around the sequence of events which children encounter as they progress through the education system from pre-school to FE. Thus in the opening chapters the importance of identifying a child as having any special educational need as early as possible is recognized. Also stressed is the need for regular assessment and reviews by a multi-professional team, which should also involve the child's parents.

For some children the formal processes of assessment would lead to the production of a Statement of Special Educational Needs. We will say more about Statements later.

Turning to the issue of integration, the Warnock Committee stressed the desirability of retaining a 'continuum of provision' ranging on the one hand from education in a mainstream class with very minimal additional support, to home tuition at the other. Having such varied possibilities should enable the system to meet as many different needs as possible. The Report did emphasize that where possible, children with special educational needs should attend mainstream school but it did not advocate the closure of all special schools. Three kinds of integration were identified:

1. THE DIFFERENT FORMS OF INTEGRATION.

7.7 The first form of integration relates to LOCATION of special educational provision. Locational integration exists where special units or classes are set up in ordinary schools. It also exists where a special school and an ordinary school share the same site.(. . .)

7.8 The second form of integration which we have identified relates to its SOCIAL aspect, where children attending a special class or unit eat, play and consort with other children, and possibly share organised out-of-classroom activities with them.(. . .)

7.9 The third and fullest form of integration is FUNCTIONAL integration. This is achieved where the locational and social association of children with special needs with their fellows leads to joint participation in educational programmes. It is the closest from of association, where children with special needs join, part-time or full-time, the regular classes of the school, and make a full contribution to the activity of the school.(. . .)

From: *The Warnock Report*, pp. 100–1, Department of Education and Science 1978

The later chapters of the Report discuss the transition from school to FE and life in the community. Detailed consideration is given to the roles and responsibilities of a range of professions involved in policy and provision.

Having compiled all the evidence and made a lengthy list of recommendations, the Committee realized that the government was likely to be overwhelmed by the scale and comprehensiveness of the proposed changes. To avoid this three priority areas were indicated:

1 provision for pre-school children;

2 school-leavers;

3 teacher training.

Look at the three priorities identified above and taking each one, find out about any changes which have occurred between 1978 and today.

From the Education Act 1981 to the Education Reform Act 1988

Statements

Following the publication of the Report there was a period of further consultation at the end of which the Education Act 1981 was passed by Parliament. The Act introduced many of the recommendations made by the Warnock Committee, most notably Statements. A later Circular 1/83 gave guidance about the format and content of Statements. Having opened with some factual information about the child, the Statement was to consist of four other sections:

1 the identification of the child's special educational needs;

2 the development of the strategies for meeting these needs;

3 the naming of the place most appropriate to carrying out these plans;

4 the compilation of evidence submitted by the various professionals and by the parents in order to decide on provision.

This approach is quite different from the one we outlined earlier. It has as its central concern the individual child, rather than the nature of the disability or learning difficulty. For example, two children who are blind might have different needs which can be met in different ways.

 Arrange to interview some parents whose children have been given a Statement and find out their views both about the content of the document and about the procedures which they had to follow.

The Education Act 1981 also supported the Committee in supporting the concept of mainstreaming, although qualifying conditions were imposed; as the quote below iillustrates:

2 Provisions of special education: duties of local education authorities etc.

(2) Where a local education authority arrange special educational provision for a child for whom they maintain a statement under section 7 of the Act it shall be the duty of the authority, if the conditions mentioned in subsection (3) below are satisfied, to secure that he is educated in an ordinary school.

(3) The conditions are that account has been taken, in accordance with section 7, of the views of the child's parent and that educating the child in an ordinary school is compatible with—

(a) his receiving the special educational provision that he requires;

(b) the provision of efficient education for the children with whom he will be educated; and

(c) the efficient use of resources.

From: The Education Act 1981

The problems

The new system did not become fully operational until 1983 and quite soon after its introduction some of the weaknesses became apparent. For example there were wide variations in policies between LEAs regarding the issuing of Statements and educating children with special needs in mainstream schools. These are evident in the statistics compiled by a pressure group, the Centre for Studies on Integration in Education (CSIE).

Figure 7.2

Proportion of pupils with statement in England and Wales

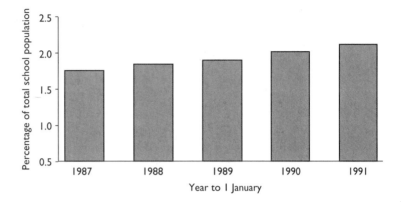

Critical comments also came from other sources. For example, in 1989 the Australian researcher Gillian Fulcher pointed out the dangers of having a policy which can legitimately label up to 16 per cent of the school population as having special educational needs. She based her arguments on comparisons with practices in other countries.

Before any organized opposition developed, however, policy and provision was altered radically by the Education Reform Act 1988.

The Education Reform Act 1988 – implications for learners with disabilities and learning difficulties

The Education Reform Act 1988 brought important changes to state-funded education. The focus of the Act can be summarized in two words: curriculum and control.

Since their return to power in 1979, the Conservative government have been concerned to improve standards in education and to make the best use of resources, some of which they felt were being wasted by ineffective teachers and inefficient LEAs. In line with Conservative political philosophy, successive governments felt that their objectives could be reached by introducing elements of the 'market economy' into education in the form of greater competition and greater choice. All of these concerns can be seen in the provisions made by the Act.

These changes to mainstream education have possible consequences for children with disabilities and learning difficulties. On the one hand the National Curriculum's clear definition of what all children are entitled to could be beneficial since in the past many special schools were criticized for their lack of concern with the mainstream curriculum and for their low educational standards.

On the other hand there are problems relating to the appropriateness of the

Figure 7.3

Levels of attainment at three key stages

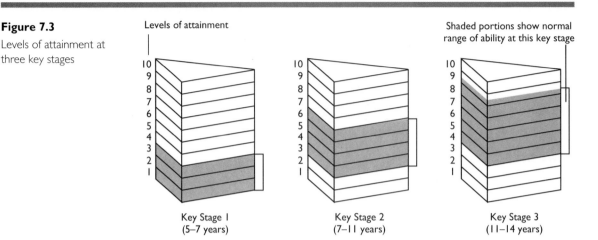

Levels of attainment

Shaded portions show normal range of ability at this key stage

Key Stage 1
(5–7 years)

Key Stage 2
(7–11 years)

Key Stage 3
(11–14 years)

National Curriculum for some children. Perhaps the most serious worry relates to the potential consequences of testing and the publication of results. For example, if a child with a learning difficulty is being educated in a mainstream school and his/her results in the SAT are poor, their performance could bring down the average score for the class group/school. When this information is published the impression given to the local community could be that standards in that particular school are inferior to those of a neighbouring one, and so parents might choose not to send their children to it. In view of this, and believing that the performance of children with disabilities and learning difficulties might depress the aggregated scores, schools might be more reluctant to admit them in the first place.

In fairness the Education Reform Act does offer an alternative in that, at the discretion of the headteacher, the child can be exempt from the National Curriculum and the associated testing. However, if this happens, it perhaps suggests that the education of these children is less important than that of others.

The second dimension of the Act is about changing the basis of control in education. In line with the government's view that too much money is spent on LEA bureaucracy, the Act introduced a mechanism whereby schools could move out of LEA control. By holding ballots with parents, schools could move to grant-maintained status – they could 'opt out' of the LEA. By doing so they would become totally responsible for managing their own affairs, particularly their finances.

This has potentially serious consequences for children with disabilities and learning difficulties. Currently many benefit from the support provided by the LEA in a variety of ways such as in-class support from non-teaching assistants and peripatetic teachers (i.e. who travel to a child's home to teach). This is provided free. Thus, if a school chooses to leave the LEA, it could not expect those services to continue without charge. Yet if the support is provided by the school itself, clearly some children might be more 'costly' to a school than others. If this is the case, schools which have moved to grant-maintained status might not wish to recruit children whose attendance will result in such additional 'costs'.

It is early days yet and there is no evidence to suggest that the possibilities we have outlined above are taking place. However, it will be necessary to monitor the situation carefully if the progress made since 1978 is to continue.

Arrange to visit a school and discuss with appropriate teachers how their work with children with disabilities and learning difficulties has been affected by the 1988 Act. If you are studying within a school context, do this for your own school.

Education policy since 1988

There are a number of other more recent developments which are also likely to have effects on the system in the future.

The Parent's Charter

As part of its policies to encourage competition and to introduce the practices of the marketplace into as many aspects of social life as possible, the Conservative government has issued a number of 'Charters' which try to clarify the rights of the various participants in the service. Within education the government issued the *Parent's Charter: You and Your Child's Education* in 1991. Soon after, in early 1992, parents of children with special educational needs were given their own version simply entitled *Children with Special Needs: A Guide for Parents*. Its aims and content are set down in a summary on the first page:

> If your child has special educational needs because of disability or other learning difficulties, you and your child have a right to an education which meets these needs – in an ordinary school where possible. All children, including children with special educational needs, should have the opportunity to follow all the subjects of the National Curriculum up to the best of their ability.

> Department for Education 1992

What is your view of these ideas?

Having made parents more aware of their rights, it will be interesting to see if many resort to the courts to pursue their cases if they feel that they have been treated unfairly. This situation has become common in the USA following the passing of Public Law 94–142: The Education of All Handicapped Children Act, in 1975. It is also important to note that there have been further changes since the publication of the *Charter* which could have a significant bearing on this point. We discuss these later.

The work of the Audit Commission

With its concern both for standards and also for value for money the government asked the Inspectorate and the Audit Commission to work together to provide information about policy and provision for children with special educational needs. In fact three publications produced jointly appeared in quick succession:

1 *Special Educational Needs: Access to the System;*

2 *Getting in on the Act: Provision for Pupils with Special Educational Needs – the National Picture;*

3 *Getting the Act Together: Provision for Pupils with Special Educational Needs – A Management Handbook for Schools and Local Education Authorities.*

The comments in these publications are based on a survey in twelve local areas. They reported that many aspects of policy and provision needed attention. For example, some time was spent looking at the procedures surrounding the issuing of Statements. They found great variations in the typical time needed to compile a Statement (in some cases the period was so long that any strategies suggested were outdated because the child had developed), and also in their content. In some cases, the content was too vague and general, making it difficult to judge the impact of the provision agreed.

The government acted quickly to introduce ways of improving the situation with several action strategies.

Publication of Choice and Diversity: A New Framework for Schools

Just one month after the joint DfE/Audit Commission reports listed above, a further government White Paper was launched and whilst its focus was on the total system, it contained a three-page chapter about special educational needs. The most significant proposal was that special schools were to be allowed to seek grant-maintained status. In the light of this the chapter discussed the possible changes in financial responsibilities should many special schools decide to 'opt out'. It indicated that the LEAs would retain responsibility for assessments, Statements, and for a range of support services.

Passing of the 1993 Education Act

The plans outlined in the White Paper were enshrined in the Education Act 1993. As well as the opportunity to move to grant-maintained status, other changes related to the appeals procedure made by parents unhappy with the educational provision made for their child.

In the past the role of the LEA in the procedure was unsatisfactory in that in the first instance it was the LEA itself which gave judgement on an appeal – which might have been brought by a parent against its own policies. The new system offered an LEA the possibility of acting as an intermediary in any disputes between parents and the schools – a more neutral position. In addition there was to be a tribunal whose membership would comprise people from outside the LEA.

It remains to be seen how these changes will benefit the children in the long term, but there was some opposition to the Act. In particular the lack of funding specifically allocated to support children with disabilities and learning difficulties is seen as a major weakness. Equally of concern is the apparent lack of recognition for those children who need support but who do not have a Statement.

Publication of The Code of Practice on the Identification and Assessment of Special Educational Needs 1994

In 1993 the government issued a draft of the guidance it intended to give to schools and LEAs about the actual day-to-day operation of the new procedures. This was intended to improve the efficiency of the system, and to take into account many of the issues raised since 1981.

Much attention was focused on the identification of pupils with disabilities and learning difficulties. If it is suspected that a child is experiencing problems there are a number of stages through which action is to be taken. An example of a school-based stage (Stage 1) is given in Figure 7.4. Stage 1 is the initial expression of concern by a parent, teacher or other professional.

Figure 7.4

School-based stages: stage 1

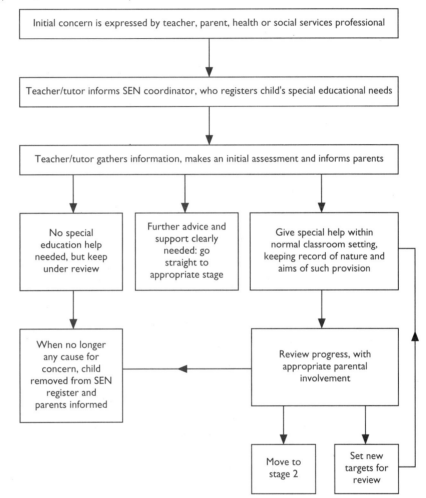

These stages placed greater responsibilities on the schools and on their teachers. In order to eliminate the delays highlighted by the DfE/Audit Commission, a timetable was prescribed. If parents experienced delays, they could use this information to bring an appeal against the school and LEA.

Another intention was to change the nature of the Statement: it would become much more like the 'Individualized Education Programme' (IEP) used in the USA since 1975. These set specific objectives to be attained within a particular timescale. Again, if the objectives are not met, parents could have stronger grounds on which to base an appeal.

Following a short period of consultation about the draft, the Code was distributed in Spring 1994, with the intention of putting it into operation in the following Autumn.

Contact the Department for Education Special Educational Needs Publications Section (address on p. 227) to obtain your own copies of the Code of Practice and the associated guide for parents. (There is no charge for these.) When you have read them list the strengths and weaknesses of the new system.

Mainstreaming and support for children with disabilities and learning difficulties

Since the inclusion of children with disabilities and learning difficulties into mainstream schools has been a theme throughout this chapter, it is appropriate if we offer a brief summary of some of the advantages and disadvantages of segregated special schools before moving on.

Reflect on what you have read in this chapter and what you already know about children with disabilities and learning difficulties. Draw up a list of the advantages and disadvantages of including these pupils in mainstream schools. Then compare your list with ours.

Table 7.4	The advantages and disadvantages of special schools
Advantages	Disadvantages
High ratio of staff to learners	Living with others with disabilities and so lack of 'normal' reference group
Use of special teaching techniques	Impact of having to live away from home for those attending residential schools
Availability of special resources (e.g. for therapy)	Sense of stigma from attending a special school
Less pressure on learners – can build confidence	Environment too protective and caring
A caring, small community	Sometimes lacks emphasis on educational purposes

Within a mainstream school it is possible to provide support in several ways although each brings with it a number of problems. Identify five ways in which support for learners with disabilities and learning difficulties can be provided and a possible problem associated with each. Compare your ideas with another person.

Refer to Table 7.5 to help you with this activity.

Post-compulsory education

Further Education

As with other sectors, education and training after leaving school has undergone

Table 7.5	Five strategies
Action	*Problem*
Withdrawing from certain lessons	But which lessons? what about any 'stigmatizing' effect on the child leaving the lesson?
Support for an individual child	What expertise and training is necessary for the support worker? what happens if others in the class are in need of help?
Support for a class	What about co-operation/conflict with the class teacher? where does responsibility begin and end?
Support for the teacher	Who provides this – a special needs department?
Whole school support	Will all departments accept responsibility if the discrete special needs section is disbanded?

many changes in recent times and these have implications for learners with disabilities and learning difficulties. Chapter 3 shows that there has been a move towards creating a more vocationally oriented system with industry having a greater influence over the curriculum and qualifications. Even before these changes there was a lot of evidence showing the struggle that learners with disabilities and learning difficulties had in finding and keeping jobs.

In the face of the changes, many groups campaigned to try to ensure that the needs of this group of people were not overlooked. Many colleges did make good progress in meeting special needs, but this was in a context of continuing criticism of the qualifications and skills of those entering the labour market.

In 1991, in response to this, the government published a White Paper called *Education and Training for the 21st Century* in which it outlined further changes. These were later to become policy in the Further and Higher Education Act 1992. The Act allowed FE colleges to leave LEA control; there were to be closer links with industries in the local area via the Training and Enterprise Councils (TECs), which would also have some responsibility for allocating funds. Overall control would be vested with a newly created Further Education Funding Council (FEFC).

Each of these measures had an important bearing on learners with disabilities and learning difficulties. For example, severing the links with the LEA meant that colleges could no longer rely on some of the central services, support and coordination formerly offered without charge. Equally the LEA could no longer ensure that the newly independent colleges were allocating an appropriate level of resources to this work.

Moreover the interests of the TECs in ensuring that the colleges trained people for jobs was demonstrated in the intention to allocate funding according to the students' success rate in getting jobs (called Output-Related Funding). The implication for college funding of having students who have difficulties finding jobs is clear.

However, the best hope for the future lay with the creation of the FEFC. Indeed one of its early acts was to create a special committee chaired by Professor John Tomlinson to examine policy and provision in the area of special needs. The Committee encouraged those interested to submit evidence which would be considered and incorporated into its final report (1996).

There were also attempts to safeguard the existing levels of provision. These were helped by using the government's *Charter for Further Education*, published in 1993, which contained a section about the rights of learners with disabilities and learning difficulties.

> You can also expect information from each college about its **approach to students with learning difficulties or disabilities**, including:
>
> - the **courses** available (including separate courses), together with the **qualifications or other results** they lead to
>
> - any special arrangemetns to record and publish achievements
>
> - any additional **support** available, such as extra staff or special equipment
>
> - arrangements for **access** to buildings
>
> - the college's first **point of contact** for learning difficulties and disabilities issues
>
> Charter for Further Education, HMSO 1993

In order to help you consider some of the issues involved in supporting learners with disabilities and learning difficulties in FE, we have devised a short case study. Read it and then list all the items which you think would have to be taken into account to support Karen's education and training. Think especially about the extra costs she will be faced with. Do you think it would be possible for a college to meet all Karen's needs? Do you think every college should be able to meet needs such as these?
Our list is given on p. 228.

Case study

Following a serious accident when she was a child, Karen is a tetraplegic. She has very limited use of her upper limbs but this is sufficient to allow her to operate her electric wheelchair. Her education immediately after the accident was in a residential special school some distance away from her home. Having obtained passes at GCSE in seven subjects at Grade C and above, she has returned home to study BTEC National at her local FE college. Her subjects relate to Travel and Tourism, the area in which she hopes to find a job. As part of the course there are visits to places of relevance to the course, both in Britain and abroad, and there is also a short period of work placement.

On the basis of your list and ours at the end of the chapter, devise a checklist of points to be examined if FE colleges want to meet the needs of students with disabilities and learning difficulties.

If you are working in a college context, investigate how your college meets the standards you have just developed.

In their book *A Struggle for Choice*, Corbett and Barton identify three themes important for learners with disabilities and learning difficulties in FE:

1 equal opportunities;

2 empowerment;

3 rights.

Their debate centres upon the idea of 'choice' and the transition from adolescence to adulthood. If you want to find out more about how these students with special needs train for, find, and keep jobs, have a look at their book.

Higher Education

Figure 7.5

Working together to maximize learning potential

Within the HE sector there are some important differences in the kinds of learners involved. Unlike FE, where there could be a large group of individuals with learning difficulties arising from impaired intellectual functioning, the students in HE can be placed into just a few groups. These are now used on the standard UCAS application form and comprise students who:

• are blind/partially sighted;

• are deaf/partially hearing;

• are mobility impaired;

• have a specific learning difficulty (dyslexia);

- have a hidden disability;

- have multiple disability;

- have medical conditions (e.g. asthma/epilepsy).

In recent times there has been a lot of concern about the participation rates of some groups in HE, and a number of reports (e.g. Ball 1990) have suggested that the system needs to do more to meet the needs of working-class people, women and people from ethnic minorities. Sadly, disabled people have been neglected in this access literature.

As with FE, the government issued a White Paper in 1991. *Higher Education: A New Framework* gave the outline of the changes later to be included in the 1992 Further and Higher Education Act. This ended the distinction between the older universities and the newer polytechnics (the latter then changed their names to become universities). Funding for the sector was to be made the responsibility of one body, the Higher Education Funding Council (HEFC). Northern Ireland, Scotland and Wales each had their own equivalent.

In its guidance to the HEFC, the government had indicated that the HEFC should give some attention to disabled students. Accordingly in England an Advisory Group was established and it became responsible for allocating the £3 million which was made available for this work in both 1993 and 1994. Universities had to bid for funds to support particular projects. In 1993–94 thirty-eight projects were financed and forty-nine in 1994–95. However the basic issue of finding a way to finance permanently those institutions which made provision for disabled students remains. The items on which expenditure is necessary will emerge in your next exercise. Before you attempt that, however, something must be said about the students.

It is rather paradoxical that whilst finance for students generally has become more of a problem since the introduction of top-up loans in 1990 and the subsequent freezing of the mandatory LEA grant, the situation of disabled students has improved. In 1990, to deflect criticism about the impact of top-up loans on disabled students, the government introduced some important changes. Instead of a single additional payment there were to be three allowances to cover the additional costs associated with having a disability (e.g. having to make greater use of a telephone or to use taxis rather than public transport); the purchase of special equipment (e.g. computer, cassette recorder), and the need to buy non-medical personal support (e.g. deaf students might need a communicator). The amounts available have been increased in line with the rate of inflation.

There are still some problems though. For example part-time students are excluded; some full time students are also excluded as a result of the application of the parental means test. Difficulties are also created by the varying practices employed by the different LEAs (e.g. some require proof of expenditure before payment).

 As with FE, we are asking you to look at a case study and to identify those issues which you think need to be considered if the individual is to enter university and complete the course successfully. You might find it helpful to group the items into categories relating to entry and admissions, study support, and other items. Think also about the costs and about who pays.

Our suggestions are given on p. 228.

Case study

Jenny has been blind since birth. To aid her mobility she uses a guide dog. She goes to a local school and entered the sixth form to study modern languages. Teachers predict that she will obtain high grades in GCE 'A' level exams. At university she would like to study French but she has no strong preferences about other subjects. At the moment, she has no firm career plans.

Many universities and colleges of HE produce special information booklets for disabled people. Obtain a few of them. Look at what they say about the facilities available and make a list of each institution's strengths and weaknesses.

You can also obtain useful information from SKILL (the address appears below), although since this is a small charity you must send a stamped-addressed envelope.

There is a lack of information about disabled students in HE both in terms of the numbers involved and also in terms of the experiences of the students. The study by Hurst (1993) offers a limited view of access to HE in that it concentrates only on the experiences of people with impaired mobility. In future, information about numbers should improve as a result of the changes to the UCAS application form.

Conclusion

The aim in studying education and training in this area should be to recognize the worth of every human being. The problems of learners with disabilities and learning difficulties go beyond schools and education and into wider society. Education is an important arena in which there is the opportunity to bring people together irrespective of factors such as religion, ethnic origin, and disability. Ultimately this could make an important contribution to changing attitudes.

Suggestions for further reading

Sources specific to this chapter
Addresses of organizations active in this field which you could write to for more information are:

Department for Education Special Educational Needs
Publications Section SEN
DfEE
Freepost 435
London
EC1B 1SQ

SKILL
National Bureau for Students with Disabilities

336 Brixton Road
London
SW9 7AA

RNIB
224 Great Portland Street
London
W1N 4AA

RNID
19–23 Featherstone Street
London
EC1Y 8SL

National Association for Special Educational Needs
(NASEN)
2 Lichfield Road
Stafford
ST17 4JX

Recommended texts for further reading include Barton (1989), Booth *et al.* (1992), Bennett and Cass (1989) and Riddell and Brown (1994).

Answers

The World Health Organization's definition of terms (for the exercise on p. 206) is as follows:

- impairment – refers to any loss or abnormality of psychological, physiological or anatomical structure or function;

- disability – refers to any restriction or lack (resulting from an impairment) of ability to perform an activity in a manner or within the range considered normal for a human being;

- handicap – refers to a disadvantage for a given individual, resulting from an impairment or disability, that limits or prevents the fulfilment of a role that is normal depending on age, sex, and social and cultural factors for that individual;

- special educational needs – this was the term used following publication of the Report of the Warnock Committee (see p. 214) and was in use until the early 1990s;

- disabilities and learning difficulties – this is the current description.

Some of the items which you should have listed for the exercise on p. 224 include:

- daily travel to and from college;
- access to all facilities;
- meeting personal care needs (feeding, visits to the toilet, etc.);
- assessment and examinations;
- use of special equipment;
- disability awareness for teaching staff, support staff and other students;
- issues about visits and work placement;
- careers advice.

Our list of points which need to be considered for the exercise on p. 227 is:

Admissions and entry
university policy
choice of course;
choice of institution;
availability of information (appropriate format);
availability of specialist information;
visits and interviews;
completing the UCAS application.

Study support
mobility around the campus;
access to the curriculum;
brailling facilities/readers;
library resources/pre-recorded cassettes;
maps and diagrams;
assessment and examinations;
teaching and learning methods;
disability awareness;
special equipment;
work placements/foreign residence.

Other matters
finance;
living accommodation;
social life;
careers advice.

Did you spot the 'trick' item? When students study a foreign language it is usual for them to spend a period resident in the appropriate country – in Jenny's case this would be France. This then raises a number of issues to do with the guide dog – especially the quarantine regulations.

Bibliography

Acker, S. (1981) 'No women's land: British sociology of education 1960–1979', in *Sociological Review*, 29, pp. 77–104.

Adler, M.E. *et al.* (1989) *Parental Choice and Educational Policy*, Edinburgh: University of Edinburgh Press.

Ainley, P. (1985) *From School to YTS*, Oxford: Oxford University Press

Ainley, P. (1990) *Vocational Education and Training*, London: Cassell.

Ainley, P. (1993) *Class and Skill: Changing Divisions of Knowledge and Labour*, London: Cassell.

Aitkin, M. *et al.* (1981) 'Teaching styles and pupil progress: a re-analysis', in *British Journal of Educational Psychology*, vol. 51, pp. 170–86.

Alexander, R., Rose, J. and Woodhead, C. (1992) *Curriculum Organization and Classroom Practice in Primary Schools*, London: DES (The 'Three Wise Men' report).

Alexander, R. (1992) 'Floodlights, fanfares and facile factors', *Guardian,* 11 February l992.

Alston, J. (ed.) (1992) *The Royal Albert: Chronicles of an Era*, CNRW, Lancaster: University of Lancaster.

Arnot, M. (1994) 'Male hegemony, social class and women's education', in L. Stone (ed.) *The Education Feminism Reader*, London: Routledge.

Ashworth, P. (1992) 'Being competent and having "competencies"', in *Journal of Further and Higher Education*, vol. 16, no. 3, pp. 8–17.

Ashworth, P. and Saxton, J. (1990) 'On competence', in *Journal of Further and Higher Education*, vol. 14, no. 2, pp. 3–25.

Audit Commission/HMI (1992) *Getting in on the Act: Provision for Pupils with Special Educational Needs - The National Picture*, London: HMSO.

Audit Commission/HMI (1992) *Getting the Act Together: Provision for Pupils with Special Educational Needs - A Management Handbook for Schools and Local Education Authorities*, London: HMSO.

Bailey, C. (1988) 'The challenge of economic utility', in B. Cosin *et al. School, Work and Equality*, Milton Keynes: Open University Press.

Ball, Sir Christopher (1990) *More Means Different*, London: Royal Society of Arts.

Ball, S. (1981) *Beachside Comprehensive: A Case-Study of Secondary Schooling*, Cambridge: Cambridge University Press.

Barnes, C. (1991) *Disabled People in Britain and Discrimination: A Case for Anti-Discrimination Legislation*, London: Hurst.

Barton, L. (ed.) (1989) *Integration: Myth or Reality*, Lewes: Falmer Press.

Barton, L. (ed.) (1988) *The Politics of Special Educational Needs*, Lewes: Falmer Press.

Bash, L. and Coulby, D. (1991) *Contradiction and Conflict, The 1988 Education Act in Action*, London: Cassell.

Bash, L. and Coulby, D. (1989) *The Education Reform Act: Competition and Control*, London: Cassell.

Bates, I. and Riseborough, G. (1993) *Youth and Inequality*, Milton Keynes: Open University Press.

Bennett, N. and Cass, A. (1989) *From Special to Ordinary Schools: Case Studies in Integration*, London: Cassell.

Bennett, N. *et al.* (1976) *Teaching Styles and Pupil Progress*, London: Open Books.

Bernstein, B. (1975) *Class Codes and Control*, vol. 3, London: Routledge & Kegan Paul/Paladin.

Bernstein, B. (1960) 'Language and Social Class', in *British Journal of Sociology*, vol. 9, no. 3.

Bilton, T. *et al.* (1987) *Introductory Sociology*, London: Macmillan.

Blackburn, R. and Jarman, J. (1993) 'Changing inequalities in access to British universities', in *Oxford Review of Education*, vol. 19, no. 2.

Bogdanor, V. (1979) 'Power and perception', in *Oxford Review of Education 5*, pp. 157–68.

Booth, T. and Potts, P. (eds) (1983) *Integrating Special Education*, Oxford: Blackwell.

Booth, T. and Swann, W. (eds) (1987) *Including Pupils*

with Disabilities, Milton Keynes: Open University Press.

Booth, T. *et al.* (1992) *Curricula for Diversity in Education*, London: Routledge.

Booth, T. *et al.* (1992) *Policies for Diversity in Education*, London: Routledge.

Booth, T. and Coulby, D. (1987) *Producing and Reducing Disaffection: Curricula for All*, Milton Keynes: Open University Press.

Bourdieu, P. and Passeron, J.C. (1977) *Reproduction in Education, Society and Culture*, London: Sage.

Bowles, S. and Gintis, H. (1976) *Schooling in Capitalist America*, London: Routledge.

Brandis and Henderson (1970) *Social Class, Language and Communication*, London: Routledge & Kegan Paul.

Brandt, G. (1986) *The Realization of Antiracist Teaching*, Lewes: Falmer Press.

Brice-Heath, S. (1986) 'Questioning at home and at school: A comparative study', in M. Hammersley, (ed.) *Case Studies in Classroom Research*, Milton Keynes: Open University Press.

Broadfoot, P. (1988) 'Profiles and Records of Achievement: a real alternative', in *Educational Psychology*, vol. 8, no. 4, pp. 291–7.

Brown, G. and Atkins, M. (1988) *Effective Teaching in Higher Education*, London: Routledge.

Bryan, B. *et al.* (1987) 'Learning to resist: black women and education', in G. Weiner and M. Arnot *Gender Under Scrutiny*, London: Hutchinson, pp. 90–100.

Bryan, B., Dadzie, S. and Scafe, S. (1985) *The Heart of the Race: Black Women's Lives in Britain*, London: Virago.

Burman, E. and Parker, I. (1993) *Discourse Analytic Research*, London: Routledge.

Burtonwood, N. (1986) *The Culture Concept in Educational Studies*, Windsor: NFER-Nelson.

Byrne, E. 'Inequality in Education - discriminal resource allocation in schools?', in R. Meighan 'Education and sex roles', *Educational Review*, vol. 27, no. 3, June 1975, pp. 179–92.

Campling, J. (1981) *Images of Ourselves*, London: RKP.

Carby, H. (1982) 'White women listen! Black feminism and the boundaries of sisterhood', in Centre for Contemporary Cultural Studies, *The Empire Strikes Back*, London: Hutchinson.

Carr, W. and Kemmis, S. (1986) *Becoming Critical*, Lewes: Falmer Press.

Castles, S. (1981) *Structural Racism: Ethnic Minorities in Western Europe*, Geneva: World Council of Churches.

Castles, S. and Kosack, G. (1973) *Immigrant Workers and Class Structure in Western Europe*, London: Oxford University Press.

Chitty, C. (1989) 'CTCs: A strategy for elitism', in *Forum*, vol. 31, no. 2.

Chitty, C. (1992) *The Education System Transformed*, Manchester: Baseline Books.

Clark, A. (1993) *Diaries*, London: Weidenfeld & Nicholson.

Clark, B. (1987) *The Academic Life: Small Worlds, Different Worlds*, Princeton: The Carnegie Foundation for the Advancement of Teaching.

Clarricoates, K. (1987) 'Dinosaurs in the classroom', in Arnot and Weiner *Gender and the Politics of Schooling*, London: Hutchinson.

Cline, S. and Spender, D. (1987) *Reflecting Men*, London: Deutsch.

Coard, B. (1971) *How the West Indian Child is made Educationally Sub-normal in the British School System*, London: New Beacon Books.

Cockburn, C. (1987) *Two Track Training*, London: Macmillan.

Cockett, R. (1994) *Thinking the Unthinkable*, London: Harper Collins.

Cohen, L. and Manion, L. (1980) *Research Methods in Education*, London: Croom Helm.

Cole, M, (1989) *The Social Contexts of Schooling*, London, New York: Falmer Press.

Corbett, J. and Barton, L. (1992) *A Struggle for Choice: Students with Special Needs and the Transition to Adulthood*, London: RKP.

Corrigan, P. (1981) *Schooling the Smash Street Kids*, London: Macmillan.

Craft, M. and Craft, A. (1983) 'The participation of ethnic minority pupils in further and higher education', in *Educational Research*, vol. 25, no. 1.

Cross, M. (1991) *Ethnic minorities in the labour market: an overview of training issues*, Warwick: University of Warwick.

Daines, J. *et al.* (1982) *Changes in Student Participation in Adult Education*, Nottingham: Nottingham University.

Dale, R. (1985) *Education, Training and Employment*, Milton Keynes: Open University Press.

Dale, R. (1989) *The State and Education Policy*, Milton Keynes: Open University Press.

Dale, R. *et al.* (1990) *The TVEI Story*, Milton Keynes: Open University Press.

Davies, A., Holland, J. and Minhas, R. (1992) *Equal Opportunities in the New ERA, Hillcole Group Paper 2*, London: Tufnell Press.

De Lyon, H. and Migniuolo, F. (1989) *Woman Teachers*, Milton Keynes: Open University Press.

Deem, R. (1988) *Women and Schooling*, London: RKP.

Department for Education (1992) *Children with Special Needs: A Guide for Parents*, London: HMSO.

Department for Education (1992) *Choice and Diversity: A New Framework for Schools*, London: HMSO.

Department of Education and Science (1978) *Special Educational Needs: The Report of the Warnock Committee*, London: HMSO.

Department of Education and Science (1991) *Education and Training for the 21st Century*, London: HMSO.

Department of Education and Science (1991) *Higher Education: A New Framework*, London: HMSO.

Department of Employment (1991) *The National Record of Achievement: a Business Guide*, London: HMSO.

Department of Employment (1992) *Progress: Training Credits - A Report on the First 12 Months*, London: HMSO.

Department of Education and Science (1988) *TGAT: A Report*, London: HMSO.

Department for Education (1993) *The National Curriculum and its Assessment*, London: HMSO.

Donald, J. and Rattansi, A. (eds) (1992) *'Race', Culture and Difference*, London: Sage/Open University Press.

Douglas, J.W.B. *et al.* (1964) *The Home and The School*, London: Panther.

Doyle, W. and Carter, K. 'Academic tasks in the classroom', in M. Hammersley (1986) *Case Studies in Classroom Research*, pp. 133–55.

Drew, D. and Gray, J. (1990) 'The fifth year examination achievements of black young people in England and Wales', in *Educational Research*, vol. 32, no. 3.

Drew, D. and Gray, J. (1991) 'The black-white gap in examination results: a statistical critique of a decade's research', in *New Community*, vol. 17, no. 2.

Driver, G. (1980) *Beyond Underachievement*, London: Commission for Racial Equality.

Dubberley, W. (1988) 'Social class and the process of schooling – A case study of a comprehensive school in a mining community', in A. Green and S. Ball *Progress and Equality in Comprehensive Education*, London: Routledge.

Durkheim, E. (1956) *Education and Sociology*, New York: The Free Press.

Egerton, M. and Halsey, A.H. (1993) 'Trends by social class and gender in access to higher education in Britain', in *Oxford Review of Education*, vol. 19, no. 2.

Egglestone, S.J. *et al.* (1986) *Education for Some: The Educational and Vocational Experiences of 15-18 year old Members of Minority Ethnic Groups*, Stoke-on-Trent: Trentham Books.

Equal Opportunities Commission (1989) *Gender Issues: The Implications for Schools of The Education Reform Act 1988*, London: EOC.

Eysenck, H.J. (1971) *Race, Intelligence and Education*, London: Temple Smith.

Fairclough, N. (1989) *Language and Power*, London: Hutchinson.

Fetterman, D. (1989) *Ethnography Step by Step*, California: Sage.

Figueroa, P. (1991) *Education and the Social Construction of 'Race'*, London: Routledge.

Finch, J. (1984) *Education as Social Policy*, London: Longman.

Flanders, N. (1970) *Analysing Teacher Behaviour*, Reading: Addison Wesley.

Fletcher (1984) *Education in Society*, Harmondsworth: Penguin.

Fontana, D. (1981) *Psychology For Teachers*, London: Macmillan.

Foucault, M. (1975) *Discipline and Punish*, Harmondsworth: Penguin.

Freire, P. (1972) *Pedagogy of the Oppressed*, Harmondsworth: Penguin.

French, J. and French, P. (1993) 'Gender imbalances in the primary classroom', in P. Woods and M. Hammersley *Gender and Ethnicity in Schools: Ethnographic Accounts*, Milton Keynes: Open University Press.

Friedman, M. (1980) *Free to Choose*, London: Secker & Warburg.

Frow, M. and Alibhai-Brown, Y. (1993) *Race Through the '90s*, London: BBC and CRE.

Fulcher, G. (1989) *Disabling Policy*, Lewes: Falmer Press.

Fuller, M. (1980) 'Black girls in a London comprehensive school', in R. Deem (ed.) *Schooling for Women's Work*, London: Routledge & Kegan Paul.

Fulton, O. 'Women catch up', in *The Times Higher Educational Supplement*, 16 July 1993.

Further Education Unit (1987) *Marketing Adult Continuing Education*, London: FEU.

Galton, M. *et al.* (1980) *Inside the Primary Classroom*, London: Routledge.

Galton, M. *et al.* (1980) *Progress and Performance in the Primary Classroom*, London: Routledge.

Galton, M. *et al.* (1983) *Moving From the Primary Classroom*, London: Routledge.

Gaskell, J. (1992) 'Inside the business education classroom', in *Gender Matters From School to Work*, Milton Keynes: Open University Press.

Gibbs, G. (1990) *Improving Student Learning Project Briefing Paper*, Oxford: Oxford Centre for Staff Development.

Gill, D. and Levidow, L. (eds) (1987) *Antiracist Science Teaching*, London: Free Association Books.

Gillborn, D. (1990) *'Race', Ethnicity and Education: Teaching and Learning in Multiethnic Schools*, London: Unwin-Hyman.

Glaser, B. and Strauss, A. (1967) *The Discovery of Grounded Theory*, Chicago: Aldine.

Glass, D.V. (ed.) (1954) *Social Mobility in Britain*, London: RKP.

Gleeson, D. (1989) *The Paradox of Training*, Milton Keynes: Open University Press.

Gleeson, D. (ed.) (1990) *Training and Its Alternatives*, Milton Keynes: Open University Press.

Goacher, B. *et al.* (1988) *Policy and Provision for Special Educational Needs: Implementing the 1981 Education Act*, London: Cassell.

Goldthorpe, J., Llewellyn, C. and Payne, C. (1980) *Social Mobility and Class Structure in Modern Britain*, Oxford: Clarendon Press.

Goodson, I. (1990) 'Nations at risk' and 'National Curriculum', in *Politics of Education Association Yearbook 1990*, pp. 219–32.

Graddol, J. and Swann, J. (1989) *Gender Voices*, Oxford: Blackwell.

Graham, D. (1993) *A Lesson For Us All?* London: Routledge.

Gray, J. and Satterly, D. (1981) 'Formal or informal: a re-assessment of the British evidence', in *British Journal of Educational Psychology*, vol. 51, pp. 187–96.

Gray, J. and Jesson, D. (1989) 'The impact of comprehensive reforms', in R. Lowe (ed.) *The Changing Secondary School*, Lewes: Falmer Press.

Gray, J., Jesson, D., Pattie, C. and Sime, N. (1989) *Education and Training Opportunities in the Inner City (Youth Cohort Study)*, Sheffield: Training Agency.

Greater London Training Branch (1984) *The New Training Initiative 1981–1984*, London: GLC.

Green, A. (1988) 'Lessons in standards', in *Marxism Today*, pp. 24–31.

Gundara, J. (1982) 'Lessons from history for black resistance in Britain', in J. Tierney (ed.) *Race, Migration and Schooling*, Eastbourne: Holt, Rinehart, Winston.

Hakim, C. (1987) *Research Design*, London: Allen & Unwin.

Halpin, D. (1992) 'Staying on and staying in: Comprehensive schooling in the 1990s', in M. Arnot and L. Barton (eds) *Voicing Concerns: Sociological Perspectives on Contemporary Educational Reforms*, Wallingford: Triangle.

Halsey, A.H. *et al.* (1991) *Every Child in Britain*, Channel 4.

Halsey, A.H., Heath, A.F. and Ridge, J.M. (1980) *Origins and Destinations*, Oxford: Clarendon Press.

Hammersley, M. (1990) *Schoolroom Ethnography*, Milton Keynes: Open University Press.

Hammersley, M. (1991) *What's Wrong With Ethnography?*, London: Routledge.

Hammersley, M. and Woods, P. (1984) *Life in School: The Sociology of Pupil Culture*, Milton Keynes: Open University Press.

Haralambos, M. and Holborn, M. (1990) *Sociology: Themes and Perspectives*, London: Collins Educational.

Hardy, J. '"Race", Schooling and the 1988 Education Reform Act', in C. Vieler-Porter, M. Flude and M. Hammer (eds) (1990) *The Education Reform Act 1988: Its Origins and Implications*, Lewes: Falmer Press.

Hargreaves, A. and Woods, P. (1984) *Classrooms and Staffrooms: The Sociology of Teachers and Teaching*, Milton Keynes: Open University Press.

Helsby, G. (1991) 'TVEI pilots in profile', in D. Hopkins *TVEI at the Change of Life*, London: Multilingual Matters.

Heron, E. 'The monstrous regiment advances', in the *The Times Educational Supplement*, 12 April 1991.

Higher Education Statistics Agency (1991) *Universities Statistical Record*, Cheltenham: Higher Education Statistics Agency.

Hilgard, E.R. (1975) *Introduction to Psychology*, New York: Harcourt, Brace & Jovanovich Inc.

HMI (1990) *Standards in Education 1988–9: The Annual Report of the Senior Chief Inspector*, London: HMSO.

HMI (1991) *The City Technology College, Kingshurst, Solihull,* London: DES.

hooks, b. (1989) *Talking Back: Thinking Feminist – Thinking Black*, London: Sheba.

Hopkin, J. (1990) 'Equal opportunities in the 1990s: reconstructing equal opportunities in schools after the 1988 Education Act', in *Forum*, vol. 32, no. 3.

Horner, M.J. (1969) 'Fail: bright women', in *Psychology Today*, November.

Hughes, M. and Kennedy, M. (1985) *New Futures: Changing Patterns of Women's Education*, London: RKP.

Humphries, S. and Gordon, P. (1992) *Out of Sight: The Experience of Disability 1900–1950*, Plymouth: Northcote House.

Hurst, A. (1993) *Steps Towards Graduation: Access to Higher Education and People with Disabilities*, Aldershot: Avebury Press.

Husband, C. (ed.) (1982) *'Race' in Britain: Continuity and Change*, London: Hutchinson.

Illich, I. (1973) *Deschooling Society*, Harmondsworth: Penguin.

Immigrants Advisory Council (1964) *Commonwealth Immigration Second Report*, (Cmnd 2266), London: HMSO.

Inner London Education Authority 'Ethnic background and examination results, 1985 and 1986', in Inner London Education Authority (1987) *Research and Statistics Report*, London: ILEA.

Inner London Education Authority (1981) *School Examination Results in the ILEA 1979 and 1980*, ILEA RS 787/81.

James, M. (1993) 'Evaluation for policy', in R. Burgess *Educational Research and Evaluation*, Lewes: Falmer.

Jenkins, R., Rt Hon. (1966) *Address Given by the Home Secretary to a Meeting of Voluntary Liaison Committees*, London: NCCI.

Jenkins, R. (1988), 'Discrimination and equal opportunity in employment: ethnicity and 'race' in the United Kingdom', in D. Gallie (ed.) *Employment in Britain*, Oxford: Blackwell.

Jensen, A.R. (1969) 'How much can we boost IQ and scholastic achievement?', *Harvard Educational Review*, vol. 39, no. 1.

Jesson, D. and Gray, J. (1991) *Pupil Performance in Context*, Sheffield: University of Sheffield.

Jones, T. (1993) *Britain's Ethnic Minorities*, London: Policy Studies Institute.

Jones, K. (1993) 'Whose English?', in *Forum*, vol. 35, no. 2.

Joseph, K. (1976) *Stranded on the Middle Ground: Reflections on Circumstances and Policies*, London: Centre for Policy Studies.

Judd, J. 'Are girls scared of exams? Discuss' (Llewellyn Smith) in the *Independent on Sunday*, 23 June 1991.

Judd, J. and Borrill, R. 'Parents rush for test books', in the *Independent on Sunday*, 13 January 1991.

Keat, R. and Abercrombie, N. (1991) *Enterprise Culture*, London: Routledge.

Kelly, A. *et al.* (1987) 'Traditionalists and Trendies', in G. Weiner and M. Arnot *Gender Under Scrutiny*, London: Hutchinson.

Kelly, G.A. (1955) *The Psychology of Personal Constructs*, New York: Norton.

Kelly, T. (1983) 'The historical evolution of adult education in Great Britain', in M. Tight *Opportunities for Adult Education*, Milton Keynes: Open University Press.

Kenway, J. and Willis, S. (1990) *Hearts and Minds: Self-esteem and the Schooling of Girls*, Lewes: Falmer Press.

Kessler, S. *et al.* (1985) 'Gender relations in secondary schooling', in *Sociology of Education*, 58.

King, R. (1978) *All Things Bright and Beautiful?*, Chichester: Wiley.

Koestler, A. (1955) *The Trail of the Dinosaur and Other Essays*, London: Collins.

Kumar, V. (1993) *Poverty and Equality in the UK: The Effects on Children*, London: National Children's Bureau.

Lawton, D. (1989) *Education, Culture and the National Curriculum*, London: Hodder & Stoughton.

Lee, D. *et al.* (1990) *Scheming for Youth*, Open University Press.

Lee, G. and Wrench, J. (1987) 'Race and gender dimensions of the youth labour market: from apprenticeship to YTS', in G. Lee and R. Loveridge (eds) *The Manufacture of Disadvantage*, Milton Keynes: Open University Press.

Lee, J. (1989) 'Social class and schooling', in M. Cole (ed.) *The Social Contexts of Schooling*, Lewes: Falmer Press.

LeGrand, J. (1982) *The Strategy of Equality*, London: Allen & Unwin.

Leicester, M. and Lovell, T. (1992) 'Antiracist Higher Education: A survey to identify good practice', (unpublished report) in M. Leicester (1993) *Race for a Change in Continuing and Higher Education*, Buckingham: SRHE and Open University Press.

Llewellyn, M. (1980) 'Studying girls at school: the implications of a confusion', in R. Deem (ed.) *Schooling for Women's Work*, London: RKP.

Lobban, G. (1987) 'Sex roles in reading schemes', in G. Weiner and M. Arnot *Gender Under Scrutiny*, London: Hutchinson.

Lodge, D. (1988) *Nice Work*, London: Secker & Warburg.

Loring, J. and Burn, G.(eds) (1976) *Integration of Handicapped Children into Society*, London: RKP.

Mac an Ghaill, M. (1988) *Young Gifted and Black*, Milton Keynes: Open University Press.

Mac an Ghaill, M. (1989) 'Coming of age in 1980s England: reconceptualizing black students' schooling experience', *British Journal of Sociology of Education*, vol. 10.

Mann, K. (1992) *The Making of an English 'Underclass'?: The Social Divisions of Welfare and Labour*, Milton Keynes: Open University Press.

Martin, J. and Roberts, C. (1984) *Women and Employment: A Lifetime Perspective*, London: HMSO.

Marton, F. (1981) 'Phenomenography: describing conceptions of the world around us', *Instructional Science*, 10.

Marx, K. and Engels, F. (1970) *German Ideology*, London: Lawrence & Wishart.

Maslow, A. (1954) *Motivation and Personality*, New York: Harper & Row.

Maslow, A. (1967) 'Self-actualization and beyond', in J.F.T. Bugental (ed.) *Challenges in Humanistic Psychology*, New York: McGraw Hill.

McPherson, A. and Willms, J.D. (1989) 'Comprehensive schooling is better and fairer', in B. Cosin *et al.* (eds) *School, Work and Equality*, London: Hodder & Stoughton.

Mead, G.H. (1934) *Mind, Self and Society*, Chicago: University of Chicago Press.

Measor, L. (1984) 'Gender and the sciences', in M. Hammersley and P. Woods *Life in School*, Milton Keynes: Open University Press

Mee, G. and Wiltshire, H. (1978) *Structure and Performance in Adult Education*, London: Longman.

Meighan, R.A. (1981) *A Sociology of Educating*, London: Holt.

Miles, S. and Middleton, C. 'Girls' education in the balance', in M. Flude and M. Hammer (1990) *The Education Reform Act 1988*, London: Falmer Press.

Miles, M.B. and Huberman, M.A. (1984) *Qualitative Data Analysis*, California: Sage.

Miles, R. (1982) *Racism and Migrant Labour*, London: Routledge & Kegan Paul.

Miles, R. (1993) *Racism after 'Race Relations'*, London: Routledge & Kegan Paul.

Milner, D. (1975) *Children and Race*, Harmondsworth: Penguin.

Milner, D. (1983) *Children and Race Ten Years On*, London: Ward Lock.

Mirza, H.S. (1992) *Young, Female and Black*, London: Routledge.

Moon, G. (1990) *New Curriculum, National Curriculum*, London: Hodder & Stoughton.

Moon, B. (1983) *Comprehensive Schools: Challenge and Change*, Windsor: NFER-Nelson.

Moore, S.A. 'Certain ageism', in the *Guardian*, 13 August 1993, p. 11.

Morris, J. (1991) *Pride Against Prejudice*, London: The Women's Press.

Mortimore, P. and Blackstone, T. (1982) *Disadvantage and Education*, London: Heinemann.

Mullard, C. (1982) 'Multiracial education in Britain: From assimilation to cultural pluralism', in J. Tierney (ed.) *Race, Migration and Schooling*, Eastbourne: Holt, Rinehart, Winston.

Murray, C. (1990) *The Emerging British Underclass*, London: The Institute of Economic Affairs.

Nash, R. (1973) *Classrooms Observed: Teachers' Perception and Pupil Performance*, London: Routledge.

National Commission on Education (1993) *Learning to Succeed: A Radical Look at Education Today and a Strategy for the Future*, London: Heinemann.

National Curriculum Council (1989) *From Policy to Practice*, London: DES.

National Curriculum Council (1992) *Starting Out with the National Curriculum*, York: NCC.

Newman-Turner, A. (1991) 'Constructing a curriculum for equality', *Forum*, vol. 34, no. 1.

Nicholson, J. (1984) *Men and Women: How Different Are They?* Oxford: Oxford University Press.

North West Records of Achievement Working Group (1992) *Achievement: Assessing, Recording and Reporting Achievement, and Planning Individual Development in Education and Training*, Wigan: TVEI.

Nuttall, D., Goldstein, H. *et al.* (1989) 'Differential school effectiveness', in *International Journal of Educational Research*, vol. 13.

OFSTED (1993) *Access and Achievement in Urban Education*, London: HMSO.

OFSTED (1993) *Boys and English 1988-1991*, London: HMSO. -

Oliver, M. (1990) *The Politics of Disability*, Basingstoke: Macmillan.

Olivier, C. (1989) *Jocasta's Children*, London: Routledge.

Percy, K. *et al.* (1983) 'Post initial education in the North West of England: models of provision, barriers to provision', in M. Tight *Opportunities for Adult Education*, Milton Keynes: Open University Press.

Peters, R.S. (1965) 'Education as initiation', in R.D. Archambault *Philosophical Analysis and Education*, London: RKP.

Phizacklea, A. and Miles, R. (1980) *Labour and Racism*, London: Routledge.

Plowden Report (1967) *Children and Their Primary Schools*, London: HMSO.

Pole, C. (1993) *Assessing and Recording Achievement: Implementing a New Approach in School*, Milton Keynes: Open University Press.

Pollard, A. (1986) 'Coping strategies and the multiplication of differentiation in infant classrooms', in M. Hammersley (ed.) *Case Studies in Classroom Research*, Milton Keynes: Open University Press.

Pollard, A. (1985) *The Social World of the Primary School*, London, New York: Holt, Rinehart & Winston.

Popper, K. (1959) *The Logic of Scientific Discovery*, London: Hutchinson.

Powell, J.P. (1986) 'Small group teaching methods in higher education', in D. Bligh (1986) *Teach Thinking by Discussion*, SRHE and NFER, Guildford: Nelson.

Pratt, J. (1985) 'The attitudes of teachers', in J. Whyte *et al. Girl Friendly Schooling*, London: Methuen.

Provenzo, E.F. (1991) *Video Kids: Making Sense of Nintendo*, Cambridge, Mass: Harvard University Press.

Rampton Report (1981) *West Indian Children in Our Schools*, London: HMSO.

Randall, G. (1987) 'Gender differences in pupil–teacher interaction in workshops and laboratories', in G. Weiner and M. Arnot *Gender Under Scrutiny*, London: Hutchinson.

Rattansi, A. (1992) 'Changing the subject? Racism, culture and education', in J. Donald and A. Rattansi (eds) *'Race', Culture and Difference*, London: Sage/Open University Press.

Reed, C. 'Second class superstars', in the *Guardian*, 22 November 1990.

Rees, T.L. and Atkinson, P. (eds) (1982) *Youth Unemployment and State Intervention*, London: Routledge & Kegan Paul.

Reid, I. (1989) *Social Class Differences in Britain, Third Edition*, London: Fontana.

Rex, J. and Tomlinson, S. (1979) *Colonial Immigrants in a British City: A Class Analysis*, London: Routledge & Kegan Paul.

Reynolds, J. and Saunders, M. (1987) 'Teacher responses to curriculum policy: beyond the "delivery" metaphor', in J. Calderhead (ed.) *Exploring Teachers' Thinking*, London: Cassell.

Reynolds, D. and Cuttance, P. (1992) *School Effectiveness: Research, Policy and Practice*, London: Cassell.

Reynolds, D. and Sullivan, M. (1987) *The Comprehensive Experiment: A Comparison of the Selective and non-Selective Systems of School Organization*, Lewes: Falmer Press.

Riadell, S. and Brown, S. (eds) (1994) *Special Educational Needs Policy in the 1990s: Warnock in the Market Place*, London: Routledge.

Rieser, R. and Mason, M. (eds) (1991) *Disability in the Classroom: An Equal Rights Issue*, London: ILEA.

Robbins Report (1963) *Report of the Committee on Higher Education*, London: HMSO.

Rogers, C. (1982) *A Social Psychology of Schooling*, London: Routledge.

Rogers, C. (1951) *Client-centred Therapy*, Boston: Houghton Mifflin.

Rogers, R. (1980) *Crowther to Warnock: How Fourteen Reports Tried to Change Children's Lives*, London: Heinemann.

Rosenthal, R. and Jacobson, L. (1968) *Pygmalion in the Classroom*, New York: Holt, Rinehart & Winston.

Rutter, M. *et al.* (1975) 'Children of West Indian Immigrants III: Home circumstances and family patterns', in *Journal of Child Psychology and Psychiatry*, vol. 16, no. 1.

Rutter, M., Maughan, B., Mortimore, P. and Ousten, J. (1979) *Fifteen Thousand Hours*, London: Open Books.

Sadker, M. and Sadker, D. 'Sexism in the classroom', in *Psychology Today*, March 1985.

Sallis, J. (1988) *Schools, Parents and Governors*, London: Routledge.

Sarre, P. (1989) 'Recomposition of the class structure', in C. Hamnett, L. McDowell and P. Sarre *Restructuring Britain: The Changing Social Structure*, London: Sage.

Sarup, M. (1990) *Education and the Ideologies of Racism*, London: Routledge.

Scarr, S. *et al.* (1983) 'Developmental status and school achievements of minority and non-minority children from birth to 18 years in a British Midlands town', in *British Journal of Developmental Psychology*, vol. 1, no. 1.

Schultz, T.W. (1961) 'Investment in human capital', *American Economic Review*, vol. 51.

Scott, M. (1988) 'Patriarchy in school textbooks', in R. Dale *et al. Frameworks for Teaching*, London: Hodder & Stoughton.

Serbin, L. (1984) 'Teachers, peers and play preferences: an environmental approach to sex typing in the preschool', in S. Delamont *Readings on Interaction in the Classroom*, London: Methuen.

Sharp, R. and Green, A. (1975) *Education and Social Control*, London: RKP.

Sharpe, S. (1976) *Just Like a Girl*, Harmondsworth: Penguin.

Siraj-Blatchford, I. (1990) *The experience of black students in initial teacher education*, Warwick: University of Warwick/Department of Education.

Skeggs, B. (1994) 'Situating the production of feminist ethnography', in M. Maynard and J. Purvis *Researching Women's Lives*, London: Taylor & Francis.

Skellington, R. (1992) *'Race' in Britain Today*, London: Sage/Open University Press.

Smith, D. *et al.* (1993) 'Mission impossible? Access and the dash for growth in British higher education', in *Higher Education Quarterly*, vol. 47, no. 4, pp. 316–33.

Smith, D.J. and Tomlinson, S. (1989) *The School Effect: A Study of Multiracial Comprehensives*, London: Policy Studies Institute.

Smith, D. (1992) *Understanding the Underclass*, London: Policy Studies Institute.

Smithers, A. and Robinson, P. (1989) *Increasing Participation in Higher Education*, London: British Petroleum Educational Service.

Spender, D. (1983) *Invisible Women*, London: Women's Press.

Spender, D. (1985) *Man Made Language*, (2nd edn), London: RKP.

Spens Report (1939) *The Spens Report*, London: HMSO.

Spours, K. and Young, M. (1990) 'Beyond vocationalism', in D. Gleeson (ed.) *Training and Its Alternatives*, Milton Keynes: Open University Press.

Stanworth, M. (1984) 'Girls on the margin', in A. Hargreaves and P. Woods *Classrooms and Staffrooms*, Milton Keynes: Open University Press.

Statham, J. and Mackinnon, D. (1992) *The Education Fact File (*2nd edn*)*, London: Hodder & Stoughton.

Stone, L. (1993) *The Education Feminism Reader*, London: Routledge.

Swann, J. (1992) *Girls, Boys and Language*, Oxford: Blackwell.

Swann, W. (1992) *Segregation Statistics English LEAs 1988-1991*, London: CSIE.

Swann Report (1985) *Education For All: The Report of the Committee of Inquiry into the Education of Children from Ethnic Minority Groups*, London: HMSO.

Taylor, A. (1994) 'Schools can make a difference', in *Forum*, vol. 36, no. 1.

Taylor, P. (1993) 'Minority ethnic groups and gender in access to higher education', in *New Community*, vol. 19, no. 3.

Thomas, K. (1990) *Gender and Subject in Higher Education*, Milton Keynes: Open University Press/SRHE.

Thompson, J.L. (1980) *Adult Education for a Change*, London: Hutchinson.

Thompson, L. (1994) 'Opening doors to a learning society: the Labour Party Green Paper', in *Forum*, vol. 36, no. 1.

Thorndike, E.L. (1911) *Animal Intelligence*, New York: Macmillan.

Thorne, B. (1993) *Gender Play*, Milton Keynes: Open University Press.

Tierney, J. (ed.) (1982) *Race, Migration and Schooling*, Eastbourne: Holt, Rinehart, Winston.

Tizard, J. (1984) 'Positive action in technician training', in A. Wickham (1986) *Women and Training*, Milton Keynes: Open University Press.

Tizard, B. *et al.* (1988) *Young Children at School in the Inner City*, London: Lawrence Erlbaum.

Tizard, B. and Hughes, M. (1986) *Young Children Learning: Talking and Thinking at Home and at School*, London: Fontana.

Tough, A. (1983) 'Self planned learning and major personal change', in M. Tight *Adult Learning and Education*, Croom Helm.

Troyna, B. (ed.) (1987) *Racial Inequality in Education*, London: Tavistock.

Troyna, B. (1993) *Racism and Education*, Milton Keynes: Open University Press.

Troyna, B. and Hatcher, R. (1991) 'Racist incidents in schools: A framework for analysis', in *Journal of Education Policy*, vol. 6.

Urry, J. (1989) 'Social class in Britain', in M. Cole (ed.) *The Social Contexts of Schooling*, London, New York, Philadelphia: Falmer Press.

Wade, B. and Moore, M. (1993) *Experiencing Special Education: What Young People With Special Educational Needs Can Tell Us*, Milton Keynes: Open University Press.

Wakeford, N. (1993) 'Beyond Educating Rita: mature students and Access', in *Oxford Review of Education*, vol. 19, no. 2.

Walford, G. and Miller, H. *City Technology College*, Milton Keynes: Open University Press.

Walford, G. (1992) 'The reform of higher education', in M. Arnot and L. Barton *Voicing Concerns*, Wallingford: Triangle.

Walker, S. and Barton, L. (1983) *Gender, Class and Education*, Lewes: Falmer Press.

Walkerdine, V. (1993) 'Femininity as performance', in L. Stone *The Education Feminism Reader*, London: Routledge.

Weiner, G. and Arnot, M. (1987) *Gender Under Scrutiny*, London: Hutchinson.

Wellington, J. (1987) 'Skills for the future?', in M. Holt *Skills and Vocationalism*, Milton Keynes: Open University Press.

Wells, G. (1984) *Language Development in the Pre-school Years*, Cambridge: Cambridge University Press.

Whitty, G. and Menter, I. (1989) 'Lessons of Thatcherism: education policy in England and Wales, 1979-1988', in *Journal of Law and Society*, vol. 16, no. 1.

Whitty, G., Edwards, T. and Gerwirtz, S. (1993) *Specialization and Choice in Urban Education: The City Technology College Experiment*, London: Routledge.

Whyte, J. *et al.* (1985) *Girl Friendly Schooling*, London: Methuen.

Wickham, A. (1986) *Women and Training*, Milton Keynes: Open University Press.

Wilding, P. 'Motherless families', in *New Society*, 24 August 1972.

Willis, P. (1983) 'Cultural production and theories of reproduction', in L. Barton, and S. Walker (eds) *Race, Class and Education*, London: Croom-Helm.

Willis, P. (1977) *Learning To Labour: How Working*

Class Kids Get Working Class Jobs, Farnborough: Saxon House.

Willis, P. (1987) in D. Finn *Training Without Jobs*, London: Macmillan.

Willmott, P. and Hutchinson, R. (1992) *Urban Trends 1: A report on Britain's Deprived Urban Areas*, London: Policy Studies Institute.

Woods, P. and Hammersley, M. (1993) *Gender and Ethnicity in Schools: Ethnographic Accounts*, Milton Keynes: Open University Press.

Woods, P. (1983) *Sociology and the School*, London: RKP.

Woods, P. (1990) *Teacher Skills and Strategies*, Lewes: Falmer.

Woods, P. (1979) *The Divided School*, London: Routledge & Kegan Paul.

Woods, P. (1990) *The Happiest Days? How Pupils Cope with School*, London, New York, Philadelphia: Falmer Press.

Wragg, T. (1988) *Education in the Market Place*, London: National Union of Teachers.

Wragg, T. and Jarvis, F. (1992) *Education: A Different Version: An Alternative White Paper*, London: IPPR.

Wrench, J. (1990) 'New vocationalism, old racism and the careers service', in *New Community*, vol. 16, no. 3.

Wright, C. (1987) 'Black students – white teachers', in B. Troyna (ed.) *Racial Inequality in Education*, London: Tavistock.

Yin, R. (1989) *Case Study Research*, California: Sage.

Young, M.F.D. (ed.) (1971) *Knowledge and Control*, London: Collier Macmillan.

Young, R.M. (1987) 'Racist society, racist science', in D. Gill and L. Levidow (eds) *Antiracist Science Teaching*, London: Free Association Books.

Yuval-Davis, N. (1992) 'Fundamentalism, multiculturalism and women in Britain', in J. Donald and A. Rattansi (eds) *'Race', Culture and Difference*, London: Sage/Open University Press.

Index